TRIBES

Tribes: Challenging the Image, Shifting the Paradigm reconsiders the concept of "tribe" in political, cultural, and academic discourse, offering a dynamic alternative to outdated and damaging stereotypes.

This book critiques the popular portrayal of tribes as static, violent, or regressive, arguing instead for an understanding of tribal life as adaptive, egalitarian, and resilient. Drawing on examples from colonial history, contemporary war zones, and indigenous sovereignty movements, it explores how tribes disperse power, resist conquest, and regenerate through ritual and cultural practice. The volume challenges the misuse of "tribalism" in modern politics and repositions tribes as vital actors in global conversations about identity, governance, and resource rights. Through comparative analysis, it proposes a new paradigm that recognizes tribes as shape-shifters rather than fixed structures.

Tribes: Challenging the Image, Shifting the Paradigm is ideal for students and researchers interested in anthropology, human rights, international relations, and political rhetoric.

Lawrence Rosen is W. N. Cromwell Professor of Anthropology Emeritus, Princeton University, and Adjunct Professor of Law Emeritus, Columbia University. Named to the first group of MacArthur Award recipients, he has held fellowships at Harvard Law School, The Institute for Advanced Study, Princeton, Oxford, and Cambridge Universities.

TRIBES

Challenging the Image, Shifting the Paradigm

Lawrence Rosen

NEW YORK AND LONDON

Designed cover image: Image by the late Jimmy Pike, courtesy of Jimmy Pike Estate.

First published 2026
by Routledge
605 Third Avenue, New York, NY 10158

and by Routledge
4 Park Square, Milton Park, Abingdon, Oxon, OX14 4RN

Routledge is an imprint of the Taylor & Francis Group, an informa business

© 2026 Lawrence Rosen

The right of Lawrence Rosen to be identified as author of this work has been asserted in accordance with sections 77 and 78 of the Copyright, Designs and Patents Act 1988.

All rights reserved. No part of this book may be reprinted or reproduced or utilised in any form or by any electronic, mechanical, or other means, now known or hereafter invented, including photocopying and recording, or in any information storage or retrieval system, without permission in writing from the publishers.

For Product Safety Concerns and Information please contact our EU representative GPSR@taylorandfrancis.com. Taylor & Francis Verlag GmbH, Kaufingerstraße 24, 80331 München, Germany.

Trademark notice: Product or corporate names may be trademarks or registered trademarks, and are used only for identification and explanation without intent to infringe.

ISBN: 9781041149323 (hbk)
ISBN: 9781041149309 (pbk)
ISBN: 9781003676874 (ebk)

DOI: 10.4324/9781003676874

Typeset in Sabon
by Newgen Publishing UK

For Skip Ray
Scholar and Friend

CONTENTS

List of Illustrations   ix
Preface   xi
Acknowledgements   xix

1   The Problem of Tribes   1

2   Romancing the Tribe: History, Theory, Narrative   21

3   Shifting the Paradigm, Part I: The Tribal Ethos   71

4   Shifting the Paradigm, Part II: The Spirit of Reciprocity   114

    Interlude: Is Judaism a Tribal Religion?   149

5   Tribal Encounters: Colonialism, Corporations, and the Military   157

6   Anomalous Singularities: Tribes and Sovereignty in the Modern World   197

Afterword: "We're Still Here"   210

Index   214

O mankind,
We have created you male and female,
and appointed you races and tribes,
that you may know one another.

Quran 49:13

It is literally in my DNA to be suspicious of tribalism.
I understand the tribal impulse, and acknowledge the power of tribal
    division.
I've been navigating tribal divisions my whole life.
In the end, it's the source of a lot of destructive acts.

Barack Obama

But my Totem saw the shame; from his ridgepole-shrine he came,
And he told me in a vision of the night:
"There are nine and sixty ways of constructing tribal lays,
And every single one of them is right!"

Rudyard Kipling

ILLUSTRATIONS

1.1	Romanticized image of Canadian Natives dancing	2
1.2a	Protest by non-Natives against the fishing rights of Native Americans in the Great Lakes	3
1.2b	Cartoon illustrating opposition to Indian fishing rights	4
2.1	Marooned schoolboys in the film *Lord of the Flies* (1963) becoming savage tribesmen	27
2.2	Iroquois council portrayed in Classical style tunics	47
3.1a	Traditional raven mask from the Northwest Coast	85
3.1b	"Raven and the First Men" sculpture by Bill Reid	85
3.1c	Modern businessman portrayed as a raven figure	86
4.1	Maquinna was the chief of the Nuu-chah-nulth people (Nootka) in the 1780s–1790s	117
4.2	Picture of Inuit men sharing a wife	120
5.1	Seal of the Massachusetts Bay Colony, 1629 saying 'Come over and help us'	160
5.2	Potlatch ceremony in the Northwest Coast	164
5.3	Student at Indian boarding school forced to conform to White culture	165
5.4	Native American leader George St. Gillette cries as government takes his tribe's land in 1948 to construct a dam	166
5.5	'Friends of the Indians' assist in dividing land under the Allotment policy	167
5.6	Poster offering Indian lands to white settlers, 1911	168
5.7	Caricature of the Cherokee Removal policy	173

5.8	French colonial affairs officer oversees Berber tribal court in Morocco, 1954	175
5.9	Ecology poster	177
5.10	American soldiers meeting with Afghan tribesmen	179
5.11a	Traditional Maori warrior with facial tattoos	188
5.11b	Professor Te Kahautu Maxwell with facial tattoos and business suit	189
6.1	Signing of the Treaty of Fort Laramie, 1868	203

PREFACE

> It is the mark of an educated mind to rest satisfied with the degree of precision which the nature of the subject admits and not to seek exactness where only an approximation is possible.
>
> Aristotle

Tribes, it may seem, have returned with a vengeance. Whether as allies or adversaries when confronted on the battlefields of the Middle East and Southwest Asia or as a test of tolerance when, as in the United States, they compete through gambling casinos or tax-free smoke shops, whether because they possess vital resources sought by multinational companies or challenge the very notion of our societies' evolution, tribes have returned to trouble our self-image and view of human history.

There are some 476 million indigenous peoples (roughly 6% of the total population of the world) living in at least 5000 distinct groupings in over 70 countries, perhaps half of whom still reside in tribal settings. Thirty-percent of the earth is still occupied (and in some sense "owned") by indigenous peoples and 80% of the world's existing land biodiversity is on territories they manage.[1] The largest number of people whose national governments denominate them as "tribals" is actually in India (104 million, or about 8.6% of the country).[2] There are also over 770,000 Aborigine tribesmen (a little over 3% of the population) in Australia, 775,000 Maori (16% of the total population) in New Zealand, 580,000 tribals in Taiwan (2.5% of the nation),[3] and 1.7 million aboriginal people (5% of the nation) in Canada.

The 4.4 - 5.2 million individuals who identify as solely Native American may constitute less than two percent of the total population of the U.S., but not only are certain vital resources centered on their remaining lands but the place they occupy in the moral and cultural imagination of the nation remains disproportionately large.[4]

In addition, tribal knowledge has long been a significant contributor to the well-being of the non-tribal world: From quinine and digitalis, scopolamine to aspirin "a commonly accepted estimate in the literature indicates that a full 77% of all plant-related pharmaceutical products, or roughly 25% of the entire pharmaceutical market, contains significant elements of direct contribution from the appropriation of indigenous knowledge."[5] Moreover, as worldwide demand for electric vehicles and solar panels increases it is estimated that more than half of the rare minerals needed to power them (such as lithium and cobalt) lie on or near the lands of indigenous peoples.[6]

Yet for all their continuing importance tribes have not received much in the way of recent theorizing. The natural (or at least proprietary) domain of anthropologists for well over a century, tribes have been a potent source for our views about human society and human nature. Political pundits characterize the American and European antipathy to Muslim immigrants and our own socio-economic divide as expressions of 'tribal mentality,' while those interested in the sweep of human development contend that our psychic structure was set during some imagined tribal prehistory and that everything from corporate behavior to the psychological disruption attendant on the return to civilian life of soldiers stems from this source. But not since Marshall Sahlins' *Tribesmen*, published in 1968, and Morton Fried's *The Notion of Tribe*, published in 1975, has the category of tribes been seriously addressed as a distinct phenomenon.[7] Indeed, given its variant meanings and intellectual history many would have us abandon 'tribe' as an analytic concept altogether. The present study, while seeking to take a more cultural turn in suggesting that the concept of tribe still remains useful, does not pretend to be all-inclusive or to set aside all that has been said previously on the subject. Instead, it emphasizes some of the operative characteristics, rather than the momentary forms, which suffuse those associations we may continue to denominate as tribes, and to suggest that seen from this vantage, many of the uses to which the concept has been put by theoreticians, policy-makers, and pundits are due for rethinking.

There are two major approaches one can take in thinking about tribes, approaches that, unfortunately, many proponents have regarded as mutually exclusive. The first emphasizes the structural forms through which tribal peoples organize themselves. Here kinship, language, residence, territory, leadership designation, mutual aid, and defense arrangements are among the features taken as indicative of tribal constructs. The other approach focuses on the conceptual categories by which groups and individuals make sense of their worlds and orient their actions towards one another. It concentrates on the processes by which a people imagine their nature and interactions, the shape of the enfolding cosmos, and the logic that connects the multiple domains of their lives. Each of these analytic approaches may be infused with evolutionary, historical, and structuralist ideas, but each nevertheless focuses on either the form that tribes are said to take or their distinctive ways of imaging their world.

While supporters of each approach have wrangled, at times quite robustly, I have had the intellectual advantage of being trained by those in each camp – at Brandeis University as an undergraduate, where I studied with Elizabeth Colson (whose structural-functionalism was deeply affected by her attachments to the British scholars of the Manchester school) and, during my senior year, when I was hired as a research assistant on an evolutionist project about tribes directed by David Aberle and David Kaplan; at the University of London during my junior year, where I studied with a number of anthropologists (the faculty at that time having included Daryll Forde, Phyllis Kaberry, and Mary Douglas) who had done their fieldwork among sub-Saharan African tribes; and as a graduate student at the University of Chicago in the 1960s, where I learned from Lloyd Fallers, Clifford Geertz, and others who were central to the cultural interpretation approach. Where some (by no means all) of my teachers saw contradictions or superiorities in structural, evolutionary, or cultural theories, I have never accepted the idea that one or the other approach possessed exclusive validity. On the contrary, it has always seemed to me that much depends on the problem one is addressing and rather less on the portal through which one chooses to enter a common domain. While one approach may have advantages in certain contexts, combinations of perspectives more often serve any study well. When ideational boundaries are crossed, therefore, academics should remember, as one of my teachers pointed out, that even in the law the penalties for trespass are rather light.

All of this might sound a bit tendentious given what is to come in the following chapters. For the argument here will appear to come down solidly on the cultural side. And it is certainly true that I will be suggesting that tribes are malleable in their structural forms while maintaining certain cultural orientations that give them regularity and distinctive qualities. But I would not want that emphasis to appear as a negation of the insights gained over so many years and through so many extraordinary studies of particular tribes, or to suggest that cultural elements simply displace those relating to social structure and change. The evolutionists' idea of adaptation and the functionalists' of the relatedness of parts will suffuse this account even if, in adopting elements of each, their most ardent proponents would balk at my reluctance to accept the whole of their theories. Thus, in trying to relate multiple perspectives I ask the reader's patience and suspension of disbelief while seeking to demonstrate that these various orientations need not be at war with one another in this or any other subject with which an anthropologist may be concerned.

> To look at the symbolic dimensions of social action – art, religion, ideology, science, law, morality, common sense – is not to turn away from the existential dilemmas of life for some empyrean realm of de-emotionalized forms; it is to plunge into the midst of them. The essential vocation of interpretive anthropology is not to answer our deepest questions, but to make available to us answers that others, guarding other sheep in other valleys, have given, and thus to include them in the consultable record of what man has said.
>
> Clifford Geertz, The Interpretation of Cultures,
> New York: Basic Books, 1973, p. 30.

Indeed, when we seek to analyze social and cultural processes we are never really dealing with discrete categories. It is undoubtedly true, as Lloyd Fallers wisely noted, that getting one's thoughts in order and getting one's life in order are not the same thing, and that the logic of the one need not be identical to that of the other. But neither is that to say that they are utterly distinct. It will, therefore, also be imperative to keep in mind that setting clear conceptual boundaries between tribes and other social arrangements or between their organizational forms and their cultural orientations would be as misleading as suggesting that the processes that inform both structure and concept are entirely discreet. We deal here with continua, overlaps, form and process bleeding into one another, not the sociological equivalent of species that cannot interbreed or the relation of predator to prey. So, whether one chooses the metaphor of family resemblance or hybridization, fractal geometry, or fuzzy logic to describe tribal lifeforms, the central point remains the same: that the concept of tribe, notwithstanding its open-texture, continues to have vitality in our intellectual analysis just as it has real repercussions in the social and political world.

It may, of course, appear that the category of tribe is indeed no longer useful or that any account will include so many counterexamples as to eat up the analytic classification itself. Without simply justifying our task as one in which even inspired error may lead to greater truth, it may, therefore, be best to approach the features of tribal existence in a theme and variation sense, where each example may test both our rationale for inclusion and the validity of the insights claimed in its name. Notwithstanding the impossibility of covering all cases equally, our task will be to test the continuing value of tribe as a conceptual and analytic tool, neither reifying it nor failing to discern its characteristic traces when they cross our path.

We will begin by looking in Chapter One at the uses and misuses of the concept of tribe in popular discourse and then, in Chapter Two, at a number of the theories that have been offered over the years to explain the history and organization of tribes. Although many aspects of these accounts will be heartily criticized, in part because of their claims to total explanatory power, I will have no hesitation in subsequently purloining portions of each in ways that might displease their most ardent advocates. Indeed, I will suggest that many of the components to which they point and many of the minor themes to which they give (often muted) voice are vital to any reconsideration of the notion of tribe.

Chapters Three and Four are the heart of the matter. Here, I will suggest a series of cultural features characteristic of tribes which, when taken together, allow for a rather different paradigm to emerge. The factors to which we will have recourse affect every domain of tribal life – including, quite crucially, the roles of gender, humor, ritual, and economic ties. Again, however, I want to emphasize that mine is less a complete refashioning of existing theories than a shameless reassembling of parts I have found implicit or immersed in the works of so many of my predecessors.

A brief interlude precedes the second part of the book as we consider a specific example of how a tribal ethos may continue to suffuse a culture even if it is loosed from specific organizational forms. Thus, the issue of whether a Western religion – in this case Judaism – represents not some residue of a past life but bears into the present key aspects of a tribal orientation may help in our understanding of how tribalism retains its shape-shifting capability and its capacity to level both people and power in ways that may be more apparent once we revise our understanding of tribes.

If we take many of these same features and apply them to current issues that face us in a world where tribes continue to play a vital role, then the following chapters will be particularly challenging. In Chapter Five we will look first at the ways in which colonial regimes approached tribes, paying attention to the terms and images they set up and to which scholarship and practical politics have long been heir. States and empires have often been at loggerheads, if not indeed at war, with tribal groups. And when these militarized forces confront such entities they do so with a history of imagining what tribes are like that may be quite misguided – at least in terms of the alternative paradigm that will have been offered here. In this chapter the example of American involvement in Iraq and

Afghanistan will stand as our primary examples, but many of the features that are present in those confrontations reverberate around the history of the entire region. We will also consider the ways in which corporations have not only affected tribal life by seeking to exploit their resources but how the corporate form itself has come to be the vehicle that diverse tribes have chosen or been compelled to employ in their current political and economic lives.

Chapter Six will then ask the question: How, given a somewhat different understanding of tribes, might one envision tribal sovereignty in the presence of state power? Whether it is in the Americas, Australasia, or South and Southeast Asia, the history of tribal-state relations is easily distorted by simple stereotypes, popular slogans, and telegenic images. We will, therefore, consider some of the failed attempts at establishing tribe-state working relationships by looking at the ways in which an altered paradigm of tribes might contribute to a revised concept of sovereignty, and how such a concept might play out in various situations.

To suggest that the current work constitutes a true paradigm shift may seem more than a little pretentious. But if one goes back to Thomas S. Kuhn's actual argument about paradigm shifts in science then the present claim may not be without merit. Notwithstanding the subsequent use of his phrase in inappropriate contexts, Kuhn's argument accurately describes the period following the Second World War when the "normal science" of tribes held that they were structural in essence and each new ethnography clove to that theory. Eventually, as additional data generated anomalies that did not conform to existing expectations, the structural model not only began to fall apart but the very concept of "tribe" was largely abandoned to popular discourse. However, by reinterpreting the data it is indeed possible to change the way we envision tribes and our responses to them.

The tribes were here before the rest of us and, notwithstanding frequent predictions of their imminent demise, claims that they will be here long after we are gone cannot simply be dismissed. For the moment, the trick is to understand tribes as best we can – in their own terms and in those of our disciplines – in the hope that each will benefit from the encounter with the other. Tribes, to paraphrase the great scholar of Federal Indian law Felix Cohen, are indeed like the miner's canary: Dangerous conditions often show themselves first in their effects on tribal peoples, sounding an alert that the milieu has become poisonous to all. Throughout history tribal and non-tribal groups have had moments when they gained much from one another. Now would be a good time to reinforce that beneficial exchange which is so important to the future of us all.

Notes

1 Estimates do vary widely. See, Peter Veit and Katie Reytar, "By the Numbers: Indigenous and Community Land Rights," World Resources Institute, March 20, 2017. www.wri.org/insights/numbers-indigenous-and-community-land-rights (accessed September 7, 2025); and UN Environment Program, "Unsung Heroes of Conservation: Indigenous People Fight for Forests," April 5, 2023. www.unep.org/news-and-stories/story/unsung-heroes-conservation-indigenous-people-fight-forests (accessed September 7, 2025)

2 However, the International Work Group for Indigenous Affairs gives a figure of 120 million: see, https://iwgia.org/en/resources/publications/5798-iwgia-annual-report-2024.html. Others say that tribals, collectively referred to as Adivasi, form 10% of India's population of 1.37 billion, or 137 million. Much depends on the definition. The figure of 104 million, based on the 2011 census, is discussed in Richard Mahapatra, "More Than 50% of India's Tribal Population Has Moved Out of Traditional Habitats," *Down To Earth*, November 21, 2018. www.downtoearth.org.in/news/agriculture/more-than-50-of-india-s-tribal-population-has-moved-out-of-traditional-habitats-62208 (accessed September 7, 2025).

3 "Taiwan is also home to about 580,000 people who belong to one of 16 officially recognized tribes, descendants of Austronesian people whose presence on the island dates back thousands of years.... Recently, leaders such as Taiwanese President Tsai Ing-wen, who is a quarter [indigenous tribal] Paiwan, have promoted Taiwan's Indigenous identity. In 2016, Tsai issued the first official apology to Indigenous groups for centuries of mistreatment, including the seizure of ancestral lands and assimilation policies that banned Indigenous languages and traditions....Indigenous author Ahronglong Sakinu of the Lalaulan tribe and others have made it their mission to bring in people from the outside. Sakinu joked that the number of Han Chinese joining the community in recent years has been so much that there are now "more light faces than dark faces" in the group." Lily Kuo and Alicia Chen, "Taiwan's Han Chinese Seek a New Identity among the Island's Tribes," *Washington Post*, March 4, 2022.

4 On the difficulties related to assessing the number of Native Americans see, Andrew Van Dam, "The Native American Population Exploded, the Census Shows. Here's Why," *Washington Post*, October 27, 2023; and Ana I. Sánchez-Rivera, Paul Jacobs, and Cody Spence, "A Look at the Largest American Indian and Alaska Native Tribes and Villages in the Nation, Tribal Areas and States," United States Census Bureau, October 3, 2023. www.census.gov/library/stories/2023/10/2020-census-dhc-a-aian-population.html (accessed September 7, 2025).

As to resources:

> Indian lands contain about 30 percent of the coal found west of the Mississippi, up to 50 percent of potential uranium reserves, and as much as 20 percent of known natural gas and oil reserves. Robert Middleton, former director of the Office of Indian Energy and Economic Development, estimated, 'These lands contain over 5 billion barrels of oil, 37 trillion cubic feet of natural gas, and 53 billion tons of coal that are technically recoverable with current technologies'.

Maura Grogan with Rebecca Morse and April Youpee-Roll, *Native American Lands and Natural Resource Development*, Revue Watch Institute, 2011. www.resourcegovernance.org/sites/default/files/RWI_Native_American_Lands_2011.pdf (accessed September 7, 2025).

5   John Hunter and Chris Jones, "Bioprospecting and Indigenous Knowledge in Australia: Implications of Valuing Indigenous Spiritual Knowledge," *Bahá'í Library Online*, 2006-7, pp. 4–5. http://bahai-library.com/hunter_jones_bioprospecting_australia (accessed September 7, 2025).
6   Julia Simon, "Demand for Minerals Sparks Fear of Mining Abuses on Indigenous Peoples Lands," *National Public Radio*, January 25, 2024. www.knkx.org/2024-01-25/demand-for-minerals-sparks-fear-of-mining-abuses-on-indigenous-peoples-lands# (accessed September 7, 2025).
7   By the time of its publication in 1968 Sahlins appreciated the difficulty of his task:

> Different countries, different customs: no two tribes are the same in detail. Tribesmen, moreover, are like all people and any person: the more familiar with them one becomes the more difficult to recall one's first general impressions. So what I am about to do – which is to formulate a generalized design of tribal culture – is plainly hazardous and perhaps futile.

Tribesmen, p. 14. Robin Fox's *The Tribal Imagination*, which will be discussed later, is not about tribes as such, but, as he says, is equivalent to speaking about 'primitives,' i.e., our earlier forms of human conglomeration.

ACKNOWLEDGEMENTS

"There is no theory that is not a fragment, carefully prepared, of some autobiography."

Paul Valéry

This book arises from the conjunction of three streams of personal experience that have flowed in and out of one another's path over the course of many years. The first goes back to my undergraduate days when I discovered that I had been an anthropologist long before I could spell the word, a discovery that was consolidated by looking over the shoulders of teachers who themselves were steeped in both American and British approaches to the discipline. I was brought into anthropology by Elizabeth Colson and employed on a project about tribes by David Aberle, and through them learned the fascination and academic challenge of understanding tribal lives. That some of my teachers had done their own degrees with Franz Boas, Bronislaw Malinowski, or their immediate students might suggest that the discipline lacked true genealogical depth were it not for the fact that the quality of their insights and the sense of excitement they conveyed far outstripped the relative youth of the discipline. The scholars of the first half of the 20th century. not only discovered many of the regularities of human societies but did so without losing touch with the everyday lives of those among whom they worked – and for that I have always been their most grateful heir. My later graduate study with more culturally-oriented anthropologists is a debt that will become obvious at a number of points in this book.

The second stream flows from my engagement with tribes in Morocco. The clarity with which the men and women of these groups taught me, the humor with which they withstood my elementary ignorance, and their ready understanding of my ethnographic task brought substance to what until then had been the experience of others to which I could only attach both envy and abstract comprehension. To the Ait Youssi tribesmen of central Morocco in particular I therefore owe a very special debt for their hospitality, their patience, and their wisdom.

The final stream came when I returned several years after my anthropology degree to study law. I worked for a summer as an intern with the brilliant attorneys at the Native American Rights Fund and subsequently spent many years teaching American Indian law to both undergraduates and future lawyers. From that vantage I have seen how the very practical implications of anthropological theory, political reality, and the direct impact of law on the lives of tribal peoples have played out over the course of several centuries. Grappling with that history and its legal results from the perspectives of the tribes, the governments, and the academics has provided me with a humbling sense of the vitality and creativity of tribal peoples both in the United States and throughout the world.

Sustaining these streams of thought and experience have been institutions and individuals too numerous to thank properly. Special note must, however, be given to the School of Advanced Research in Santa Fe for the William Y. and Nettie K. Adams Fellowship, the School of Anthropology at the University of Arizona for my appointment as Resident Scholar during their centennial year, the Mellon Foundation and Center for Advanced Study in the Behavioral Sciences at Stanford University, the School of Social Sciences at The Institute for Advanced Study, Princeton, N.J., Harvard Law School for appointing me a Senior Fellow in its Islamic Law Program, the John D. and Catherine T. MacArthur Foundation for naming me to the first group of recipients of a MacArthur Award, and the many students and colleagues at Princeton University and Columbia Law School who have helped me clarify the issues addressed here. The Covid-19 pandemic interrupted my research for this book at various libraries, and I am grateful to all those who struggled to assist scholarly work like my own during such a difficult time. I am particularly grateful for help with the illustrations provided by Kathryn Dillon and Barbara Cooper who, like all the folks in Castine, Maine, have been so welcoming to a new year-rounder.

Individuals, too numerous to list, have, over many years been vital to my instruction. Among those to whom I am especially indebted are the late Ernest Gellner and David Hart (for our running conversations about segmentary tribal organization), Patrick Geary (for his thoughtful guidance about tribes in the period of Rome and Late Antiquity), Alan Mann (for always keeping me apprised of the role of human evolution in our social lives), and Abdellah Hammoudi (for his unparalleled guidance in all things North African). Clifford Geertz and Hildred Geertz brought me to Morocco, and their wisdom and kindness has been at the core of my academic life and personal gratitude ever since. A special debt is owed to Edmund (Terry) Burke III who not only shared with me the experience of working among the tribes of the Middle Atlas Mountains when we were graduate students but has, in all the succeeding years, been a constant source of insight into both history and life.

The book is dedicated to Arthur J. (Skip) Ray. Skip's knowledge about the tribesmen of North America and his commitment to having their voices heard in the courts and records of Canada has set the standard for all of us who stand in his shadow.

To one and all, my gratitude and affection: May their tribe increase!

1
THE PROBLEM OF TRIBES

In 1977 the Mashpee Indians brought suit against a municipality on Cape Cod, Massachusetts. The Indians argued that 11,000 acres of their land were sold in the 19th century without the requisite federal consent, land that had subsequently come to be worth some thirty million dollars. Following a trial that lasted forty days the court, using a definition of tribe derived from a 1901 Supreme Court case, instructed the jury to determine whether, at each of a series of specific dates, the Mashpee were in fact a tribe.[1] The jurors returned a mixed set of answers, specifying that at some times the Indians were an organized entity and at other times they were not. To be recognized as a tribe for these purposes the Mashpee had to prove that they were a structured and identifiable grouping at every one of the relevant times. But because the jury found that at some of those times the tribe was not so identified the court ruled that the Mashpee had no right to bring the suit.[2]

*

In the Middle Atlas Mountains of Morocco, some forty miles south of Fez, there is a small lake called Dayet Ifrah. When I first encountered the people living in the area I was assured that the lake was within the territory of a tribe called the Ait Seghoushen, whose lands were adjacent to those of another tribe, the Ait Youssi. But when I revisited the area only a few months later I was told that the fraction of the Ait Youssi living closest to the lake were now regarded as part of the other tribe. How, I asked, did that come about? One day, I was told, women from the Ait Youssi segment came down to the lake to fill their water jugs. But some of the men from the Ait Seghoushen told them they had no right as outsiders to the water, broke several of the jugs, and chased the women away. So, men from the Ait Youssi fraction met with the big men of the Ait Seghoushen tribe and by the time they were done talking it was settled that their section of the Ait Youssi was actually descended from an ancestor of the Ait Seghoushen. Therefore, they agreed, the Ait Youssi fraction had always *been part of the other tribe* and hence its members were entitled to use the waters after all.[3]

* *

One day in the late 1960s an anthropologist received a telephone call. The person on the other end asked if the anthropologist was indeed the one who had done research on tribes. Yes, the anthropologist answered. "Well," said the caller, "see, man, we're like up here in the hills, y' know, and we're like trying to re-tribalize – and we were wondering how we're supposed to do it."

* *

Tribes get a very uneven press. At times they have been seen as the arrangement that nurtures the 'noble savage,' a form of society wherein all that is uncorrupted in human nature finds its proper home. At other times tribes have been envisioned as the repository, if not the very source, of all

FIGURE 1.1 Romanticized image of Canadian Natives dancing.

FIGURE 1.2A Protest by non-Natives against the fishing rights of Native Americans in the Great Lakes.

that is inhuman – our species dragged back to its primal and ungodly roots, where clannishness barely kept us above a state of Hobbesian warfare.

Indeed, the very terms "tribe" and "tribal" are said by some critics to constitute derogatory, even racist, epithets.[4] One medical journal retracted an article that used the word "tribalism" to describe the isolation of medical specialists from one another, saying its use constituted a "microaggression" against indigenous peoples.[5] Each characterization has at times been used to support outside domination, whether because tribes, confined to reserves, would fare best if their self-proclaimed benefactors acted like "cultural game wardens," or because, as "irresponsible" and "childlike," they are seen as needing to be closely governed, their practices and beliefs replaced by modern science and Christian rectitude.

FIGURE 1.2B Cartoon illustrating opposition to Indian fishing rights.

Such images are, alas, still with us, whether as direct characterizations of tribal life or as a key metaphor that informs our professed understanding of both "them" and "us." At times, the image of tribes is highly romanticized, at others simply patronizing. The former has been used to justify control of their persons, the latter their land and resources. Such attitudes have not only affected the vision of and relations with many native peoples but have served as the basis for analogies projected into contemporary politics, business, and social life. We have been told that Donald Trump is a divisive "tribal warrior," that Senator Ted Cruz – who "does tribal rhetoric better than most" – demonstrated that "tribal politics, anchored in tribal media, has made knowing nothing a badge of honor."[6] A member of Congress tells us that Afghan tribes are "500 years behind civilization," a *New York Times* columnist that in America "the country's seismic demographic and cultural shifts threaten to make our tribalism permanent," and a Harvard literature professor that "maybe [the Olympics] feed our tribal instincts, stimulate the irrational basis of loyalty to our community or our country."[7] Another *New York Times* commenter, citing an anonymous Republican official who plays on the view of tribes as autocratic, reports: "'What used to be a sense of belonging,' I was told, 'devolves into primitive tribalism, absolute adherence to the leader over adherence to a code of ethics'."[8] Conservative Princeton Professor Robert George offers as the definition of "a tribalist someone who, rather than thinking for oneself, outsources one's thinking to the group," when actual tribes, as we will see, are intensely individualistic.[9] Nobel Laureate economist Paul Krugman, after Donald Trump refused to acknowledge the election of Joe Biden, characterized the Republican party as "increasingly inward-looking, engaged in ever more outlandish efforts to demonstrate their loyalty to the tribe," and asked "how long America as we know it can survive in the face of this malevolent tribalism."[10] A few days later, as the Capitol was being stormed by Trump partisans, Senate Majority Leader Mitch McConnell seemed to supply an answer when he told his Senate colleagues: "We cannot keep drifting apart into two separate tribes...with separate facts, and separate realities...with nothing in common except hostility toward each other and mistrust for the few national institutions that we still share." Indeed, some critics argue that Joe Biden failed to realize that "he needed to tell a story that would resonate in a tribal America." Similarly, David Lammy, who would become Foreign Secretary in a Labour Party government in the UK, entitled his political memoire *Tribes: How Our Need to Belong Can Make or Break Our Society*. And when the pro-separation first minister of Scotland stepped down from her post in 2023 it was reported that: "Lately the tribal nature of the independence debate in Scotland — amplified by the social media echo chamber — has made the normal functioning of politics seem next to impossible."[11]

Academics and politicians have both sought to extend their view of tribes to much broader political realms. One anthropologist has offered us the political certainty that "dictatorships have roots in tribalism," and that to retain some balance "countries with tribal culture can be ruled by despotism alone," while Senator Lindsay Graham assures us that "once you replace the totalitarian state then the governance that comes up next is most likely tribal."[12] According to the 2004 United Nations *Arab Human Development Report*, "clannism ['asabiyya] in all its forms (tribal, clan-based, communal, and ethnic)...tightly shackles its followers through the power of the authoritarian patriarchal system. This phenomenon... represents a two-way street in which obedience and loyalty are offered in return for protection, sponsorship, and a share of the spoils."[13] Indeed, we are assured that, as an unavoidable aspect of social reality, there is a strict dichotomy between individualism and "the rule of the clan," that businesses suffer when they are organized into discrete entities because "silos breed tribalism [and] go hand in hand with tunnel vision," and that "in order to harness our tribal nature it seems necessary to have an enemy as part of the motivational structure."[14] Even a rabbi, while commending that in a time of polarization each of us must attend to one another's pain, nevertheless writes: "Humans naturally incline toward the known. Our tribes can uplift us, order our lives, give them meaning and purpose, direction, and pride. But the tribal instinct can also be perilous. The more closely we identify with our tribe, the more likely we are to dismiss or even feel hostility toward those outside it. One of the great casualties of tribalism is curiosity [about others]."[15]

Science purportedly enters the picture when we are told that tribalism is ineradicably linked to our biological development, that, as E.O. Wilson declares: "The true cause of hatred and violence is faith versus faith, an outward expression of the ancient instinct of tribalism."[16] Philosopher and animal rights activist Peter Singer concurs: "If you go back in time you'll find tribes that were essentially only concerned with their own tribal members. If you were a member of another tribe, you could be killed with impunity." Religious scholar Martin Marty used the term "tribalist" to describe those individuals whose "pride in race, religion, ethnicity and gender circumscribed their vision of the American mosaic." Like many others, columnist David Brooks links the ethical and the tribal when he says that "tribal morality... narrow[s] the circle of concern to people just like us."[17] Social psychologist and Professor of Ethical Leadership Jonathan Haidt says "there's no getting around it: we are tribal primates. We are exquisitely designed and adapted by evolution for life in small societies with intense, animistic religion and violent intergroup conflict over territory."[18] We even read that sports fans are "tribes of suckers" who are played for their "basic tribal need that seems inherent to human nature,"[19] and that America is losing out to China in "our emerging world of tribes," a form of organization that expresses humankind's "primitive racial instincts."[20] Peruse the titles on the bookshelf and you will discover there is a tribe for every possible identity. There are tribes of "hackers," "'surfers," "millionaires," "fatherless girls," and even the "blissful". There are "moral tribes," "wandering tribes," "hidden tribes," and those who strayed so far as to be "lost tribes".[21] Indeed, so pervasive, though ill-defined, is "tribalism" when carried into the present cultural and political fray that it was even proposed as the term of the year.[22]

Claims about tribes are not limited to a single portion of the political or even sexual spectrum. One commenter remarks that since Western religions involve encountering "a God who revealed himself within an ecology of almost lunar desolation... [T]he call to belief was tribal, not individualistic... [such that] sexuality was an expression of faith to increase the tribe," thus rendering homosexual relations both sinful and criminal.[23] Followers of Ayn Rand's politics tell us that "the multiculturalists...hold that the basic unit of existence is the tribe [and they] reject the achievements of Western – i.e., individualistic – civilization [which] represent a way of life superior to that of savage tribalism."[24] In Britain, Conservative Party front-bencher Norman Tebbit's 'back to basics' agenda was grounded on the proposition: "Man is not just a social but also a territorial animal; it must be part of our agenda to satisfy those basic instincts of tribalism and territoriality."[25]

Columnists weigh in. Thomas L. Friedman admonishes us that the "Tribal Rule" is "Do unto Others What Has Been Done to You." Indeed, he phrases the same point as "in a tribal world it's rule or die, compromise is a sin, enemies must be crushed, and power must be held at all costs" and that in the Middle East "each tribe lives by the motto 'rule or die' – either my tribe or sect is in power or we're dead." Similarly, his colleague at *The New York Times* David Brooks tells us that fascism begins when people "mired in their own resentments…begin to base their sense of self-worth on their tribe, not their behavior."[26] Other politicians connect tribalism to immorality: "At the Catholic Prayer Breakfast in Washington, then Speaker of the House of Representatives Paul D. Ryan said: 'We see moral relativism becoming more and more pervasive in our culture. Identity politics and tribalism have grown on top of this'."[27] We have even been instructed by President Barack Obama, whose mother was a professional anthropologist, that "the obdurate nature of tribalism" to which people may naturally revert is "the source of a lot of destructive acts."[28]

This confusion of tribal images has many sources. Popular stereotypes focus on tribes as exclusionary and hostile to outsiders, while scholarly images often concern claims about human nature and the elementary structures of social organization. Anthropologists have not always been helpful. As late as the early 20th century some anthropologists continued to regard tribal societies – and indeed tribal individuals – as being of a lower order both sociologically and developmentally, terms like "savage" and "primitive" being used interchangeably with "tribal" through much of the century. Those anthropologists who went along with the colonial enterprise or were captivated by a sense that entire peoples could exist at different evolutionary stages were, however, countered by the overwhelming majority who fought strenuously for the view that tribalism was not a sign of inferiority in any organizational or biological sense. Sometimes the images, even when well-intended and seemingly innocuous, could nevertheless appear as representing levels of superiority rather than different approaches to life. Over the past century, therefore, anthropologists have promulgated a wide and contradictory set of theories about tribes. For many years (and still for a number of archaeologists and introductory textbook writers) the simple progression of band → tribe → chiefdom → state has been taken to represent humanity's evolutionary pathway. However, most of those who championed such cultural evolution in the 1960s later recanted their position, as neither the historical record nor evolutionary mechanisms could be found to support the theory. True, there are determinists, both biological and geographical, who continue to cite work of that period, and there are others who take the position that our current temperament traces directly to the pre-historic tribal organization in which the human psyche is said to have been forged.[29]

But alternative views have not been wanting. For example, it has been suggested that tribes come into being only in the face of states, rather than leading up to them. As part of his argument along these lines Morton Fried asked: "Do Tribes exist? Or are they chimeras, imaginary compounds of various and, at times, incongruous parts, societal illusions fabricated for diverse reasons, but once created, endowed with such solid reality as to have profound effect on the lives of millions of people?"[30] Others have argued that tribes are but one form of organization on a continuum that cannot be conveniently divided into discrete parts. Indeed, many of the British anthropologists who had approached tribes as a set of structural forms based on rules of descent, territorial control, and patterns of marital alliance found, as their studies shifted from Africa to the Pacific and from the "ethnographic present" to a range of historical examples, that structural forms appeared so varied that it would be best to abandon the concept of tribe altogether. Elizabeth Colson, who came to reject the term, spoke for many when she wrote: "I do not know what is meant by 'Tribal Societies.' 'Tribe' and 'tribal' are slippery terms despite various attempts to pin them down so they could be used analytically."[31]

It is this latter question – whether the analytic category of "tribe" maps directly onto a set of social forms that exist in the world or whether the very concept is misplaced – that may understandably prompt a certain degree of skepticism about the present enterprise. In the early years of anthropology few questioned the classification of "tribe." After all, were we not the spiritual descendants of the twelve tribes of Biblical times, if not heirs to the Barbarian tribesmen of European history or descendants of people ripped by slavers from their tribal homes? Were not many of the peoples encountered during the age of discovery, through the long colonial era and up to the rise of the new nations, organized as tribes? Indeed, was the story of humankind not one of Darwinian forces carried into the social realm, with tribes forming a base from which further societal evolution took place?[32] And yet the very definition of a tribe was often variable and inexact. Indeed, as in so many other aspects of anthropological theorizing, definitions – whether of "marriage", "family", or "tribe" – were initially a function of the groups studied. And since most of the early work was done on the peoples of sub-Saharan Africa, North America, and other portions of the colonial empires, such features as territory, descent, and leadership – all of which, not extraneously, bore on the purposes of missionaries, administrators, and the military – became the defining features of the concept of tribe. But when scholars began to move beyond these original regions – and when they also began to bring history back into consideration without fear of retreating into social Darwinism or a Whiggish view of history – the paradigms developed in one part of the world or political setting clearly did not apply to newly considered places or times. The result was a call among many by the mid-20th century to abandon the use of the term and concept of tribe altogether.

"The problem of tribe" (to borrow the title of a set of essays published in 1967) is, therefore, a serious one facing any scholar who proposes to reconsider the utility of "tribe" as an analytic construct.[33] On the one hand it might seem reasonable to agree with those who would have us avoid the term and the concept altogether because time has shown that tribes are too varied a grouping to be very useful – more a category of judgment than of science, like "vermin" or "art." Moreover, the term has been so tainted by colonialism and states have so thoroughly replaced tribal enclaves that terms like "ethnic" should take precedence. Thus, one may cite some 3000 "tribes" in Africa yet argue that few meet the criteria adopted here. On the other hand, we undoubtedly have groups that are quite comfortable with being denominated tribes, laws and policies that continue to treat them as such, and metaphoric extensions of the concept – including the recent use of the term as a level of biological taxonomy – whose foundation should be carefully assessed before being retained or discarded.

Indeed, it may be argued that it is not so much that our theories test the category of tribe as that tribes test many of our theories. If, for example, we are to be persuaded that our biology and psychology were formed when we lived in bands or tribes surely we need to think carefully about what those forms of social arrangement imply.[34] Similarly, if, for purposes of governance or as a consequence of military engagements, we approach native peoples or groups in contested regions of the world with a notion of what it must mean for them to be organized as tribes we need to consider whether our theories of those groupings are properly grounded or inappropriate. In each instance the way we think about these societies will form a vital test of theories that go beyond the question of tribe itself to issues about the existence and qualities of something denominated "human nature" or whether societies evolve in accordance with principles comparable to those discovered in the biological sciences.

Of course, we could approach the problem of tribe by simply asserting that we are not trying to describe something that exists in the exact form in which we portray it. We might, therefore, characterize tribes in much the way that Werner Heisenberg depicted quantum particles, as not exactly real since "they form a world of potentialities or possibilities rather than one of things or facts," excited avatars of the fields within which they exist.³⁵ Or we could claim that ours is a kind of Weberian "ideal type" analysis, one in which the general features of the things in question do not necessarily match any specific instance (much as an average may not appear as a specific number in the array) but nevertheless point to distinctive features that cover the broad range of cases, an approach that is helpful in directing attention to factors that we may also need to learn more about. Much as I admire Max Weber's work, however, I have always regarded this method as something of a cop-out. Having claimed that the subject of study is not some form of sociological accounting but actually exists in the world, either one should be able to point to its attributes and analyze them directly or make only temporary use of ideal types and then proceed to the thing itself. In this regard I am rather like the student in the 1960s British comedy skit *Beyond the Fringe* who, in the course of being tutored by the analytic philosopher G. E. Moore, keeps mentioning concrete examples, only for the master finally to say, with obvious exasperation, "you're rather fond of the real world, aren't you, young man?"

Fond I may be, but not in all ways. For one alternative "real world" way of approaching tribes seems to me equally limited. Here what one would do is to look for features that cohere in a discernible pattern. So, for example, one would take all the factors that can be gathered from every available ethnography – marital patterns, territorial arrangements, rules of descent, etc. – run them through a program that seeks correlations, and come up with a constellation that could be called tribal. And, in fact, this is essentially what has been done. It is called the Human Relations Area File (HRAF), which for decades has coded aspects of societies culled from a vast number of ethnographic accounts. The problem, of course, is that codings and correlations are not self-executing much less dispositive of structural or causal relations. If one starts by assuming that there are features of tribes that are observable or that can be regarded as rule-like propositions one will have presumed that everything that is relevant is articulated, that the categories created are the only ones that matter, and that knowledge and structure are sufficient, meaning and process being secondary at best.

But even if we do not attempt an HRAF-style sweep of all tribes and all criteria the question arises, as in any study of this scope, as to how many examples constitute a basis for assessment. There is a Yiddish saying: " 'For example' is no proof." And surely a singular instance, or perhaps quite a range of instances, does not necessarily establish the validity of a broad generalization. While being careful not to make one's selection of examples a function of the interpretation one hopes to support, a delicate line must be drawn between assumptions that float above the concrete and trying to cover every instance that an alternative interpretation could possibly sustain. The goal is not to fashion a perfect definition of "tribe": As Patricia Crone notes, "A definition is not meant to exhaust a phenomenon, only to identify the constitutive feature which makes it a single phenomenon."[36] Or, to choose a different metaphor and preferable tactic, the point, in some broad Wittgensteinian sense, is to spot the family resemblances, the instances where things that might be regarded as linked by a single, essential feature may actually be connected by a series of overlapping similarities. If, as I believe to be the case here, forms and processes bleed across clusterings and a precise taxonomy of forms is a feckless pursuit, concrete examples become vital but not conclusive. Put somewhat differently, where (as we shall see), in making the best use of the concept of tribe, process takes precedence over form, it will indeed be indispensable to discuss a number of particular tribes, and the constellation of interlocking features I believe help characterize the subject. Given the revised paradigm that will be offered it is, however, not possible – nor, I believe, necessary – to be totally comprehensive as one sets about constructing an analytic framework that reorients our inquiry and upon which further interpretation may be effected.

Having said that, it will be obvious that there is one last approach that could be taken, a tactic, however, I believe to be particularly unhelpful. This viewpoint claims that all ethnography is fiction, that we can never really study another group (only ourselves studying them), and that tribes, like all other anthropological constructs, are simply in the mind, if not indeed the biases and mercantile interests of the beholder.[37] This may have the dubious advantage of avoiding difficult analysis of any sort but clearly destroys any possibility of advancing anything other than one's own self-regarding assertions. Anthropology is both a science – an organized and regularized quest for unbiased knowledge – and an interpretive enterprise – a quest for credible connections and felt meaning – and, as cautious as one must be about one's own orientations and contexts, neither the study, responsibly borne, nor its results, modestly offered, are solely reducible to statements about our personal predilections.

Native scholars, leaders, and discussants, of course, have their own views of what constitutes a tribe. For the most part, however, confidence in their own identities has not necessitated the development of overarching theories of 'what is a tribe' except when it is in reaction to definitions that trench on their legal rights and self-image. Native anthropologists have made enormous contributions to outsiders' understanding of their own communities, including, to name but a few of the Americanists, Ella Deloria (a student of Franz Boas), Alfonso Ortiz, Bea Medicine, and Edward Dozier. While many native peoples characterize their groupings by the same criteria that non-native anthropologists have stressed – territorial integrity, kinship solidarity, linguistic cohesion, etc. – accounts of their communal lives often stress precisely the features essential to the paradigm offered here: reciprocity, levelling, moral equivalence, cross-boundary borrowing, etc. Thus while it may be hard to find tribesmen who have published a comparative theory of tribes as such, it is only because of their own enrichment of tribal values that it is possible for outsiders to attempt the consolidated view of tribes presented here.

It is, then, the argument of this book that the concept of tribe remains a useful one – descriptively, analytically, and (depending on one's viewpoint, of course) politically. The problem with the problem of tribe, it will be suggested, is that, for all the insights that have been produced, previous theories of tribes have significant limitations. As we will see, those that have been based on biological assumptions are either unfalsifiable or do not accord with all that is known, while those that focus entirely on the organizational structure of such groups cannot account for the variation in forms because structure itself is not the key feature of tribal organization.

To the contrary, the present study will argue for an alternative approach to tribes, one that emphasizes their capabilities rather than their momentary shapes. If one does not think about tribes as an evolutionary step, a restricted set of structural forms, or the crucible in which human nature, having once been cast, continues to determine our perceptions and relationships, a quite different way of envisioning tribes and their current import presents itself. For if we think of tribes as a family of socio-political entities it is not in their structural manifestations but in the capacities that allow them to adapt to varied circumstances that their distinctive features may be sought. Seen in this fashion tribes may be regarded as more like amoeba than crystals, entities whose shape-shifting abilities rather than settled architecture are vital to their nature and success. We will see this when we return to the Mashpee case, when we probe the ways in which tribes like the Moroccan ones sketched above respond to other tribes and the state in whose environs they operate, and when groups appear to be "retribalizing" in a modern world where their adaptive endowments may or may not prove advantageous.

Tribes are inherently fascinating. They challenge our ability to comprehend their qualities no less than to construct explanations of their trajectory. They may seem to possess the most tenuous of arrangements even as they have outlasted many states and empires; they may appear to cover a deep-seated anarchy while achieving a remarkable degree of orderliness; they may seem to bury the individual in the "stale cake of custom" only for the individual to be no less vital and creative than in any other societal arrangement; and they may appear to be as rigid as the rules of chess when, in fact, every move, every stratagem, every artful gesture or ritual reprise calls for a level of thought and execution whose success or failure ultimately depends on the resourceful acts of each participant.

The brief examples we have just seen, like those that will be mentioned throughout this study, demonstrate that, contrary to popular stereotypes, tribes are not, therefore, simply territorial, exclusionary, and pugnacious. Rather, their boundaries, both physical and cultural, are open-textured, their warfare routinely limited, and their genealogies frequently adapted to changing needs. A series of general features thus informs what might be called the "tribal ethos," among which are a deep ambivalence towards power coupled with a variety of ritual mechanisms by which individuals are cut down to size and the scope of their powers significantly limited. Whether through witchcraft accusations, strategic gossip, or didactic trickster stories, the sources of dominance in one sphere are not allowed to develop into permanent control over all other domains. In many cases, too, it is one's enemy who must ratify the choice of a momentary leader, as the adversary in one context is the necessary trade partner, supplier of mates, or martial ally in the next. Indeed, in this tribal ethos and its indispensable twin, an elaborated spirit of reciprocity, no individual is regarded as morally superior to any other, situation and circumstance being of far greater import than a system of ethical absolutes. Shifting the paradigm might also have some practical implications. If, given such features, we regard our own military personnel as bonded like tribesmen might the experience of actual tribes in reintegrating their warriors to peacetime society hold out lessons for us?[38] And without simply romanticizing them or ignoring counter examples, might the qualities of tribal orientations also hold lessons in how better to attend to our environmental concerns?

Such features do not mean that tribes are perfectly adapted or inherently democratic any more than that they are devious or unchanging. To the contrary, given their shape-shifting quality tribes, as the examples thus far given suggest, may reconfigure themselves through genealogical amnesia or invention, thus reinforcing their very adaptability. In other instances tribes may lose their language and religion yet retain collective identity and the features of a tribal ethos. In fact, these features may come to the fore and then recede, thus giving the impression, as in the Mashpee case, that the tribesmen have lost their identity altogether rather than having held it in reserve. And while some tribes may indeed be artifacts of state creation, in many other cases they are activated or recast, rather than conceived *ab initio*, through their interaction with larger political systems. In each instance tribes tend to be far less insular, excluding, and resistant to change than the picture outsiders may convey about them.

Nor is the image of tribalism that appears in our sporting arenas, movies, political discourse, business metaphors, and some academic theories simply benign. When extended into popular discourse the image of tribalism could be dismissed as a mere metaphor, a synonym for group solidarity that, notwithstanding overtones of separateness and intense rivalry, is really quite harmless. But when we see tribes as stumbling blocks to regional peace, representatives of divisive human instinct, hindrances to natural progression, or binding structural forms our stereotypes can have disastrous effects on a nation's choice of domestic policies and military engagements. Moreover, for the millions of tribal peoples living in over seventy countries around the world an uncritically accepted analogy may imply the inevitability of a progressive cultural sequence or that the arc of moral improvement will eventually transcend their allegedly antiquated mode of existence. The question of violence among prehistoric groups, for example, is vexed and contentious, and whether one can read back to the distant past or to more recent groupings for whom we lack written sources a history of bloodletting any approach to the issue of tribal violence demands the most serious scholarly precision. We need to keep in mind that when evolutionary psychologists, philosophers, or anthropologists characterize tribal peoples as violent they risk supplying to the malevolent a justification for the tribes' exploitation or suppression.[39]

Indeed, the denigration that arises from associating tribes with pre-modern or anti-state development has contributed significantly to our blinkered approach to tribes in key parts of the world. In Iraq, as we will see, where three-quarters of the population identify with one or another of some 150 tribes, American forces referred to tribal lands as "Indian country'" and for a number of years refused to seek them out in the belief that tribes were inconstant in their alliances and incompatible with modern democratic development. By characterizing the tribes as antithetical to nation-building the U.S. thus failed to recognize their larger role in the nation. It comes as a surprise to many, therefore, to learn that only after the tribes approached American forces in 2006-7, rather than because of the so-called military "surge," that a degree of momentary calm was achieved in Iraq.[40] In many other parts of the world – Brazil, for example – vilifying tribes as stumbling blocks to progress continues to be used as a basis for discrimination, forced integration, and the seizure of land, minerals, and medicinal resources. In each instance tribes, whatever scholarly analysis may yield, continue to play a critical role in the politics and self-view of those who interact with them.

We in the West are often disposed to call squabbling groups tribal, to think of them as insular, exclusionary, and pre-(or anti-)modern, the individual as submerged in the collective, and custom as stultifying repetition. The opposite is closer to the truth. Tribes commonly borrow from each other, claim no ethical superiority among their highly individualistic members, engage in ritual reversals and structured joking that ease stress, and possess numerous devices for dissipating what they see as the deleterious effects of concentrated power. We may extend the adverse images of tribes to any situation of exclusivity. But it is important to remember that however one sees metaphors – as efficient because they are "a shortcut to meaning," as disambiguating even though they are "knowledge existing in several states and without contradiction," or simply as convenient because "they are much easier to see than the real thing" – we should also keep firmly in mind that "metaphors are dangerous. They are not to be trifled with."[41] When we analogize our opponents' politics or the perceived inevitabilities of human nature and history as transcending a "tribal stage" we should, therefore, recall U.S. Supreme Court Justice Benjamin Cardozo's warning that "metaphors are to be narrowly watched, for starting as devices to liberate thought they end often by enslaving it."[42]

"History wasn't counting on our still being here," says the director of the Navajo Nation Museum. In order to survive, tribes have often had to draw on their ability to remold themselves. But shape-shifting is not a sign of weakness. Rather, it is a mode of awareness that one's social environs are susceptible to constant flux. Tribalism is a solution rather than a problem. Understanding what tribes were, what they are, and why they still matter is, therefore, a subject that continues to be worthy of our most thoughtful academic and political consideration, as well as our most serious humanitarian respect.

Notes

1 *Montoya v. United States*, 180 U.S. 261 (1901).
2 *Mashpee Tribe v. New Seabury Corp.*, 592 F.2d 575 (1st Cir. 1979).
3 For a fuller description of this example see, Clifford Geertz, Hildred Geertz, and Lawrence Rosen, *Meaning and Order in Moroccan Society*, New York: Cambridge University Press, 1979, pp. 53–57.
4 See, e.g., critics of the BBC/Discovery Channel series in which Bruce Parry visits a number of such groups. The series, filmed from 2005–2007 under the title "Tribe," was marketed in the United States as "Going Tribal." For the debate on the term 'tribe,' see the BBC radio broadcast of July 30, 2017. By contrast, see the TED talk by Seth Godin, "The Tribes We Lead," claiming that the internet has revitalized 'tribes' as common interest groups and agents of change. www.ted.com/talks/seth_godin_on_the_tribes_we_lead (accessed September 7, 2025).
5 The authors of the article, both on the staff of Harvard Medical School, felt compelled to then publish an abject apology for their use of the word. Batya Swfit Yasgur, "What an Editor Learned after a Journal Paper Was Deemed Insensitive," *Medscape*, July 7, 2021. www.medscape.com/viewarticle/954 358?form=fpf (accessed September 7, 2025). In the original publication the

authors had cited Rosabeth Moss Kanter's characterization: "Tribalism reflects strong ethnic or cultural identities that separate members of one group from another, making them loyal to people like them and suspicious of outsiders, which undermines efforts to forge common cause across groups." Rosabeth Moss Kanter, "Is Tribalism Inevitable?" *Huffpost*, July 26, 2013. www.huffpost.com/entry/is-tribalism-inevitable_b_3661436 (accessed September 7, 2025).

6 The quotes about Trump and Cruz come from *Time*, March 14, 2016, pp. 41 and 43; the final quote is from Roger Cohen, "The Know-Nothing Tide," *New York Times*, May 16, 2016.

7 The first reference is to Rep. Dana Rohrabacher (R. CA). The others are: Charles M. Blow, "A Nation Divided against Itself," *New York Times*, June 20, 2013; and Louis Menand, *New Yorker*, August 6, 2012. See also, "In My Tribe – Sports in America," *Sports Illustrated*, Nov. 28, 2011.

8 Peter Wehner, "What's the Matter with Republicans?" *New York Times*, September 30, 2019.

9 Robert P. George, "A Princeton Professor's Advice to Young Conservatives," *New York Times*, September 22, 2024.

10 Paul Krugman, "How the Republican Party Went Feral," *New York Times*, January 4, 2021.

11 David Clegg, "Tribal Politics Weighed on Scotland's Nicola Sturgeon," *Washington Post*, February 16, 2023.

12 Philip Carl Salzman, "Tribes and States," *Inference: International Review of Science*, vol. 2, no. 1 (February 9, 2016), p. 10; and his *Culture and Conflict in the Middle East*, Amherst, NY: Humanity Books, 2008. Elsewhere he writes: "The Middle East is a place where doing harm and being cruel to others is regarded as a virtue and a duty. Middle Easterners see their world as a zero-sum game in which there are winners and losers. They believe that others conspire to advance their own interests, so each must conspire to protect his own against the conspiracies of others. Middle Easterners see their political environment as a war of all against all, with only their closest friends as potential allies." Philip Carl Salzman, "The Middle East: Tribal Culture and Premodern States," *Middle East Forum*, January 17, 2020. He concludes: "Tribal culture was an ingenious human creation. Its time has passed." Philip Carl Salzman, "Tribes and States." Senator Graham's remark is from an interview of July 13, 2015: www.washingtonpost.com/postlv/politics/campaign-close-up-sen-lindsey

13 United Nations Development Programme, *Arab Human Development Report 2004*, p. 145. https://arab-hdr.org/wp-content/uploads/2004/12/ahdr-report_2004-en-full.pdf (accessed August 1, 2025). The report continues: "Clannism implants submission, parasitic dependence, and compliance in return for protection and benefits. More damagingly still, clannism is the enemy of personal independence, intellectual daring, and the flowering of a unique and authentic human entity. It blocks the energies that lead to growth and a mature, self-reliant intellect. It must do this to ensure its own smooth functioning and to guarantee its sway. The reproduction of this phenomenon across society turns it into an array of suffocating institutions that reward loyalty and discount performance. One is good so long as one's loyalty is guaranteed; it does not matter, naturally, if one's performance is poor; and woe betide clan members whose loyalty falters, however good their performance."

14 The "rule of clan" quote is from Mark S. Weiner, *The Rule of the Clan*, New York: Farrar, Strauss and Giroux, 2013, and his "The Paradox of Modern Individualism," *Cato Unbound*, March 10, 2014; the quote about "silos" is in Gillian Tett, *The Peril of Expertise and the Promise of Breaking Down*

Barriers, New York: Simon & Schuster, 2015; and the quote about "harnessing tribal nature" is in Arnold Kling, "Human Nature vs. Libertarian Ideals," *Cato Unbound*, March 12, 2014, www.cato-unbound.org/2014/03/12/arnold-kling/human-nature-vs-libertarian-ideals (accessed September 7, 2025).

15 Sharon Brous, "Two Lessons from an Ancient Text that Changed My Life," *New York Times*, January 19, 2024.

16 Edward O. Wilson, *The Meaning of Human Existence*, New York: Liveright, 2014. See also, his *The Social Conquest of Earth*, New York: Liveright, 2013. *Washington Post* columnist Michael Gerson is not the only one to employ Wilson's assumptions about human nature as it resulted from our evolutionary history when he writes that "tribalism is our default value - the 'our' here covering all *Homo sapiens*. The ability to quickly and intuitively distinguish 'us' from 'them' - likely someone from another tribe intent on taking resources or lives - was a tremendous evolutionary advantage on the plains of Africa." Michael Gerson, "Tribalism Triumphs in America," *Washington Post*, September 18, 2017. See also Amy Chua, *Political Tribes: Group Instinct and the Fate of Nations* (New York: Penguin, 2018) and my review of her book in Lawrence Rosen, "Are Our Politics Really 'Tribal'?" *The American Interest*, vol. 13, no. 6 (May 2018).

17 David Brooks, "I'm Normally a Mild Guy. Here's What's Pushed Me Over the Edge," *New York Times*, May 29, 2025.

18 Jonathan Haidt, "The Age of Outrage," *City Journal*, November 15, 2017, www.city-journal.org/html/age-outrage-15608.html (accessed September 7, 2025).

19 Kevin Carey, "College Sports, Enriched by Loyal Tribes of Suckers," *The Chronicle of Higher Education*, May 23, 2014, p. A48.

20 Joel Kotkin, "Rise of the Hans: Why a Dominant China Could Spark Tribal Warfare," *Foreign Policy*, January 17, 2011. Another columnist writes: "A know-nothing tide is upon us. Tribal politics, anchored in tribal media, has made knowing nothing a badge of honor." Roger Cohen, "The Know-Nothing Tide," *New York Times*, May 16, 2016. Kenan Malik writes: "The real problem is neither Muslim disloyalty nor rampant Islamophobia. It is, rather, the emergence of a tribalized society in which people have an increasingly narrow sense of belonging....[T]he consequences of tribalism can be devastating." Kenan Malik, "Britain's Dangerous New Tribalism," *New York Times*, July 10, 2015. See also, Anna Simons, "Getting Tribes: A Corrective," *The American Interest*, vol. 14, no. 1 (September 7, 2018).

21 On 'hidden tribes' see, "The Hidden Tribes of America," https://hiddentribes.us (accessed September 7, 2025).

22 "As Fissures Between Political Camps Grow, 'Tribalism' Emerges as The Word of 2017," Fresh Air Program, National Public Radio, December 6, 2017.

23 Richard Rodriguez, "Is the God of Jews, Christians and Muslims a Homophobe?" *Los Angeles Times*, June 15, 2016.

24 Peter Schwartz, "Introduction" to Ayn Rand, *Return of the Native: The Anti-Industrial Revolution*, New York: Plume, 1999, p. ix.

25 Quoted in Slavoj Žižek, *The Universal Exception*, London: Bloomsbury, 2006, p. 175.

26 The first quote is from Thomas L. Friedman, "Tilting the Playing Field," *New York Times*, May 30, 2004; his second, from "The American Civil War, Part II," *New York Times*, October 2, 2018, is repeated as "tribal mentality: rule or die" in his "Iran is Crushing Freedom One Country at a Time," *New York Times*, December 3, 2019, and the third comes from his "Tribes With Flags," *New York Times*, March 22, 2011. He repeats these themes again in "Have

We Reshaped Middle East Politics or Started to Mimic It?" *New York Times*, September 14, 2021. The first Friedman quote is also used word for word by Michael Walzer, "The New Tribalism," *Dissent*, Spring 1992, pp. 164–71, at 169. The David Brooks quote is from his "Are We On the Path to National Ruin?" *New York Times*, July 12, 2016. Brooks also writes: "Crude tribal dividing lines inevitably arouse a besieged, victimized us/them mentality. This mentality assumes that the relations between groups are zero sum and antagonistic. People with this mentality tolerate dishonesty, misogyny, and terrorism on their own side because all morality lays down before the tribal imperative." David Brooks, "The Danger of a Dominant Identity," *New York Times*, November 18, 2016. He repeats himself, after the start of the Israel-Hamas conflict, in "Scorn in the American Story," *New York Times*, October 14, 2021, when he says: "It feels as if we're teetering between universalist worldviews that recognize our common humanity and tribal worldviews in which others are just animals to be annihilated." David Brooks, "Searching for Humanity in the Middle East," *New York Times*, October 26, 2023. See also, Frank Bruni, "Our Tribalism Will Be the Death of Us," *New York Times*, January 27, 2022. Michael Gerson strikes a similarly inapposite characterization of actual tribes when he notes that "America is currently cursed, not only with tribal politics, but with tribal morality." Michael Gerson, "America is Cursed with Tribal Morality," *Washington Post*, November 27, 2017. Brooks, in particular, plays up the notion of tribalism's connection to authoritarianism: "Tribalism is in the air, on the left as well as on the right. It is based on a scarcity mentality, the idea that life is a zero-sum war between us and them. It emphasizes division and conflict, not solidarity and cohesion. It draws out the authoritarian tendencies in any movement." David Brooks, "The Future of the American Left," *New York Times*, May 3, 2018. See also, Michael Walzer, "The New Tribalism," *Dissent*, Spring 1992, pp. 164–71, at 171 ("The standard rule of intertribal relations is: do unto others what has been done to you."). David Brooks' fellow conservative and *National Review* editor Rich Lowry, however, takes a 'positive' view of tribalism, asserting that it is the basis for national sentiment and solidarity. See, Rich Lowry, *The Case for Nationalism: How It Made Us Powerful, United, and Free*, New York: Broadside Books, 2019.

27 Michael Gerson, "Trump Exposes the Hypocrisy of Christian Republicans," *Washington Post*, May 28, 2018. Similarly: "In recent years, however, happiness has been elusive for this dyspeptic nation, in which too many people think and act as tribes and define their happiness as some other tribe's unhappiness." George F. Will, "The Pursuit of Happiness is Happiness," *Washington Post*, September 14, 2021.

28 In Jeffrey Goldberg, *The Atlantic*, March 2016. Another columnist writes: "Following Trump's election Obama mused: 'Maybe people just want to fall back into their tribe'." Peter Baker, "How Trump's Election Shook Obama: 'What if We Were Wrong?'" *New York Times*, May 30, 2018. Again, during the coronavirus pandemic Obama said, apropos the Trump administration: "What we're fighting against is these long-term trends in which being selfish, being tribal, being divided, and seeing others as an enemy—that has become a stronger impulse in American life." Richard Hall, "'Selfish, Tribal and Divided'," *The Independent*, May 9, 2020. See also, Akbar Ahmed, Frankie Martin, and Amineh Ahmed Hoti, "Re-Tribalization in the 21st Century, Part 1," *Anthropology Today*, vol. 39, no. 5 (October 2023), pp. 3–6; and "Re-Tribalization in the 21st Century, Part 2," *Anthropology Today*, vol. 39, no. 6 (December 2023), pp. 6–10.

29 Jared Diamond (*Guns, Germs, and Steel: The Fates of Human Societies*, New York: W.W. Norton, 1997) as still relying on rejected anthropologists' evolutionism. A similarly simplistic view of societal evolution can be found in numerous popular works, such as Francis Fukuyama, *The Origins of Political Order: From Prehuman Times to the French Revolution*, New York: Farrar, Strauss and Giroux, 2011.
30 Morton H. Fried, *The Notion of Tribe*, Menlo Park, CA: Cummings Pub. Co., 1975; and his "On the Concepts of 'Tribe' and 'Tribal Society'," in June Helm, ed., *The Problem of Tribe*, pp. 3–20.
31 Elizabeth Colson, "Political Organization in Tribal Societies: A Cross-Cultural Comparison," *American Indian Quarterly*, vol. X (1986), pp. 5–20, at 5, and her "Contemporary Tribes and the Development of Nationalism," in June Helm, ed., *The Problem of Tribe*, pp. 201–6. See also Edmund Leach, "Tribal Ethnography: Past, Present, Future," in Elizabeth Tonkin, et al., eds., *History and Ethnicity*, London: Routledge, 1989, pp. 34–47; and Maurice Godelier, "The Concept of Tribe: Crisis of a Concept or Crisis of the Empirical Foundations of Anthropology?" *Diogenes*, vol. 21, issue 81 (1973), pp. 1–25.

Much the same was said about attempts at defining marriage: "I am left in the position of claiming that if we are not to condemn ourselves forever to the tautologies of functionalist explanations we must come to realize that marriage as an isolable phenomenon of study is a misleading illusion." Pierre Riviere, "Marriage: A Reassessment," in Rodney Needham, ed., *Rethinking Kinship and Marriage*, London: Tavistock, 1971, pp. 57–74; "So 'marriage,' too, is an odd-job word: very handy in all sorts of descriptive sentences, but worse than misleading in comparison and of no real use at all in analysis." Rodney Needham, "Remarks on the Analysis of Kinship and Marriage," 1971, pp. 1–34, at 7–8.
32 Charles Darwin, *The Descent of Man*: "As man advances in civilization, and small tribes are united into larger communities, the simplest reason would tell each individual that he ought to extend his social instincts and sympathies to all members of the same nation, though personally unknown to him. This point being once reached, there is only an artificial barrier to prevent his sympathies extending to the men of all nations and races." He continues:

"When two tribes of primeval man, living in the same country, came into competition, if the one tribe included...a greater number of courageous, sympathetic, and faithful members, who were always ready to warn each other of danger, to aid and defend each other, this tribe would without doubt succeed best and conquer the other.... A tribe possessing the above qualities in a high degree would spread and be victorious over other tribes; but in the course of time it would, judging from all past history, be in its turn overcome by some other and still more highly endowed tribe. Thus the social and moral qualities would tend slowly to advance and be diffused throughout the world.
See also, Freeman Dyson, "Biological and Cultural Evolution: Six Characters in Search of an Author," *Edge*, February 19, 2019."
33 June Helm, ed., *The Problem of Tribe*.
34 See, e.g., Peter J. Richerson and Robert J. Boyd, "The Evolution of Subjective Commitment to Groups: A Tribal Instincts Hypothesis," in Randolph M. Nesse, ed., *Evolution and the Capacity for Commitment*, New York: Russell Sage Foundation, 2001, pp. 186–220.
35 See generally, Werner Heisenberg, *Physics and Beyond: Encounters and Conversations*, New York: Harper & Row, 1971.

36 Patricia Crone, "Tribes and States in the Middle East," in her *From Arabian Tribes to Islamic Empire*, Aldershot, UK: Ashgate, 2008, p. 356.
37 Morton H. Fried, *The Evolution of Political Society*, New York: Random House, pp. 42–44. See also, Edmund Leach, "Tribal Ethnography: Past, Present, Future," in Elizabeth Tonkin, et al. (eds.), *History and Ethnicity*, London: Routledge, 1989, pp. 34–47. But see, Raymond Firth, "*Fiction and Fact in Ethnography*," 1989, pp. 48–52.
38 See the discussion in this regard at Chapter Three of this book.
39 Steven Pinker, *The Better Angels of Our Nature*, New York: Penguin, 2015; and Napoleon Chagnon, *Noble Savages*, New York: Simon and Schuster, 2013. For references to critiques of both authors, see Survival International, "The Myth of the 'Brutal Savage'," www.survivalinternational.org/articles/3289-brutal-savages (accessed September 8, 2025).
40 Lawrence Rosen, "Anthropological Assumptions and the Afghan War," *Anthropological Quarterly*, vol. 84, no. 2 (March/April 2011), pp. 535–58. These issues will be discussed in greater detail in Chapter Six on tribes and the military.
41 On metaphors, see, e.g., H. Allen Orr, "DNA: The Power of the Beautiful Experiment," *New York Review of Books*, July 9, 2016.
42 *Berkey v. 3d Ave. Ry Co.*, 244 N.Y. 84, 94 (1926).

2
ROMANCING THE TRIBE
History, Theory, Narrative

"A well-thought-out story doesn't need to resemble real life. Life itself tries with all its might to resemble a well-crafted story."
Isaac Babel

"Once we come to see that many of our best theories are idealizations, we will also see why our best chance of understanding the world must be to have a plurality of ways of thinking about it."
Kwame Anthony Appiah[1]

When it comes to studying the concept of tribe sometimes there is too little history, sometimes too much. There is too little, of course, because hardly any information, particularly of a written nature, is available from the thousands of tribes that have existed over thousands of years. Archaeology can help, but artifacts do not speak for themselves and, as we will see, the prehistoric dots are usually characterized and connected by one or another (often contradictory) theory, rather than being self-evident. Similarly, when it comes to thinking about tribes we may have too much history precisely because, myths and prejudices aside, we have had a wide range of competing theories over the years that claim to account for tribal structure, function, and evolutionary role. Indeed, the way the story is told may, as Isaac Babel suggests, be more a function of how we think the story must have played out than an inherently neutral set of facts. And, as Anthony Appiah suggests, while we may benefit from multiple theories that start with a rather idealized model we do not simply want to end with a disparate collection of stories.[2] To help sort out the various theories of tribe and analyze their implications it may, therefore, be useful to group them into several categories: those that focus on the tribes' place in the evolution of human social and psychological structure, those relating to organizational forms, and those that consider tribes in the light of history.

Tribal Evolution

The standard evolutionary story goes something like this:

When our species was in its infancy – perhaps when we still resided on the savannahs of Africa, certainly by the time we had spread across most of the globe – we lived in small-scale, close-knit groupings that, for a variety of reasons relating to our evolutionary history, local ecology, behavior of neighboring groups, and patterns of exchange, came together, fitfully or routinely, to accomplish purposes it was difficult or dangerous to achieve alone. Indeed, in this *long durée* of our species, when we lived in small clusters and made our living primarily as scavengers, foragers, hunter/gatherers, or fishermen, our brains are said to have taken on the form that has remained largely unchanged, with whatever dispositions may accompany that initial structure – a tendency to fashion tools that could also serve as weapons, appreciation of a mysterious handprint on the wall of a cave – to which we continue to remain heir.

But how were such groupings to be recruited and maintained? Kinship clearly had its merits, including the relative control over patterns of learning, maintenance of resources within the collectivity, and (assuming proximity and willingness) a reliable supply of necessary aid. The range of ways one can classify kin and arrange systems of descent are, of course, highly variable, but the general principles used in tracing such ties as well as in organizing tasks and relationships would have added a vital degree of regularity and predictability in a very uncertain world. One can even move beyond nearby kinfolk and resources by establishing alliances with other groups, exploiting marital ties and fictive kinship, forging strategic adoptions and pragmatic inheritance rules, and arranging trade, defense, and raiding to obtain that which is not available from one's immediate kin or locale. The pattern has ancient roots: "Fossil evidence shows that as far back as 130,000 years ago, it was not unusual for our ancestors to travel more than a hundred and fifty miles to trade, share food and, no doubt, to gossip and whinge [complain] about each other."[3] From this generalized evolutionary account several branching explanations now emerge.

One variant suggests that forms of organization constitute our species' mechanism for evolutionary adaptation in much the same way biological processes achieve the same purpose in plant and animal species. Thus, for individuals to group together with others – whether in more circumscribed or expansive arrangements – contributes to both personal and group survival. Indeed, if, as social animals, our modes of organization prevail only if they serve our collective success then the story of our form of life is one in which the arrangement of our ties to one another has been indispensable to our survival as a species. Here a plentiful supply of speculation abounds. The writings of Robin Fox, continuing a line of commenters running from Lewis Henry Morgan and Fredrich Engels to the present socio-biologists and some genetic determinists, encapsulates much of the approach of those who believe that our tribal disposition was formed during this early hominin development and continues to inform our behavior to the present. In Fox's own words:

> [H]uman nature is fundamentally tribal.... [W]e have not changed physically in any significant way since the end of the Paleolithic era in which we were formed. The tribal imagination then remains the default system...We do not lose anything in evolution, even if we do sometimes reduce it to a Whisper.... The tribalism I am interested in does not change; it exists in our heads, and we constantly reproduce it in our societies, whatever stage of development they have achieved.... We shall never be freed from the tribal imagination.[4]

For Fox, however, there was a 'radical break' that occurred in the 5th century BCE in Athens that did make possible "a society different in kind from the tribal." Nevertheless, he argues, the tribal keeps reappearing: "The 'perennial appeal of tribalism'...both to the masses and to the elites, is often overpowering. When things are looking bad for us, we cry out for a savior – a doctrine and a leader – to return us to the unthinking security of tribal society and the tribal mentality."[5] This claim takes on current political tones from such commenters as *The New Yorker*'s Adam Gopnik, who writes: "The default condition of humankind is not to thrive in broadly egalitarian and stable democratic arrangements that get unsettled only when something happens to unsettle them. The default condition of humankind, traced across thousands of years of history, is some sort of autocracy."[6]

But there are discrepancies in this interpretation of our evolutionary story. Fox is never precise in his usage of "tribe."[7] No less tellingly, (1) if the concept of tribal is to mean more than some generalized clustering there is no hard evidence to support the claim that humans are programmed to group together in some specifically "*tribal*" sense; (2) if (as will be argued here) tribes are not primarily organizational forms but characterized by distinctive cultural orientations, then much more is in need of specification than some simplified tribal "mentality" or "imagination", and (3) if this purported biological disposition once existed, its history might well be one of "relaxed evolution," in which a feature that no longer serves a function for the species as a whole is (to borrow Fox's own metaphor) so low a whisper as to be inaudible. Contrary to Fox's claim that traits never just vanish the evidence is clear that they do. As biologist David Lahti, reporting on a study supported by the National Evolutionary Synthesis Center, concludes: "All traits will eventually disappear if they have no function."[8] And to speak of the "unthinking security of tribal society" as if individuals were simple automata without the author offering some factual support is at best speculative and at worst disparaging. Indeed, merely attributing the necessary function of tribalism to some generalized solidarity is far too vague to support the claim of a tribal instinct. Moreover, Fox's own criterion for a reliable scientific claim (for which he relies, uncritically, on Karl Popper) is that it be falsifiable, a criterion neither he nor other proponents of this interpretation are capable of achieving.[9] Nevertheless, the notion that we have been "hard-wired" by evolution to be "tribal" has entered much of the contemporary (especially American) way of seeing the world.[10]

Corollaries to this evolutionary story abound. Epigenetics holds that phenotypic modifications can be inherited, such that a change may occur in the expression of a gene even if there is no alteration in the underlying DNA. So, for example, an individual who carries certain alleles may be more prone to depression if, in addition, he or she was subjected to abuse as a child. Similarly, anxiety, addiction, and fear conditioning may also be exacerbated if there is a baseline genetic propensity towards such expression. Clearly, this problematizes any strictly genetic conception of the self.[11] But to draw a line between any of these factors and the qualities of a distinctly *tribal* orientation – or any other specific social organizational form or process – is an extreme to which no one has, thus far, demonstrated an appropriate connection.

The idea of "dual inheritance," however, might be prone to just such an extension. Here, the idea is that culture and biology interact, such that learned behavior may produce adaptive benefits that in turn may alter the selection of genetically transmitted traits. Thus, as learned information is transferred from one individual to another, those who are better able to store and relate such information may have a selective advantage. Mechanisms analogous to those informing biological evolution – the disproportionately large effect one individual can have in a small population being akin to genetic drift, or random occurrences leading to substantive change appearing to mimic the process of mutation – may start from the cultural rather than the biological end of the feedback loop.

Critics of the dual inheritance theory, however, point out that accumulated cultural change occurs too rapidly to become adequately inscribed in genetics and that the actual mechanisms involved in cultural change and biological alteration are too dissimilar to be covered by simple analogies. For this theory to be truly persuasive one may, at the very least, have to show the creation of new neurological pathways which in turn can be inherited and – more to the present point – correlate with *specific* cultural or organizational features. Robert Paul's gloss on dual inheritance theory suggests that kin-based assistance and extra-kin cooperation – which he calls "tribal" – play a crucial role in the process of cultural change. But neither he nor others are able to point to mechanisms of "evolution" comparable to those in biology or – to reiterate the point that bears on the current undertaking – to establish a causal connection between *particular* adaptations and *particular* socio-cultural processes and resultant forms, like those of tribes. The outcome is an intriguing feed-back possibility for biology and culture but not a demonstration that the same biological promptings lead to specific cultural concepts or social forms.[12]

Social and cognitive accommodations are not the only aspects of human life that are said to have been involved in the evolutionary process. Various authors have suggested, for example, that religion developed as an adaptive device for group coherence and individual constraint, or that moral propositions have had organizational and leadership advantages over the course of human history.[13] Certainly the style of religions may vary with the social structure. As Marshall Sahlins amusingly noted:

> When we were pastoral nomads, the Lord was our shepherd. We were His flock, and He made us to lie down in green pastures, and led us beside the still waters. When we were serfs and nobles, the Lord was our king. Sat regnant on the throne of heaven, His shepherd's crock now a jeweled scepter… Finally we are businessmen – and the Lord is our accountant. He keeps a ledger on us all, enters there our good deeds in black and debits our sins in red. The Lord useth double-entry bookkeeping.[14]

That religious ideas should connect in some fashion with socio-cultural organization is an obvious truism: That the trajectory of development points in a given direction is, at best, speculative, and the idea that one can identify societies by simple indices of "complexity" is certainly debatable. After all, an aboriginal tribe in Australia may have a bounded technology but also possess a multi-section marital rule system that would cross the eyes of an untutored mathematician. Just as in other claims of cultural evolution neither the mechanisms nor the causal sequences are sufficiently clear to warrant the use of the concept of "evolution".

The allure of evolutionary theories in social life lies, in part, in the prospect of penetrating to the core of human nature, a quest that tempts many scientists notwithstanding David Hume's warning that: "Any hypothesis that pretends to discover the ultimate original qualities of human nature ought at first to be rejected as presumptuous and chimerical."[15] If "evolution" is equated with Darwinian "descent with modification" one may even be tempted, as William H. Durham is, to state: "I take *cultural evolution* to refer to the proposition that all human cultural systems are related by descent to a common ancestral culture."[16] Culture, seen from this approach, works not with "total plasticity" but is still so effective in transmitting useful knowledge that "if natural selection increasingly turned control, so to speak, over to culture, it was because culture, as a general rule, did a better job."[17] Once again, though, the cultural history this presumes is not merely speculative and the mechanisms unproven but the idea of a single starting point may owe more to our own style of creating origin myths than to demonstrable events. George Eliot, in her novel *Daniel Deronda*, understood this well: "Men can do nothing without the make-believe of a beginning. Even science, the strict measurer, is obliged to start with a make-believe unit.... No retrospect will take us to the true beginning; and whether our prologue be in heaven or on earth, it is but a fraction of that all-presupposing fact with which our story sets out."[18]

A related approach to the quest for essential human nature looks to particular qualities said to be inscribed in our deepest genetic makeup. Here, one of the enduring propositions about human beings concerns our reputed proclivity towards violence, with our species' evolutionary history and 'tribal' lives once again being synonymous with this presumed disposition. E. O. Wilson is only one of many who, in his words, has argued that: "Human nature has not changed. Modern groups are psychologically equivalent to the tribes of ancient history. As such, these groups are directly descended from the bands of primitive humans and prehumans.... Our bloody nature...is ingrained because group-versus-group was a principle driving force that made us what we are.... Research has shown that tribal aggressiveness goes well beyond Neolithic times."[19] The end product, he continues, is "an unstable mix of innate emotional responses...a mind that is continuously and kaleidoscopically shifting in mood – variously proud, aggressive, competitive, angry, vengeful, venal, treacherous, curious, adventurous, tribal, brave, humble, patriotic, empathetic and loving."[20] The brain development of early hominins, who are frequently portrayed as brutal hunters, is thus said to have settled the pattern to which we are the present heirs. William Golding's *Lord of the Flies* is the literary centerpiece of this presumption, while the infamous Robbers Cave psychological experiment purported to prove that stripped to its essence boys would group up and turn on opponents.

Columnist David Brooks again weighs in: "In my view, if you leave people naked and alone, they do what their evolutionary roots tell them to do, which is revert to tribe. And so they pick a bad form of community, which is tribalism."[21] In his speech accepting the Nobel Peace Prize President Barack Obama may have put this viewpoint most succinctly when he said: "War, in one form or another, appeared with the first man." Even those scholars who claim that biology alone is not destiny and that culture plays a role in the evolution of human behavior commonly start from this presumed developmental base.[22] It is here, especially as it concerns the question of inherent human violence, where there has been much dispute.

On one side stand those who insist that early hominins and later hunter/gathering and fishing cultures are not, in fact, nearly so violent as they are made out to be. To a growing number of investigators survival of a species is more often due to the development of friendliness and cooperation: Sheer aggressiveness, even in canines or bonobos, is less successful than working together.[23] A number of scientists also dispute the statistics and selectivity of the examples employed by those arguing for the innate violence of humankind.[24] Indeed, many scholars suggest that it is only with the rise of

FIGURE 2.1 Marooned schoolboys in the film *Lord of the Flies* (1963) becoming savage tribesmen.

agriculture and the concomitant protection of assets that warfare becomes prominent, while others point to the practices of relatively small-scale communities moving as necessary to avoid the violence and control of state structures (their own communities being comparatively peaceful), and still others argue that coercion through warfare is the hallmark not of tribes but of ranked chiefdoms.[25] To the extent that archaeology and historical records offer support it is their contention that violence is often ritualized, that it is comparatively limited, and that the tyranny of small numbers may make early societies appear more violent than would be true if we had more extensive data.

On the other side stand those who argue that the archaeological and ethnographic records show that prehistoric and contemporary small groups are rife with violence and that it is largely due to the Western history of viewing such societies as uncorrupted by the excesses of civilization that we often refuse to face this uncomfortable fact.[26] Some commenters point to fights over resources as the basis for this violent behavior. Others, most notably anthropologist Napoleon Chagnon, argue that violence among tribal groups has served primarily as a vehicle for gaining access to mates: "I am simply arguing that conflicts of reproductive interests occur commonly in band and tribal societies and that these often lead… to intergroup conflicts that we traditionally consider to be warfare."[27] Based on his work in the Amazon region, Chagnon thus claimed that 45% of the Yanomami tribesmen had engaged in at least one killing, and many on numerous occasions. But his statistics – and indeed his underlying methodology – have been repeatedly shown to be seriously flawed.[28] Nevertheless, other commenters have uncritically picked up on his conclusions. Steven Pinker, for example, argues that humans are far less violent now than when we lived in tribal groupings, but his claims only underscore how much interpretations in this realm depend on the reading of sparse examples and the story one brings to the enterprise.[29] Indeed, his assumption that behavioral psychology demonstrates, as no studies of human nature ever had before, that our present dispositions stem from their formation in prehistoric times is at best conjectural. As the British philosopher Mary Midgley, described as Britain's "foremost scourge of 'scientific pretension'," notes: "Pinker's method fails because we don't know any Stone Age sociology."[30] Similarly, Jared Diamond argues that our tribal predecessors lived in a state of constant warfare and have only become less ferocious with the advent of agriculture and the monopolization of violence by the state. Yet, once again, broad assertions based on singular examples that are themselves highly questionable pervade Diamond's work and render his conclusions untenable.[31]

One of the biases present in studies of human violence is the lack of equal consideration of its opposite, namely peacemaking. Sir Henry Maine could assert that "War is as old as mankind, but peace is a new invention."[32] However, neither he nor others of similar persuasion offer convincing evidence in support of that claim. Warfare, as more recent studies have shown, tends to be more costly than the benefits gained, stimulates the development of complex institutions only when combined with peacemaking, and may be of value to some individual warriors but not to society as a whole.[33] As Douglas Fry notes: "Individuals and social groups across cultural contexts go to great lengths to avoid and minimize violence."[34] Numerous examples can, in the words of one analyst, be drawn from "New Guinea, northwest coast societies, the Andamans, and East Africa of successful replacement of enmity with friendship involving the acceptance of liability, apology, and joint mourning, followed by singing, dancing, small feasts, and gift exchange.... In many exogamous societies, marriages were contracted after warfare with enemy groups to rebuild ties for future trade and exchange."[35] Indeed, among the tribes of the Amazon enemies are generally referred to as potential affines. Thus while revenge is the category into which many Westerners place inter-tribal warfare it may be better to think of such matters as ones of perceived balance that needs to be restored. That may better explain what some tribesmen in Southwest Asia mean when they say, "I took my revenge after a hundred years – and I took it too soon." That sense of a world that needs to be brought back into balance may also inform the hostile encounters with European invaders. Bernard Bailyn, referring to the early colonial period in Virginia, thus notes that for the Indians:

> The fear was not simply that they might face brutal attacks but, in a deeper sense, that the equilibrium of their lives would be permanently upset, subject to shattering disturbances. Their response was not only to defend themselves but to retaliate in ways that would restore the balance of their lives. They would return violence for violence, but they did not need or seek the annihilation of their enemies. Their wars were rarely genocidal. What they fought for, however savagely and cruelly, was the restoration of the equilibrium of forces, human and spiritual, that formed the inner stability of their world.[36]

Since arguments about violence in hunter-gatherer/tribal societies often rely on the evidence derived from recent excavations one might think that the archaeologists could solve many of the issues concerning human aggression and cultural evolution. But, not surprisingly, they, too, do not all see eye-to-eye, notwithstanding some marked alterations in recent years in the discipline's broader consensus. Proponents of human cultural evolution place a good deal of reliance on the questionable claims of those archaeologists who interpret the remains they have discovered as furthering the idea of innate violence among small-scale societies. So, for example, we are told that the 10,000-year-old remains of twenty-seven individuals at Nataruk, Kenya demonstrate that massacres occurred early in our species' development.[37] As one of the investigators put it: "I've no doubt it is in our biology to be aggressive and lethal, just as it is to be deeply caring and loving." But others interpret the evidence differently. Thus, at a comparable prehistoric site in Japan archaeologists found that over a span of many centuries the rate of violent death was very low indeed.[38] Because such archaeological sites are few in number, because it may matter if one is dealing with a tribe or a hereditary chiefdom when such distinction is almost impossible to determine from material items, because forensic analyses of the human remains are subject to a good deal of speculative interpretation, and because commenters often mix examples of societies that may be taken to represent enormously different levels of complexity (possessing no shared concept of "complexity" in the first place), such claims about rates of violence risk being suffused with prior assumptions about tribal peoples and their purported representation of innate human qualities.[39] Indeed, if one is going to speak of violence, killing is not the only index: intimidation, enslavement, etc. would at least have to be included. Moreover, as has been noted, the archaeological record is often not read as indicating the extent and nature of peacemaking as opposed to violence.[40] When linked to claims that animal studies reveal humankind's essentially violent nature the projections from prehistory, by their denial of how varied our ancestors were and how much they continued to change over the course of thousands of years, are indeed deserving of Marlene Zuk's characterization of such claims as "Palaeofantasy."[41] That warfare and ritual violence were present among many indigenous peoples is hardly surprising.[42] That it should be taken as proof of human nature, as a definitive statement about the relation of violence to levels of cultural development, or be used as a basis for justifying claims of superiority and rights of control over others' lives and resources is to take the data far beyond their carrying capacity. And linking isolated examples to an evolutionary theory is less about science than about the uses of the past to support the story of ourselves we imagine to be true about ourselves.[43]

Whether it concerns human violence, economic advancement, or organizational complexity, the justifying typology of evolutionary stages formerly used by many archaeologists has, in fact, largely given way to a more processual approach. The earlier sharp division between one 'evolutionary level' and the next has yielded to a much more nuanced picture, one in which many societies exhibit a mixture of traits that were previously assigned to quite separate stages. Many archaeological sites now appear to expose not categorical shifts but long-term, intermingled, and very gradual alterations. Thus diverse groups – such as those living on the Great Plains of North America and in the Cherokee villages of the 18th century – could, at different times of the year, coalesce and disperse in such a way as to be more like familial bands at one moment and more like tribes (in the older taxonomic scheme) at another, rather than representing just one structural form at all times.[44]

Any simple equation of tribal with nomadic or hunter-gathering is also misplaced: Not only have most tribes been agricultural for centuries but many have shifted their economic base over time with relatively little strain.[45] Similarly, the evidence continues to mount suggesting that sharp breaks – such as the purported "Agricultural Revolution" of the Neolithic period – were actually neither unidirectional nor did they obliterate many of the features that characterized those societies that gradually shifted, say, from nomadism to cultivation and domestication. Indeed, there was a period of at least four thousand years between the time many plants were domesticated and the appearance of villages, thus indicating that sedentarism was not – at least initially – the preferred settlement pattern even for agriculturalists.[46] It also now appears that there was no sharp break that placed egalitarianism and Rousseauian peace on one side of the divide and private property and warfare on the other.[47] As we will see in greater detail later, human history appears not as a series of all-encompassing, sharply bounded steps but a sliding scale of back-and-forth forms and processes, one in which an elaborating repertoire rather than a restricting vocabulary may best describe the course of change.[48]

Theories of cultural evolution that seek to penetrate to the core of human nature are, of course, not the only goal of such models. Indeed, for many analysts the mainstream evolutionary story of tribes continues by suggesting that over time it is the organizational forms they represent that is crucial. Human social, political, and economic organization, in this view, has become more elaborated and more adapted to changing circumstances even if, in their general design, they exhibit a significant range of variability. So, while there is no necessary reason why tribes must take on a particular organizational shape the ways in which they have, in any local variant, actually come to do so is seen, especially for those who pay special attention to issues of ecology, as the result of a close interaction between how they work their environments and how they organize their relationships. For example, Cheyenne social organization is said to have tracked the habits of the buffalo, a key source of sustenance, through the dispersal of settlements during part of the year, collecting the separated families when the scattered animals also gather, and organizing, through cross-cutting affiliations, a style of hunting that insured no one violated the collective interest by favoring his own localized band. This was not simply a political or ecological "solution": Kinship, ritual, and cosmology all connected in this pattern. From an evolutionist's perspective this represents either an example of a group that is staged between a less complex form of organization (an extended family or band) and a more complex form (such as a hereditary, ranked chieftainship) or as a particular adaptation that nevertheless represents a social or technological advance over a prior arrangement. Either way, the emphasis is on the process by which humans have come to group together and (as we will see in a later chapter) the key role that patterns of reciprocity were said to have played in that process.

For many scholars tribal organization is thus envisioned as interacting with, rather than simply resulting from, a particular environmental context. However, some anthropologists have seen the relation of biology, environment, and society in much more directional and causal terms. Julian Steward, for instance, argued that the unilinear cultural evolution espoused (as we shall see in a moment) by Leslie White was wrong to claim that its laws are universal and that cultural evolution has operated through set stages of development. To Steward the environment sets limits and possibilities for societies, and though less complex groups are more susceptible to its parameters there is no singular path every group must follow. But Steward's own emphasis on certain 'core' features as more important for development remained imprecise, and his claims of causation based on a few comparisons did little to further understanding of the different levels of integration of cultural features to which he laid claim.[49]

There were also those anthropologists within the discipline's culture and personality movement who found attractive Freud's theory that as humans gave up their natural instincts for civilization, the moral dilemma of being both prey and hunter led to the neurosis, repression, and perpetual psychic ambivalence that accompanies a more complex society. Yet with no way of proving this historical claim or the psychic "deficiencies" of still extant tribals the theory, like the use of anthropology to establish broad patterns of our species' psychological course, largely passed from the mainstream of the discipline.

It was, in part, as a reaction against such unilineal and psychological theories of cultural evolution that many anthropologists by the mid-20th century sought other ways of reconciling cultural and biological evolution. The British had largely rejected any such consideration, fearful that such speculative history would lead down the slippery slope to social

Darwinism and Whigish visions of the progress of civilization.[50] In the United States the intellectual history of the discipline stemmed from other roots. Franz Boas, the forefather of American anthropology, was deeply opposed to theories about the grand sweep of history, cultural evolution included, favoring instead the particularistic histories of individual cultures. Indeed, his fear that evolutionary theories necessarily lead to claims of greater and lesser superiority of cultures informed both his academic opposition to race-based explanations of human history and his political opposition to policies based on such claims.[51] It took another half century before other American anthropologists sought a way to conceive of cultural evolution without directional progress. In addition to its intellectual content, this development was, to a significant degree, prompted by – or at least found compatibility with – the political views of those proclaiming it.

The attempt to reintroduce evolution to cultural studies as a variant of the 19th century theory was centered primarily around Leslie White and his students at the University of Michigan in the early 1960s. White argued that as societies gain ever more control of energy resources they become more structurally differentiated and functionally specific.[52] Deeply affected by his trip to the Soviet Union in 1929, White came to favor a materialist view of human history, one in which "the technological factor, exercised and expressed in the tools and processes of subsistence, protection from the elements, and defense from enemies determines the social system."[53] Like Karl Marx, Friedrich Engels, and anthropologist Lewis Henry Morgan before him, White argued that cultural features – including art, religion, morality, and philosophy – were a function of the material base, culture itself being "an organization of energy transformations" such that "a culture is high or low depending upon the amount of energy harnessed per capita per year."[54] Rejecting the importance of environment in favor of technology, White's approach has continued to be cited favorably by those, like Jared Diamond, who place far more emphasis on environment than was the case for White himself.

It is true that White and many of his followers were, throughout the cold war period in the United States, the subjects of surveillance by J. Edgar Hoover's Federal Bureau of Investigation.[55] And it is true that he and most of his students were well to the left on the American political spectrum. Though not unaffected by their political views, the theoretical orientation of the Michigan cultural evolutionists was, however, not simply a function of their personal politics. It was largely on intellectual grounds that Marshall Sahlins and Elman Service thus distinguished between what they called specific and general evolution. General evolution, they said, involves increased complexity, organization, and technological sophistication; specific evolution involves different modes of integrating these factors. The former can imply a straight-line set of steps through which all advanced cultures pass (the famous *band→ tribe→ chiefdom→ state* progression), while the latter suggests that the developmental line of any particular society might differ from that of another in its course, speed, and result. Thus, for one society the progression may pass through each of a series of stages; for another, those steps may be jumbled, reversed, or skipped. Regardless, from this perspective, they argued, what is crucial to any case of cultural evolution, whether general or specific, is the presence of greater structural complexity and greater functional specificity.

The new cultural evolutionists, like their mentor Leslie White, even proposed certain "laws." For example, Elman Service, following Leon Trotsky rather than Karl Marx, argued that in some instances a society may give evidence of a "privilege of backwardness."[56] According to this "law," ancient Egypt, for example, was unable to progress because of a stultified bureaucracy and an arcane writing system few were allowed to master, whereas another society could leap over that stage of development by utilizing a simpler and more accessible system of communication and a more flexible and adaptable system of government. (In Trotsky's case, this meant one could skip over socialism and go straight from capitalism to communism.) In each instance, following Leslie White, it was argued that it is the capture of greater sources of energy that is substantially responsible for propelling whatever distinctive alterations occur. For White and his followers, each societal development was called an instance of cultural *evolution* and not mere change or alteration because the adaptations were said to be advantageous to collective success, to say nothing of individual survival.

Critics of this form of evolutionism have pointed to a number of shortcomings in the theory: that there is no scientific relationship between the capture of energy and the size or complexity of a culture, that one form of organization cannot be unmistakably marked as more "efficient" than any other, that adaptation does not necessarily lead to stability, and (the concept of specific evolution notwithstanding) individual societies seldom are as bounded and distinct as the theory demands. White's knowledge of biological evolution was also limited. His major book, *The Evolution of Culture*, makes no mention of radiocarbon dating – discovered in 1949, the same year White's book was published – or of Watson and Crick's discovery of DNA and the double helix in 1953, which, like newly discovered dating techniques, was not even mentioned in the 1959 edition of White's book. Nor is there mention of the discoveries of the Australopithecines' ability to make and use tools, which radiocarbon dating was beginning to establish in the early 1950s. Thus White and others involved in the debate over cultural and social evolution were operating with a very incomplete idea of the mechanisms of biological evolution and were, like others of the day and notwithstanding their scientific presentation, rendering their positions in terms of unprovable generalizations rather than replicable procedures. Morton Fried's version of cultural evolution – that tribes only come into existence in the face of state structures and his use of a typology based on singular features, limited archaeological data, and in direct contradiction of information showing tribes to exist without the development or impact of states – though flawed, did draw attention to the role of the state in many tribes' histories.[57] But as the overall deficiencies of each form of cultural evolutionary theory emerged, attachment to the Michigan school's evolutionism, in particular, soon waned. Indeed, almost all of White's followers eventually abandoned the theory altogether – Sahlins quipping that his own thinking 'had evolved' – and cultural anthropologists at large lost interest in the subject as it failed to generate new insights.[58]

Undoubtedly the evolutionary model of tribalism has yielded valuable understandings: that social and political forms are part of our species' adaptive toolkit, that our ability to conceptualize abstractly and communicate complex propositions constitutes a selective advantage, and that cultural variations keep alive the capacity to adapt to changing conditions. At the same time this model has serious flaws. It may be too much to say, with biologist Stephen Janes, that: "Evolution is to the social sciences as statues to pigeons – a convenient place to deposit ill-digested ideas." But it is nevertheless true that, unlike biologists, the cultural evolutionists have not succeeded in going beyond correlational conjectures to demonstrate conclusively the mechanisms by which such evolution is said to take place. Moreover, the evolutionists and neo-evolutionists would have been closer to the mark had they stressed the keystone of their own theory, namely variation. For tribal forms, as we will see, are rich in their capacity to display variation and to exploit the advantages of essential ambivalence.

Cultural evolutionists and socio-biologists have, notwithstanding the risk of inappropriate anthropomorphism, also suggested that genetic similarities to other primates account for the course of our species' social trajectory. But genetic overlap is hardly persuasive. After all, we share 98.4% of our genetic code with gorillas, but that small difference is enough for them to be in the zoo and us outside.[59] (We even share 26% of our genes with yeast, 18% with certain weeds, and nearly half with fungi – which may explain a lot about faculty meetings!) To take only one of the biologically-based claims about the evolution of culture: The evidence shows that "the prevalence across mammalian species of displays, instead of contact aggression and ritualized tournaments [or] 'total war,' suggest that restraint is a more successful evolutionary strategy than engaging in unbridled aggression."[60] Population growth, control over greater amounts of energy, elaborated divisions of labor, or increased levels of immunity to various pathogens may certainly play a key role in survival. But when posed as the precise mechanisms through which cultures evolve these ostensible processes are hardly equivalent to natural selection, mutation, genetic drift, or genetic flow – much less a detailed accounting of DNA – through which biological evolution takes place. For those who argue that cultures are subject to evolutionary forces the fact that culture involves passing on knowledge acquired by one generation to the next shows that Lamarck's discredited biological theory that acquired traits can be inherited is, at least metaphorically, actually much closer to being the rule in the domain of culture. Others, like Daniel Dennett, may argue that the transmission of information ("memes," in Richard Dawkins' terminology) are selected for in much the same way as biological traits and become incorporated into our neurological system.[61] But, once again, any demonstration that the parallel to biological evolution is anything more than metaphoric remains unsubstantiated.[62]

It is not, of course, necessary to specify precise evolutionary mechanisms in order to pinpoint crucial evolutionary processes: Though living at the same time, Darwin knew nothing of Gregor Mendel's breakthrough study of plant genetics, yet he discovered key aspects of the process of species evolution. Nevertheless one may still ask: (a) why assume that our subsequent evolution ("punctuated" or of long gestation) has not produced patterns that supersede those of our "tribal instincts"; (b) why assume that a particular form of organization (the tribal) is the mold in which our psyche was cast when smaller groupings, like families and bands, or larger non-segmented structures whose deep history we know practically nothing about, could as well be the generative social form; and (c) why have we been unable to specify the operative mechanisms if what is at work is actual *evolution* and not simply change, variation, development, or alteration? To say that cultural evolution means advancing "along a trajectory of increasing complexity" begs the question. Yet somehow, we seem to suppose, since evolution is well-established in the scientific community, that the evolution of cultures *must* be true in some fashion given that we are evolved animals and culture is an integral part of who we are.[63] But without further specification it is also indisputable that the cultural evolutionists have not – or at least not yet – made their case. Notwithstanding the advances that may be attributed to the efforts of these scholars, we cannot rely on the present state of this set of theories to say that we possess some 'tribal instinct,' that tribes are stages in the development of complexity rather than clusters of features that do not have sharply defined boundaries, or that the material or geographical base is the most important among the factors that contribute to that array of characteristics.

And so we have to look elsewhere for additional guidance.

Social and Political Organization

If the stories about the evolution of human cultures often betray an eagerness to attach themselves to the scientifically accepted version of biological evolution, the stories about how tribes are put together and operate draw their source of professed legitimacy from – and have greatly contributed to that source itself – the recognition that all societies, whatever their level of complexity, are orderly. That simple proposition may seem unexceptionable, but it was not always regarded as so. Indeed, it is to the everlasting credit of scholars like Lewis Henry Morgan, who in 1871 showed that a tribe is "a completely organized society," and the structural-functional anthropologists of the first half of the 20th century, who showed that so-called "primitive" or "savage" peoples are not examples of Hobbesian chaos or childlike behavior, and that we have been able to move away from visions that were often in service of colonial or commercial domination of tribal lands and lives.[64] Indeed, in the process of establishing that all societies possess some order the studies of tribal peoples raised questions about the place of kinship, territory, language, and authority in tribal life, each of which warrants closer attention.

Kinship and Tribal Organization

Kinship has always been at the heart of the matter for anthropologists studying tribes. Not only was kinship a core feature of the definitions of tribe for most of the discipline's history but it was the concentration on kinship systems that ultimately created a problem. When we were Americanists and Africanists we found informants who gave us genealogies that could be readily transformed into diagrams showing descent in one line or another (or, like "ourselves," in both lines). But as more examples from more diverse places were gathered "exceptions" to behavior being ordered by descent and filiation could not simply be set aside as occasional glitches or kinks.[65] Two studies were especially important in this respect.

In 1954, Edmund Leach published *Political Systems of Highland Burma*. In it he argued that the hill people he was studying could switch back and forth between two systems of identification and affiliation, one quite egalitarian and one hierarchical. Indeed, he argued that both were themselves ideals that individuals could choose to model themselves after, for different purposes and at different times, rather than set structures. This, as the British would say, threw a spanner in the works of structural-functional anthropology: It suggested not only that multiple choices were available within a single culture and that the symbols and meanings of relationship were more malleable and important than ostensible structures, but that context and individual choice rather than strict rules of relationship were crucial to the system. While Leach and others used the term "tribe" to characterize the people of upland Southeast Asia, his use of the term, rather than that of "peasants" or some other category, was consistent with the nomenclature of the day, even though it was of questionable pertinence. Nevertheless, Leach did focus attention on identity and political structure and demonstrated that kinship was open to manipulation as circumstances varied.[66]

Only five years later – though with no reference to Leach – Fredrik Barth published *Political Leadership among Swat Pathan*. He, too, placed the decisions of individuals at the forefront of understanding Pakistani tribalism. Stressing that there is great "freedom of choice," that allegiance should be viewed "not as something which is given to groups, but as something that is bartered between individuals," that "most statuses and rights are usually defined by contractual agreements," and that "group commitments may be assumed and shed at will," Barth switched the focus from structures as determinative to a view in which relationships are "systematically manipulated to build up positions of authority, and the variety of politically corporate groups which result."[67] As Leach had indicated for the Burmese, kinship, too, became an instrument to be differentially applied, not a rigid set of rules governing all relationships.[68] Although neither author denied that there were expressed norms of kinship in each society, both implied that such norms constitute a tool rather than a straitjacket and are, therefore, of a piece with the more dynamic picture of the groups involved than previous modes of analysis embraced.

With the way now open to a more processual view of kinship and social organization other anthropologists stepped in. A number of students of North American native cultures emphasized the importance of personal decision-making, as when Robert F. Spencer noted that "aboriginal society consisted of aggregates of individuals that formed bands and villages. Membership and residence in either depended pretty much on the choice of the individual; the size of the group could expand or contract depending on local circumstances."[69] Just as the centrality of kinship to the definition of a tribe became strained when more examples were added to the literature, so, too, many ethnographers had noted the use of fictive kinship as a device for extending and even relativizing the image of kinship as a (if not *the*) governing principle of tribal societies. Writing about native Greenlanders, Mark Nuttal says: "[P]eople can deactivate kinship relationships if they regard them as unsatisfactory....[They] can choose much of their universe of kinship....While the flexibility of the kinship system allows individuals to choose who they want to have as relatives (or who they do not wish to have as a relative), it does not give them license to decide how they should behave with that person."[70]

> Whatever is construed genealogically may also be constructed socially. One may be kin to another by being born on the same day (Inuit), by following the same tabus (Araweté), by surviving a trial at sea (Truk), or on the ice (Inuit), even by mutually suffering from ringworm (Kaluli). For the New Guineans of the Nebilyer Valley kinship is produced by the transmission of *kopong*, 'grease' or 'fat,' found in father's semen, mother's milk, or by food-sharing, commensality, or eating from the same land. In this way, the children or grandchildren of immigrants may be fully integrated as kinfolk. On the Alaska North Slope, the Iñupiat will name children and sometimes adults after dead persons, never the birth parents. Kinship statuses are not set by the begetters of persons but by their namers. Indeed, it is the child who chooses the characteristics of birth, including where he or she will be born and of what sex.
>
> Marshall Sahlins, *What Kinship Is – And Is Not*,
> Chicago: University of Chicago Press, 2013, pp. 2, 68, 5–6, 4–5

Ibn Khaldun, discussing Arab genealogies in the 14th century, had long since pointed to the manipulation of descent when he argued that *nasab* (kinship, linage, genealogy) "is a fictitious matter, it has no truth... its function is association and solidification" of identity.[71] Much later, E. E. Evans-Pritchard could note of the Nuer's open-ended structure that outsider "persons of Dinka [tribal] descent form probably at least half the population of most [Nuer] tribes," while Marshall Sahlins could state that kinship is often the idiom in which tribesmen construct their political and economic arrangements, thus exemplifying "the general propensity of tribal peoples to cloak alliances of convenience in kinship garb."[72] Indeed, Sahlins underscored that in many tribes " 'descent'...is a political ideology and not a mere rule of personal affiliation," that "in specific cases the constraints of a mode of descent may be buried and covered over, [thus being] proved no match for countervailing circumstances," and that rather than "a direct recognition of existing practices...a descent dogma...is quite capable of reinterpreting contradictions of membership in its own terms."[73]

> Elaborate genealogies are, in this respect, a vast portfolio of possible connections, most of which remain in the shadows but could, if necessary,

> be summoned. The more turbulent the social environment, the more frequently groups fission and recombine, the greater the likelihood that more of the portfolio of shadow ancestors will come into play. The Berbers are said to be able to construct a genealogical warrant for virtually any alliance of convenience necessary to politics, grazing rights, or war.
>
> James C. Scott, *The Art of Not Being Governed: An Anarchist History of Upland Southeast Asia*, Yale University Press, 2009, p. 233

A number of other ethnographers joined their findings and interpretations to a more processual view of kinship. Roy Wagner, in his studies of the Daribi tribesmen of New Guinea, followed Evans-Pritchard in referring to kinship as an "idiom" rather than a "principle," such attachments constituting "the ideological expression, or idiom, of normative patriliny."[74] Modes of alliance, he argued, remain more constant than incidental assemblages, kinship being only one dimension of group creation. Roger Keesing, working out from his study of Malaita in the Solomon Islands, joined a number of others in arguing that the focus should shift to "action groups, not merely jural categories like 'descent groups'."[75] J. van Velsen and others associated with the Manchester School of anthropology and African studies, arguing that relationships were situational rather than strictly determined by kinship rules, could, therefore, say that "the norms of society do not constitute a consistent and coherent whole. On the contrary, they are often vaguely formulated and discrepant. It is this fact which allows for their manipulation by members of a society in furthering their own aims, without necessarily impairing its apparently enduring structure of social relations. Situational analysis therefore lays stress on the study of norms in conflict."[76] Morality and individual choice thus gained particular attention. Clyde Kluckhohn, for example, wrote that "Navaho morality is ... contextual rather than absolute," a position supported by Marshall Sahlins who indicated that, "In the tribal framework, a given act is not in and of itself good or bad whomever it might concern; it depends on exactly whom it does concern."[77] Other examples joined the literature. David Schneider and John Roberts could argue, apropos a southwestern American Indian tribe: "Basic in Zuni integration, then, is the individual as the nexus of a pattern of relationships and not monolithic corporate descent groups balanced against one another."[78] Indeed, as Harold Scheffler suggested, "unilineal descent groups (or lineages and clans) [are not necessarily] groups by virtue of their descent ideologies."[79] And as anthropologists began to follow tribesmen to the cities a number of them began to apply network analysis, having found that tracing kinship and focusing on traditional social structure was inadequate for understanding the urban experience.[80]

Increasingly, then, anthropologists started to see the relation of choice and descent to broader ecological and political factors. Daniel Gross, for example, argued that the seasonal movement from villages to nomadic foraging groups among many central Brazilian groups indicates that they possess two distinct social structures applicable at different times of the year.[81] Fred Gearing, who made a similar argument for the Cherokee, concluded: "In a word, a human community does not have a single social structure; it has several."[82] Others, noting that norms are often in conflict, argued for a "situational analysis" of social relations.[83] And while the ostensible rules of marriage figured greatly in structural-functional accounts, anthropologists increasingly concluded, as did Dean Snow from his study of the Penobscot, that "dynamic group membership turnover is typical of tribal societies. While some tribes might successfully maintain strict rules of endogamy, most do not."[84] Similarly, James Woodburn says of the Hadza of Tanzania: "Social groupings are flexible and constantly changing in composition. Individuals have a choice of whom they associate with in residence, in the food quest, in trade and exchange, in ritual contexts. People are not dependent on *specific* other people for access to basic requirements. Relationships between people, whether relationships of kinship or other relationships, stress sharing and mutuality but do not involve long-term binding commitments and dependencies."[85] And somewhat along the same lines, Gary Witherspoon could say of the Navajo: "[T]he relationship between two particular kinsmen is not fixed and changes with time and context, for most relationships are constantly being defined and redefined ... according to the ebb and flow of social life."[86]

Clearly the range of variation in the structuring and import of kinship among the world's tribes is very wide indeed: It is undeniable that clan membership (as among many North American tribes) can be strictly determined by descent, and that incest taboos and marital restrictions may remain extremely strong. But even within such groupings the range of personal maneuver is far from confined and apparent boundaries are far more flexible than early anthropological studies tended to assume. The result of modern kinship studies has not been to deny the importance of kinship in tribal groupings but to open up kinship as allowing choice, strategic application, and alternative mechanisms of association.

Within Bounds? Territory and Language

Territorial distinctiveness has long constituted a second leg for the way tribes are characterized. Indeed, the broader question of the boundedness of cultures has been the subject of debate in anthropological theory for well over a century. To Franz Boas and his students tribes lived within highly porous borders such that maps needed to show multiple domains for diverse uses rather than sharply delineated boundaries. Robert Lowie underscored the point: "In defiance of the dogma that any one culture forms a closed system, we must insist that such a culture is invariably an artificial unit segregated for purposes of expediency." Similarly, Alfred Kroeber, whose culture-area concept was envisioned as clusters rather than exclusion zones, spoke of any one area as invariably "integrated" with elements of other cultures.[87] Edmund Leach, too, had concluded his Burmese study by arguing that "it is largely an academic fiction to suppose that in a 'normal' ethnographic situation one ordinarily finds distinct 'tribes' distributed about the map in orderly fashion with clear-cut boundaries between them."[88] As Ira Bashkow notes: "Drawn lines appear to block things from passing across them, and they appear to create discrete domains, when in reality, cultural boundaries are less like barriers than they are like thresholds or frontiers that mark the movement across them and even create the motivation for relationships with what lies beyond."[89] Indeed, tribesmen clearly value objects from distant areas, whether it is the mountain Arapesh studied by Margaret Mead who prize material goods from lowland areas of New Guinea or North American tribesmen who were only too eager to trade with newly arrived Europeans. In Akbar Ahmed's concise summation: "Tribes cross borders all the time."

Moreover, Westerners, having equated territory with cultural and political distinctiveness, often placed indigenous peoples in a double-bind: On the one hand the tribes had to demonstrate possession of a distinct domain and, on the other, having had their land taken from them by the colonizing power, they were unable to show that they did have dominion over such land. This became a particular problem, for example, in the Mashpee case referred to earlier when the court set aside the issue of land to focus on proof of continued existence as a legally cognizable tribe, thereby depriving the plaintiffs of the opportunity to show what lands they controlled in favor of a much vaguer concept of cultural continuity. Unable to make the argument about such land ownership they were handicapped in utilizing the court's vision of territory as part of their assertion of identity, however much their primary claim to distinctiveness did not, for them, turn solely on that issue.

Like other supposed indicators, therefore, the stereotype of tribes as socially or territorially circumscribed mistakes the permeable for the impassable.[90] Tribes may commonly be associated with a given locale, but the use rights of such territory may be divisible at different times of the year or for various usages among several tribal groups. In many cases, as Francis Jennings puts it, "The [American] Indian did not wander; he commuted."[91] Among Northwest Coast tribes, for example, a given territory may be used by one tribe for ritual purposes and by another for resources; among the Walbiri of Australia, clans, once thought to be territorially distinctive, move easily across various domains, admixture among the various clans also being quite normal.[92] This does not, of course, preclude each having a sense of territory, but when coupled with the emphasis on use rights (to be discussed later) it does underscore the divisible nature of claims to a given site.[93]

> Sometimes it is difficult to know to which tribe a certain territory belongs; or members of one tribe may have hunting rights over country held by another...Contrary to popular belief tribal territories and boundaries are, or were, relatively flexible. Also, people are not invariably afraid to move across the territory of an adjacent tribe. As a rule they have grounds for fear only if they deliberately or inadvertently interfere with a sacred site.
> Ronald M. Berndt and Catherine H. Berndt,
> *The World of the First Australians*, Chicago:
> University of Chicago Press, 1964, p. 34

Ownership, territory, and property may also concern things that are intangible. Among the Australian aborigines, for example, every child inherits a set of song couplets that confirm rights to a territory described by the song. This Dreamtime, with its cadences indicating types of terrain, not only helps in finding one's way over vast distances but secures recognition that one does have a territorial base of one's own and is therefore not a threat when crossing a frontier.[94] Among the Kwakiutl a ritual bowl includes the exclusive right to obtain the fruit that is used to fill it, while sacred bundles among some Plains Indians could be bought and sold by individual possessors.[95] Elsewhere, as among many Middle Eastern and Southwest Asian tribes, territory is defined predominantly not by the resources it contains but by the people who have populated it, such that exclusive claims to reckoning a genealogy become an instrument for asserting access to certain relationships, rather than absolute entitlement to the terrain.[96]

The image of tribes as the jealous guardians of a prescribed territory is, then, misleading in several key respects. For all their assertions of attachment to mother earth and the sites of their ancestors graves tribes often move around a great deal, traverse one another's domains, and carry their culture with them as they move. What matters is that they be able to do so of their own free will. What colonialism and the pressures of other groups does is force them to move without it being of their own choice. Place, in this conceptual universe, is a terrain for engagement, not simply reducible to a "blood and soil" obsession. That is what some ethnic and national groups are characterized by when they imagine themselves tribal, but it is not the characteristic emphasis of actual tribes. For "real" tribes blood is indeed fluid and soil recalls Gertrude Stein's quip, "what use are roots if you can't take them with you." Of course, there is a great deal of variation here and I do not mean to suggest that "pure" tribes regard land as fungible, only that their cultures are portable, that such portability is an important aspect of their survival adaptation, and that when they become fixed to one place they may have to maintain the ethos of movement in other ways – by separate dream quests, physical separations, etc. – that recall the vital importance of being able to move and still be oneself. Such flexibility may also account for why groups of native peoples can feel they are still themselves when elsewhere and at the same time have some difficulty adapting to unchosen places since they have not brought their culture with them by their own design.

Since territory normally correlates with some sort of sovereignty – the ability to apply one's own laws within its reaches – location would seem to be integral to political organization, and certainly that is often the case. But while European powers in particular came to equate boundaries with legitimate authority other states used a variety of indicators as the basis for claiming sovereign control over tribal regions. For example, the claim by Morocco to the territory of the former Spanish Sahara is based on the region's tribes being the source of several early Moroccan dynasties and their having paid taxes to and recognized the spiritual dominance of successive Moroccan sultans. However, tribesmen might not only have split their recognition of the sultan into a series of actions but often exhibited different elements of this seeming allegiance at different times while rarely submitting to the full list of sovereign powers (including jurisdiction and military service), thus further problematizing the tribal concept of territory as a basis for claiming sovereignty in the first place.[97] Moreover, tribal members may not only be dispersed: They may maintain an interest in some aspects of the tribe's activities or resources even though living in a village or city, and they may apply the conceptualizations of diverse groupings with considerable ease. The sheer fact that control may, therefore, be partible, that timing and purpose may play a key role in usufructuary rights, and that exclusive dominion may not be the factor that a given tribe takes as central to even its own identity further underscores how problematic territoriality has been as a basis for political claims or social theory.

Like territory the role of language has also been taken as an important indicator of a tribe by many analysts. The older notion was "one language, one culture," individual tribes being regarded as consonant with a given culture. As Judith Irvine notes: "For 19th-century linguists, missionaries, and colonial administrators it was a common assumption that language was the index of ethnic distinctiveness – that Africans, and all other human beings for that matter, had exclusive cultural identities, grounded in linguistic difference."[98] Though referring specifically to West Africa her remarks highlight the role that colonialism played in correlating language with tribal differentiation:

> Language, ethnicity, and territory were supposed to coincide, and to define population units on an administratively manageable scale – not too small, and not too large. Whatever shapes African societies had taken previously, and however variable or multifarious their populations' ways of speaking, the moment of colonization is when they were given that particular inflection that turns cultural traditions and genealogies into 'ethnicity,' turns linguistic practices into named 'languages' corresponding (supposedly) to ethnic groups, and interprets multilingualism as a secondary effect.[99]

Operating from this intellectual and political backdrop, anthropological linguists commonly drew maps of tribal groupings based entirely on the language they spoke. But, like territory, linguistic units are not hermetically sealed.[100] As in the criterion of territoriality, earlier anthropologists, Edward Sapir most notably, often knew better than to draw a simple equation of language and tribe. Ira Bashkow summarizes the findings:

> Contrary to our naive view of dialects as discrete entities, the isoglosses of distinct features often fail to coincide; instead, they form tangled patterns of crisscrosses and loops, making it impossible to establish a definitive line of demarcation between dialects. Indeed, isoglosses rarely coincide even at the boundaries of languages, in which the patterns they form resemble stretched-out bundles or tangled skeins more than they do thick redrawn lines.[101]

Thus, not only is it open to question when a dialect arises to the level of a separate language, but closer study reveals that many tribesmen are multilingual as a result of trade relations and intergroup marriage. Jared Diamond reports that in one New Guinea tribe he found most people spoke between eight and twelve languages, one man speaking fifteen.¹⁰² As another scholar notes:

> We can get some sense of how prevalent multilingualism may have been from the few hunter-gatherer peoples who survive today. "If you look at modern hunter-gatherers, they are almost all multilingual," says Thomas Bak, a cognitive neurologist who studies the science of languages at the University of Edinburgh. "The rule is that one mustn't marry anyone in the same tribe or clan to have a child – it's taboo. So every single child's mum and dad speak a different language." In Aboriginal Australia, where more than 130 indigenous languages are still spoken, multilingualism is part of the landscape. "You will be walking and talking with someone, and then you might cross a small river and suddenly your companion will switch to another language," says Bak.¹⁰³

The noted art historian Erich Gombrich was thus wrong on numerous counts when, describing humanity's earliest development, he wrote:

> These tribes differed little from one another, either in appearance or in language. They spoke different dialects, which they could all understand if they chose. But they very rarely did. For, as is often the case, these close-related, neighbouring tribes were unable to get on with one another. They spent all their time exchanging insults and ridicule, when actually they were jealous of each other.¹⁰⁴

The question, then, may not, as Dell Hymes points out, be one of a particular language but of "the communicative relationships among persons and groups." He cites studies of Australian aboriginal groups that have distinct languages but lack a defined territory or distinctive customs, as well as tribes in east Africa where the ability to communicate across localized groupings may depend not on the language itself but the style, the code, the implications each group may or may not attend to similarly. Accordingly, Hymes called for abandoning language as a defining feature of a tribe in favor of the far more interesting question of how language is used: "Let us cease to think of languages as if they should reflect some primitively given demarcation of the world, and learn to think about them instead as instruments of human action."¹⁰⁵

Indeed, the porous boundaries of territory and language are vital to the ways in which members of a culture construe their own lives as they encounter those of others. There is, as Ira Bashkow points out, "this paradoxical aspect of boundaries: that in separating cultures, boundaries

Romancing the Tribe: History, Theory, Narrative **47**

actually facilitate the interpretation and integration of cultural difference *within* a culture" by highlighting both one's own distinctiveness and the incorporation of that which arrives from the outside.[106] Keeping these features in mind is clearly more in line with the actualities of tribal identity than the images that have guided both scholarship and popular conceptions through much of Western history.

Political Structure

Political organization was taken by many anthropologists as central to identity as a tribe. Whatever the form of leadership or representation, for these scholars the indispensable element of such group coherence and identity was the ability to govern itself and channel the behavior of its members in such a fashion as to preserve the group's wellbeing. For a long time, as we have seen, this was thought to be accomplished in tribes through the mechanism of kinship and its extensions. Many of the early anthropologists, however, characterized the political life of tribal societies either in highly romanticized terms or as archaic predecessors to more complex forms of organization.

Just as the definition of tribes imploded under increased examples, so, too, the image of their political organization became increasingly difficult for anthropologists to corral. Characterizations thus became couched in

FIGURE 2.2   Iroquois council portrayed in Classical style tunics.

terms of what tribes were not: They were "acephalous" in that they lacked headship, or they were "stateless" because they were somehow less than states, or they were "anarchic" even when that quality was promoted as desirable. Leadership became a particularly crucial index: When the formal powers of leaders were limited by occasion and purpose we were told that we were at a tribal level; when they became ensconced, much less hereditary, and individual leaders could cumulate resources beyond the requirements of survival and recompense we were told that the level of political organization had shifted to that of a chiefdom. Of special concern for tribes was the issue of segmentation.

In popular parlance tribes are commonly seen in much the same way atoms were once regarded – as unitary, unfractionated, irreducible. But just as the atom was revealed to be composed of many sub-units, so, too, tribes came to be regarded as a congeries of segments that could be put together in a variety of ways. To a number of anthropologists, however, the process was virtually mechanical: Kinship rules, even if manipulated, provided the primary outline and the segments fell into line accordingly. That the constituent elements were seen as doing so autonomously solved several problems. First, the theory demonstrated that no centralized authority was necessary for a society to operate. In that regard it proved for some that anarchy was not only theoretically possible but actually existed among such groups as the Nuer (for E. E. Evans-Pritchard), the Berbers of the High Atlas Mountains (for Ernest Gellner), and virtually all early human groupings (for David Graeber). Secondly, the existence of uncentralized governance could reveal, in certain cases, the crucial role of intermediaries – whether religious or drawn from voluntary associations that cross-cut kinship groups – who performed the function of maintaining peace that states try to manage through the monopolization of force. The only problem was that, upon closer inspection of actual cases, assembling segments proved far less neatly rule-bound than the theory claimed.

A good example in this regard is provided in the work by Paul Dresch in Yemen. There, he argues, not only is the evolutionary theory misplaced – since states may provoke tribal attachment, rather than the other way around – but tribes do not possess corporate qualities or remain unified and solidary across time. Indeed, what Dresch calls "fragmented answerability" is but a process of constantly maneuvering among possible levels of affiliation. "[T]he individualism of the tribal scheme," he notes, "was predicated, and still is, on its indefinite divisibility." In the context of a centralizing state like Yemen, he concludes, "tribes are not simply things, groups, or forces in this context. They are part of a system of ideas that can be reworked, and no doubt will be."[107] It is not simply that new units may arise through the fissioning of existing ones – whether due to demographic pressures or resource realignment. Wholesale secession (documented as well among the Winnebago and many others) may occur as a result of sibling rivalry, personality differences, or cross-boundary affairs of the heart.[108] That such is the case in any particular historical context is, therefore, not simply a function of the moment but of possibilities that are inherent in the nature of tribes.

Put in more general terms, Sahlins notes that a descent group does "not necessarily correspond in fact to what it is alleged to be in principle....[A] descent dogma imposes itself on existing practices. It is quite capable of reinterpreting contradictions of membership in its own terms." He notes that as one moves up in greater inclusiveness the same contradictions continue: "the segmentary lineage system...[is not simply] the working out on the tribal plane of homebred rules of linearity, a linearity that in any case is not the rule at home."[109] Thus a more fruitful approach to the segmented nature of tribes is to see the pattern of ever more genealogical inclusiveness and solidarity as a template that can be used, along with other structures of interdependence, as part of the sociological toolkit that individuals and their dependent allies may draw upon as they import a sense of deeper order to a system that in its actuality – and its acceptable fictions – is generated out of the repertoire of negotiable ties common to that particular group.

Indeed, the idea that tribes are built up of oppositional units – to say nothing of the broader projection of them as oppositional in the most negative sense – misses a key point about the segmental nature of tribes. For while, as Dresch notes generally, "identity is established in part by mutual observation of opposite numbers," segmentary theorists mistook process for structure.[110] The strength of many tribes is their ability to generate multiple groupings within a single identifiable entity (often as a vehicle for achieving peace) and to connect this organizational repertoire with an ethos of the moral equivalence of units, the dispersal of power across generations and sub-groupings, avoidance of state domination, and maintenance of the capacity to adapt to changing political environs. While variable segmentation could, as we will see later, also be a weakness, tribal emphasis on the proliferation and malleability of opposed units of attachment further undercuts any image of their innate proclivity to endemic violence and unreliability.

The possibility arises, therefore, that the use of the term " 'tribe" has, on more than one occasion, been very misleading in both a political and more broadly sociological sense. Consider the case of the "Barbarian" tribes of Europe. The enigma would seem to be that the tribes defeated Rome but then somehow disappeared. Historians admit that they are perplexed. As for their advent, Derek Williams notes: "In fact the emergence of barbarian power has never been satisfactorily explained; and the absence of a clear answer has clouded the long-standing conundrum of why the western empire succumbed."[111] As for the tribes' demise, some attribute it to the success of Christianity (especially its rules of inheritance and marriage, which are said to have undermined tribal practices), while others point to the hollowing out of tribal identity through the gradual inclusion of the tribes within the ambit of Roman society.[112] Numerous Barbarians were, in fact, incorporated in the ranks of the Roman forces; indeed, many became Roman citizens and even reached the highest levels of Roman administration. But while absorption goes far to explain the disappearance of Europe's tribes it may be more accurate to say that by the time of Rome's fall these "tribes" were no longer classically acephalous tribal entities but had already been transformed into paramount chiefdomships. Some of the Germanic groups moved as small bands and may have maintained a tribal arrangement of limited leadership and emphasis on reciprocity. But most of the groups, it may be argued, were not tribes at all – at least not in the sense developed here – and probably had not been for quite some time. These units had not only been migrating across the continent for centuries but had taken on much more centralized leadership, owing perhaps to their being constantly at war, and had thus cast up leaders – some of whom became hereditary chiefs, even kings – with much more concentrated powers.[113] The coalesced groups may have appeared to scholars as tribe-like mainly because followers, as in all paramount chiefdomships, could dissolve into small groupings that were more easily incorporated into the Roman sphere. But to argue, following Morton Fried and other cultural anthropologists and archaeologists, that these "tribes" were the convenient creation of Rome is insupportable.[114] Rather, it is more likely that as paramount chieftainships the Barbarians could be more susceptible to absorption as the replacement of leadership and the benefits of Roman citizenship undercut the security offered by the devices of earlier forms of tribalism.

The characterization of numerous groupings in sub-Saharan Africa and parts of Southeast Asia presents a similar concern. Invariably denominated as "tribes" by the colonial powers, scholars also picked up on the language of the day – just as they employed terms like "savage" and "primitive," even when arguing that tribesmen were neither – until, as we have seen, their definitions were stretched to the breaking point as they encountered new information and groupings. The result is that in the current parlance of African studies, for example, one no longer uses the term tribe, replacing it instead with terms like "ethnic group". The latter term still partakes of many of the earlier indicia of the tribal (a shared language, territory, and kinship idiom) but recognizes that this is now mainly an issue of identity politics, if not of straight-out factional politics, and that state organization has suffused and displaced most elements of the tribal.[115] Rather than reconceptualizing "tribe" the choice has been to abandon the term altogether given the stigma that has at times been attached to it. Moreover, categorizing these African groups as chiefdoms and kingdoms more accurately reflects the distribution of powers over the course of the groups' histories. Yet the curious conclusion is all but unavoidable, namely that the anthropologists, victims of their own structural theories and the terminology of the day, had deluded themselves all along in speaking of many of the African examples as tribes.

The Historical Dimension

As we have seen, most anthropological studies of tribes took place at a time when the discipline's focus was on social structure and its operation. Such studies yielded an implicit challenge to the view of tribes as primitive precursors or survivals that more developed societies had transcended. However, the success of the structural-functionalists was also their undoing. Each new study of a given tribe undertaken from their perspective added to our understanding of the lives of those particular groups. But each new study also demonstrated that the exceptions to their definition of a tribe ate up the proffered rule. This devolution can be traced through the course of definitions by which anthropologists tried to grapple with the problem.

The *Encyclopaedia Britannica* of 1911 describes the "ethnological meaning" of tribe as: "any aggregate of families or small communities which are grouped together under one chief or leader, observing similar customs and social rules, and tracing their descent from one common ancestor."[116] At this time it was also common to add the ill-defined notion that tribes are "largely distinct by race from other such communities."[117] Evans-Pritchard, based on his work among the Nuer, added elements of segmentarity, when, in 1940, he suggested: "The simplest definition states that a tribe is the largest community which considers that disputes between its members should be settled by arbitration and that it ought to combine against other communities of the same kind and foreigners." He also stressed "territorial unity and exclusiveness" as well as "a sense of patriotism: they are proud to be members of their tribe and they consider it superior to other tribes."[118] Similarly, the British *Notes and Queries on Anthropology* went through a series of definitions of a tribe. In the 1951 edition the editors largely followed the Africanists of the preceding decades when they noted that a tribe is defined as "a political or socially coherent and autonomous group occupying or claiming a particular territory." By 1968 the entry in the *International Encyclopedia of Social Sciences* by I. M. Lewis not only stressed territory and political control but added such attributes as an unwritten language leading to communication that is "inevitably narrow" and a "closed system of thought" such that "tribal societies are supremely ethnocentric." To this day *The Oxford English Dictionary* replicates much of the early *Britannica* definition, which like its predecessor replaces one unknown (tribe) with another (community) when it offers as its definition of tribe: "A group of persons forming a community and claiming descent from a common ancestor." Inevitably, the definition became so strained as to be posed in terms of what it is not: "The accepted usage of 'tribe' is as a political unit larger than a clan and smaller than a nation or people."[119] And while the archaeologists in the last half of the 20th century relied heavily on the social anthropologists' definitions to read between the lines of the material cultures they excavated some of them eventually noticed that even the students of living tribes saw that a trait-list approach failed to grasp that there are "institutionalized alternatives" to any society's acceptable practices. As Philip Salzman notes:

> [t]he crucial fact, often overlooked or de-emphasized, is that every society provides alternatives – *institutionalized alternatives* – for many if not all major areas of activity: alternative organizational forms, alternative productive activities, alternative value orientations, alternative forms of property control. This results in fluidity and variability as people switch back and forth, between activities, between organizational forms, and between priorities.[120]

The history of the concept of tribe is; therefore, an almost perfect example of what Thomas S. Kuhn had described in *The Structure of Scientific Revolutions* – but minus the revolution.[121] In the case of tribes, the prevailing paradigm produced numerous examples of "normal science," that state in which investigators continue to make observations and extensions based on a model that often results in what Kuhn called "drift" and "crisis" before a new vision appears. In this instance, definitions of tribe had grown increasingly vague as the range of variation stretched the existing paradigm to the breaking point, at which juncture most anthropologists simply abandoned "tribe" as a useful category of analysis. Just as the cultural evolutionists could not get beyond generalities that had little to do with genuine evolutionary mechanisms – leading to many of its initial proponents forsaking the concept altogether – so, too, the structural-functionalists could not hold onto their definitions in the face of ever-challenging counter-examples rather than search for a new paradigm. The enterprise got a partial reprieve – but was not ultimately saved – by adding a historical dimension to the search.

While the evolutionary and structural-functional views of tribes can be seen – except by their most ardent boosters – as overlapping and set at different levels of abstraction, history has not always figured into either of their equations. Evolutionary views, of course, necessarily incorporate time, but commonly at such a grand scale as to obliterate the everyday details of any given society's course. The structural-functionalists, on the other hand, were so concerned with how a society holds together at any given moment that change and history – especially if cast in evolutionary terms – was largely pushed out of consideration.[122] They took, as it were, a micrometer cut through the societies they observed, seeing not "a surface seething with life and movement" but a steady state, an equilibrium, in which each part served to perpetuate the working of the whole.[123] So, too, the leading proponent of structuralism, Claude Lévi-Strauss, distinguished between "hot" and "cold" societies; the latter ("primitive" societies), he said, "tend to remain indefinitely in their initial state" while the former ("modern" societies) keep changing since they must cope with the contradictions generated internally by their "different forms of social hierarchy."

These theories did not, of course, exist in isolation: They were very much part of their own time and intellectual contexts. Among the many stereotypes of tribes found in the West is that they make history but have none of their own. Whether it is the Twelve Tribes of Israel, the Barbarian tribesmen who defeated Rome, the hordes that marched to the gates of Vienna, the Comanche who dominated the Great Plains, or the confederacies that burst out of Arabia to make Islam a world religion, tribes are properly credited with changing the history of many of those with whom they have made contact. At the same time, tribes are often characterized as having rather less internal history of their own: Leaders may change, the death of one commander may stop the entire tribe in its tracks, and forest dwellers may burst onto the plains where horse-culture changes their lives, but history as internal development – rather than shifting to a "more evolved" condition – is seldom attributed to tribes. Thus while viewing tribes as existing in a state of equilibrium may have credited them with endurance and orderliness, the reigning theories actually canceled history, either through the imputation of ineluctable forces or through the backhanded compliment of giving up their shapeshifting in favor of their ardent defense of the cultural pattern of the moment.

Other theories of tribes, however, have been deeply situated in one or another approach to history. One the most influential of these theories, particularly for studies of the Middle East and North Africa, is that of the indomitable Ibn Khaldun, whose cyclical account of dynastic histories depended in great part on the role he ascribed to tribes. Flourishing in the latter half of the 14th century, his contemporary appeal lies, in part, in the way his theory taps into certain Western assumptions about change. For Ibn Khaldun argued that history repeats itself in a circular pattern that links tribes to larger entities. From the cauldron of their tribal solidarity tribes, he said, come roaring out of the margins to conquer the sophisticated center of power, only to fall prey to the urbanites' luxurious and enervating ways, thereby becoming susceptible to the next tribe that repeats the pattern. Boosted by Arnold Toynbee to Western readers, Ibn Khaldun's interpretation left in its wake two key notions – that of solidarity ('*asabiyya*) based largely on kinship, and the ability to recruit larger and larger alliances through such kinship or kinship-like devices. But this part of Ibn Khaldun's approach was, in a sense, both less original than it might seem and less true to his overall theory. For Ibn Khaldun was, above all, an Arab, and, building on his own cultural background, he realized that such alliances were not automatically precipitated by genealogical connection but were dependent on a "big man" creating a network that gained some of its force and legitimacy by virtue of its being modeled, though not reliant, on a highly structured clan-based paradigm. It was the failure to grasp this point that, in turn, led more recent social scientists to apply his thinking to mistaken ends.[124]

Enter some of the discipline's most notable players. E. E. Evans-Pritchard and Ernest Gellner both relied – implicitly, in the one case, explicitly, in the other – on Ibn Khaldun's approach. They took the notion that tribes incorporate segments delimited by kinship and suggested – in Evans-Pritchard's case for the Nuer and in Gellner's for the Berbers of Morocco – that groupings coalesced at ever higher points on the genealogical charter. Evans-Pritchard could, therefore, describe the Nuer as a society in which "the political system is an equilibrium between opposed tendencies towards fission and fusion, between the tendency of all groups to segment, and the tendency of all groups to combine with segments of the same order."[125] True, Evans-Pritchard referred to kinship among the Nuer as an "idiom" – without ever fully indicating what he meant by that term – but neither he nor Gellner pursued the alleged segmentarity of these societies across time. Indeed, the aversion to history – or more precisely, the fear that it would devolve into claims of time always working in some direction – steered most British anthropologists of the period away from considering that they had caught the groups they studied at a certain moment in their histories, the result being a kind of frozen anthropological snapshot called the "ethnographic present." Sahlins, in his evolutionary phase, did at least add the factor of history when he referred to such groups as structured for purposes of predatory expansion.[126] That is, the idea of "me and my brother against my cousin" and "me and my cousin against a still more distant cousin" (and on up the genealogical ladder) could serve as a vehicle for recruitment of allies as one expanded into new territory or defended it against opponents. But neither the proponents of segmentary theory nor Sahlins, when he was still a cultural evolutionist, coupled their theories with specific historical studies.[127]

The result of leaving history out of the equation seriously undermined the structural-functionalists' equilibrium model. Raymond C. Kelly, for example, showed in *The Nuer Conquest* that Evans-Pritchard actually encountered the Nuer at a moment in their history when segments did match organization, but that if one moves backwards or forwards in time the results are quite different.[128] Indeed, the operative principle of recruitment is not one of automatic kin alliance: The role of leaders who choose to employ such a model is vital. Not infrequently, actual practice may be "me and my distant relative against my close relative – and both of us against my brother." Patricia Crone thus notes that "pre-Islamic poetry is full of complaints of kinsmen who fail to fulfil their end of the bargain," while among the Pashtun of Pakistan the term for "cousin" also means "enemy."[129] Similarly, Gellner's view – shared for a time by several others working mainly in the Arabo-Berber world – has also been shown not to work once the clock is set in motion.[130] That is, groups do not simply become organized by genealogical reckoning: Ibn Khaldun's addition – indeed supplementation – of leadership based on a wide range of recruitment devices that could then be rationalized in terms of kinship (more often than not through genealogical amnesia and creative revision of one's descent) was the part of his thought that had been left out. The good news may be that the functionalists saw the role that kinship extensions could play in the expansion and success of the group. But that same strength was also its weakness inasmuch as it also perpetuated the image of kin-based form and function as more important than the full range of devices available for alliance creation in tribal societies.

History also tends to be downplayed in the analysis of tribes when they are regarded as either the creature of other organizational forms, mainly states, or as symbiotic, if not indeed parasitic, to such larger structures. From this perspective, too, tribes are often portrayed as having no independent history of their own: They are either static by nature or whatever history they do partake of is a function of the host entity. The absence of writing in most tribal cultures may make documenting their histories difficult, but that is not the same as imagining them to be without history. Avoiding dependence on writing, as many scholars have noted, is not without its advantages: Writing may freeze a text, thus making it appear authoritative and unassailable; it may describe as enemies those who are now friends, thus preserving outdated animosities; and writing makes it easier for the state to administer, tax, and categorize people. Orality can be very exact, as anyone who has sung an old song will know, and indeed may retain far more flexibility than the written word.[131] Moreover, the lack of emphasis on history may be due to tribesmen's intense focus on persons as independent actors, such that history, as informing both inheritable character and predictable individual behavior, is deemed both irrelevant and ineffective in forming interpersonal ties. If it is the person who makes something believable that quality may be difficult to retrieve from a written text. And since each person's ties to others are distinctive history may be seen as a rather poor guide to the appraisal and creation of such ties.

Morton Fried's claim that tribes are the creation of states also plays into the view that tribes have little if any independent history of their own.[132] Undoubtedly, some colonial governments did indeed recognize certain tribesmen as leaders they could deal with or co-opt, and no doubt groupings were frequently forced into organizational and living arrangements they did not choose for themselves. But this approach ignores two features that show up when tribes are accorded histories of their own, namely that tribes frequently adapt to superordinate structures and thus survive rather than simply assimilate, and that key elements of tribal identity (as will be suggested in the following chapters) can be amalgamated even by the larger or more complex socio-political form with which they must now deal.[133]

Many of the foregoing theories partake of a common – and very significant – problem, namely that the narratives the analysts bring to their study often reveal more about the authors' own cultural and historical contexts than some timeless and objective truth about the subject. Where the data do not support a clear interpretation it is often the unwitting assumptions and credible forms of narration that fill in the lacunae, a process that has occurred throughout the history of science. It is, therefore, not only in the study of tribes that, at times, as one commenter put it: "The facts matter, but the story matters more."[134] This is particularly true of the history of tribal studies.

The story that was told about tribes – that they were adapted to a particular mode and level of existence – fit well with the assumption that they were survivals of an earlier era of social development or were revelatory of basic human nature. However, as the role of individual tribesmen became more central to the development of anthropological humanism – as, for example, in Paul Radin's *Autobiography of a Winnebago Indian* – the story of tribal lives was quietly recast as one of malleable choice rather than cultural constraint and individual maneuverability rather than collective intransigence. But this was also an era in which structural-functionalism, ethnoscience, and French structuralism all sought certainties rather than contending with the indeterminacies of social life, a period characterized by Donald Levine as "the flight from ambiguity."[135] As the discipline oscillated and divided, the humanistic and structural approaches were never truly reconciled. Instead of pursuing a reconsideration of such classic issues as the nature of tribes even those oriented towards a more cultural analysis failed to appreciate that the elements were in place for the fabrication of a new paradigm. It is towards reconfiguring these elements and shifting that paradigm to which we can now turn our attention.

Notes

1 Kwame Anthony Appiah, *As If: Idealization and Ideals*, Cambridge: Harvard University Press, 2017.
2 See, Kwame Anthony Appiah, *The Lies that Bind: Rethinking Identity*, New York: Liveright, 2018.
3 Michael Bond, *From Here to There: The Art and Science of Finding and Losing Our Way*, Cambridge: Harvard University Press, 2020, p. 7. His footnote to this passage (p. 229, n. 2) reads: "Studies of the few existing hunter-gatherer societies demonstrate the advantages of forming connections with people outside the core family group, i.e., with non-kin, such as the spread of technological innovations, social norms and knowledge about natural resources." See also, A. B. Migliano, et al., "Characterization of Hunter-Gatherer Networks and Implications for Cumulative Culture," *Nature Human Behaviour*, vol. 1, article no. 0043 (February 8, 2017). A quote from this latter source reads: "We believe that multilevel structuring already characterized Middle Stone Age populations emerging as early as 320,000 years ago, which were also known to have established trade dyads connecting sites up to 160 km apart." However, Ariane Burke, who studies Paleolithic human wayfinding, warns: "Evolutionary psychologists are cherry-picking the archaeological and ethnographic records." This is exemplified in claims that women did not explore as much as men and thus would not have established trade relations. But, she argues, the evidence for this assertion is simply missing: "The evidence that women did not travel long distances and did not use allocentric [spatial] strategies for wayfinding isn't there." Ariane Burke, "Spatial Abilities, Cognition and the Pattern of Neanderthal and Modern Human Dispersals," *Quaternary International*, vol. 247 (January 9, 2012), pp. 230–35. See also, Ariane Burke, Anne Kandler, and David Good, "Women Who Know Their Place: Sex-based Differences in Spatial Abilities and Their Evolutionary Significance," *Human Nature*, vol. 23, no. 2 (2012), pp. 133–48.
4 Robin Fox, *The Tribal Imagination: Civilization and the Savage Mind*, Cambridge: Harvard University Press, 2011, pp. 1, 6, 7, 15, and 354. Typical of such assertions is the statement by Jonathan Haidt:

> When we look back at the ways our ancestors lived, there's no getting around it: we are tribal primates. We are exquisitely designed and adapted by evolution for life in small societies with intense, animistic religion and violent intergroup conflict over territory. We love tribal living so much that we invented sports, fraternities, street gangs, fan clubs, and tattoos. Tribalism is in our hearts and minds. We'll never stamp it out entirely.... [A]s tribal primates, human beings are unsuited for life in large, diverse secular democracies, unless you get certain settings finely adjusted to make

possible the development of stable political life....A funny thing happens when you take young human beings, whose minds evolved for tribal warfare and us/them thinking, and you fill those minds full of binary dimensions. You tell them that one side of each binary is good and the other is bad. You turn on their ancient tribal circuits, preparing them for battle.

Jonathan Haidt, "The Age of Outrage," *City Journal*, December 17, 2017. www.city-journal.org/html/age-outrage-15608.html (accessed September 7, 2025). See also, Greg Lukianoff and Jonathan Haidt, *The Coddling of the American Mind*, New York: Penguin, 2018, pp. 56–59.
5 Fox, *Tribal Imagination*, pp. 323 and 326.
6 Adam Gopnik, "Fault Lines," *The New Yorker*, January 4 and 11, 2021, pp. 15–16, at 15.
7 "Speaking technically, for most of our hominid existence we lived in small bands, not in tribes conceived as political entities; but I shall use 'tribal' to cover them all, including chiefdoms." Fox, *Tribal Imagination*, p. 15.
8 D. C. Lahti, N. A. Johnson, et al., "Relaxed Selection in the Wild," *Trends in Ecology and Evolution*, vol. 24, no. 9 (2009), pp. 487–96. Researchers at the Max Planck Institute for Evolutionary Anthropology in Leipzig, for example, have shown that "most harmful Neanderthal genes have been eliminated by natural selection while useful ones have established themselves in the human population." Max Planck Gesellschaft, "History of Our Evolution in a New Light." www.mpg.de/11180454/project_humanhistory (accessed September 7, 2025). Geneticists employ the term "selective sweep" to refer to the process by which hitchhiking features are de-selected until only one version of the full set of clumped elements remains: "At every opportunity, natural selection prunes out the damaging instructions and leaves the non-coding 'junk' as well as the functional sequences, to carry themselves into the future." Nicholas P. Money, *The Amoeba in the Room*, Oxford: Oxford University Press, 2014, p. 12.
9 For the argument that falsifiability should not, in any case, be the applicable measure of a theory's validity, see Mano Singham "The Idea that a Scientific They Can Be 'Falsified' is a Myth," *Scientific American*, September 7, 2020.
10 Often, the image is one that plays well into the national myth of perpetual improvement. Thus literary critic E. D. Hirsch, Jr. writes of the founding of the United States: "The history of tribal and racial hatred is the history and prehistory of humankind. . . . The American experiment, which now seems so natural to us, is a thoroughly artificial device designed to counterbalance the natural impulses of group suspicions and hatreds. . . . This vast, artificial, trans-tribal construct is what our Founders aimed to achieve. And they understood that it can be achieved effectively only by intelligent schooling." *The Making of America: Democracy and Our Schools*, New Haven: Yale University Press, 1994, pp. 85–86.
11 "Epigenetics dissolves the boundaries of the self even further. Messages coded in the DNA can be modified in many ways - by mixing and matching DNA modules, by capping or hiding bits so that they can't be read, or by changing the message after it's been read, its meaning altered in translation. DNA was once taught as a sacred text handed faithfully down the generations. Now, increasing evidence points to the nuclear genome as more of a grab bag of suggestions, tourist phrases, syllables and gibberish that you use and modify as needed. The genome now seems less like the seat of the self and more of a toolkit for fashioning the self." Nathaniel Comfort, "How Science Has Shifted Our Sense of Identity," *Nature*, no. 574 (October 14, 2019), pp. 167–70.

12 Robert A. Paul, *Mixed Messages: Cultural and Genetic Inheritance in the Constitution of Human Society*, Chicago: University of Chicago Press, 2015. For the argument that cultural evolution proceeds through the development of neurological pathways see, Francesco d'Errico and Ivan Colagè, "Cultural Exaptation and Cultural Neural Reuse: A Mechanism for the Emergence of Modern Culture and Behavior," *Biological Theory*, vol. 13, no. 4 (December 2018), pp. 213–27; Ivan Colagè and Francesco d'Errico, "Culture: The Driving Force of Human Cognition," *Topics in Cognitive Science*, (July 22, 2018) pp. 1–19, https://doi.org/10.1111/tops.12372 (accessed September 8, 2025); Robert Turner, "Finding Likeness: Neural Plasticity and Ritual Experience," *Anthropology Today*, vol. 35, no. 3 (June 2, 2019), pp. 3–6; and Cecilia Heyes, *Cognitive Gadgets: The Cultural Evolution of Thinking*, Cambridge: Harvard University Press, 2018. See also, Dalton Conley, *The Social Genome: The New Science of Nature and Nurture*, New York: W. W. Norton, 2025.
13 See, e.g., Robert Bellah, *Religion in Human Evolution*, Cambridge: Harvard University Press, 2011; Scott Atran, *In Gods We Trust: The Evolutionary Landscape of Religion*, Oxford: Oxford University Press, 2002; Leonard D. Katz, ed., *Evolutionary Origins of Morality*, Bowling Green, OH: Imprint Academic, 2000; Barbara J. King, *Evolving God*, Chicago: University of Chicago Press, 2017; and Pascal Boyer and Brian Bergstrom, "Evolutionary Perspectives on Religion," *Annual Review of Anthropology*, vol. 37, (2008), pp. 111–30.
14 Marshall D. Sahlins, *Tribesmen*, Englewood Cliffs, NJ: Prentice-Hall, 1968, p. 96.
15 David Hume, "Introduction," *A Treatise of Human Nature* [1739].
16 William H. Durham, "Advances in Evolutionary Culture Theory," *Annual Review of Anthropology*, vol. 19 (1990), pp. 187–210, at 188 (original italics). The idea that there was some unified primordial 'culture' is at best dubious.
17 Durham, *Advances in Evolutionary Culture Theory*, p. 201.
18 George Eliot (the pseudonym of Mary Anne Evans, 1819–1880), *Daniel Deronda*, New York: Penguin Classics, 1991 [1876]. On the role of narrative in evolutionary thought see especially, Misia Landau, *Narratives of Human Evolution*, New Haven: Yale University Press, 1991.
19 E. O. Wilson, "Biologist E.O. Wilson on Why Humans, Like Ants, Need a Tribe," *Newsweek*, April 2, 2012. On the image of early hominins as brutal hunters see, Matt Cartmill, *A View to a Death in the Morning: Hunting and Nature through History*, Cambridge: Harvard University Press, 2009, pp. 1–27.
20 Edward O. Wilson, "Masters of Earth, Alone in the Universe," *Bloomberg View*, September 11, 2014. www.bloomberg.com/opinion/articles/2014-09-11/mast ers-of-earth-alone-in-the-universe (accessed September 8, 2025). See generally, Edward O. Wilson, *The Social Conquest of Earth*, New York: Liveright, 2013. See also, Andrew Bard Schmookler, *The Parable of the Tribes*, Albany: State University of New York Press, 1994 (when one tribe becomes violent all others become so as well).
21 "David Brooks on Youth, Morality, and Loneliness." https://medium.com/ conversations-with-tyler/david-brooks-tyler-cowen-religion-plurality-lonelin ess-new-york-times-diversity-eb051a4b47cc (podcast June 6, 2018) (accessed September 7, 2025).
22 See, e.g., Amy Chua, *Political Tribes: Group Instinct and the Fate of Nations*, New York: Penguin, 2019; my review of her book, Lawrence Rosen, "Are Our Politics Really 'Tribal'?" *The American Interest*, vol. 13, no. 6 (May 2018);

and Caroline Kitchener, "The Trouble with Tribalism," *The Atlantic*, October 16, 2018.

23 This is not, however, to suggest that bonobos, for example, are non-violent. Contrary to earlier claims that they settle their disputes peaceably there is clear evidence that this is not the case. See, Jason G. Goldman, "Bonobos May Not Be So Laid-Back after All," *Scientific American*, January 4, 2018; Christopher Krupenye and Brian Hare, "Bonobos Prefer Individuals That Hinder Others Over Those That Help," *Current Biology*, January 22, 2018. https://doi.org/10.1016/j.cub.2017.11.061 (accessed September 8, 2025); and Carl Zimmer, "No 'Hippie Ape': Bonobos Are Often Aggressive, Study Finds," *New York Times*, April 12, 2024, citing Maud Mouginot, et al., "Differences in Expression of Male Aggression between Wild Bonobos and Chimpanzees," *Current Biology*, April 12, 2024. https://doi.org/10.1016/j.cub.2024.02.071 (accessed September 7, 2025).

24 On species cooperativeness see, Brian Hare and Vanessa Woods, *Survival of the Friendliest*, New York: Random House, 2020. On the selectivity of data by proponents of innate human violence see, John Gray, "Steven Pinker is Wrong about Violence and War," *The Guardian*, March 13, 2015, and the sources discussed therein, especially the critique of Pinker's data by Pasquale Cirillo and Nassim Nicholas Taleb, "The Decline of Violent Conflicts: What Do the Data Really Say?" *Nobel Foundation Symposium 161: The Causes of Peace*, n.d., www.fooledbyrandomness.com/pinker.pdf (accessed September 8, 2025). About the statistical apparatus in Pinker's book, Gray observes: "Like the obsidian mirrors the Aztecs made from volcanic glass and used for the purposes of divination, these rows of graphs and numbers contain nebulous visions of an unknown future - visions that by their very indistinctness ... comfort anxious believers in human improvement." John Gray, *The Soul of the Marionette*, New York: Farrar, Straus and Giroux, 2016. See also, R. Brian Ferguson, "Pinker's List: Exaggerating Prehistoric War Mortality," in Douglas P. Fry, ed., *War, Peace and Human Nature*, Oxford: Oxford University Press, 2013, pp. 112–31, at 126 ("[Pinker's] is a selective compilation of highly unusual cases, grossly distorting war's antiquity and lethality."); R. Brian Ferguson's review of Lawrence H. Keeley's book "War before Civilization: The Myth of the Peaceful Savage," (Oxford: Oxford University Press, 1997), (also published in *American Anthropologist*, vol. 99, no. 2 (June 1997), pp. 424–25); and Augustin Fuentes, *Race, Monogamy, and Other Lies They Told You: Myths about Human Nature*, Berkeley: University of California Press, 2015, pp. 114–55. For an overview of recent research on human violence see, Elizabeth N. Arkush and Mark W. Allen, eds., *The Archaeology of Warfare*, Gainesville: University Press of Florida, 2008.

25 On the first two points see, respectively, Claudia Doyle, "Change that Came from the Plowed Field," *Max Planck Research*, March, 2017, pp. 27–33, at 27 ("before our ancestors discovered agriculture [t]here was no cause for warlike conflicts; the concept of social status was alien to them and possessions were shared."), and James C. Scott, *Against the Grain: A Deep History of the Earliest States*, New Haven: Yale University Press, 2017. On warfare in the rise of chiefdoms, see Robert L. Carneiro, *Evolutionism in Cultural Anthropology*, Boulder, CO: Westview Press, 2003.

26 See, e.g., the essays in Richard J. Chacon and Rubén G. Mendoza, eds., *North American Indigenous Warfare and Ritual Violence*, Tucson: University of Arizona Press, 2013. Margaret MacMillan (*War: How Conflict Shaped Us*, New York: Random House, 2020, p. 4) perpetuates this view in her popular

book, notwithstanding her reluctant admission that: "Much of what is known is naturally highly speculative."
27 Napoleon Chagnon, "Reproductive and Somatic Conflicts of Interest in the Genesis of Violence and Warfare among Tribesmen," in Jonathan Haas, ed., *The Anthropology of War*, Cambridge: Cambridge University Press, 1990, pp. 77–104, at 82. See also, Luke Glowaki and Richard W. Wrangham, "Warfare and Reproductive Success in a Tribal Population," *Proceedings of the National Academy of Sciences*, vol. 112, no. 2 (2015), pp. 348–53; and Penelope Eckert and Russell Newmark, "Central Eskimo Song Duels: A Contextual Analysis of Ritual Ambiguity," *Ethnology*, vol. 19, no. 2 (April 1980), pp. 191–211, at 194 ("Violence permeated many aspects of Central Eskimo life."). Others who argue for early human violence include Keith F. Otterbein, "A History of Research on Warfare in Anthropology," *American Anthropologist*, vol. 101, no. 4 (December 1999), pp. 794–805; and Keeley, *War Before Civilization*.
28 See generally, Stephen Corry, "The Emperor's New Suit in the Garden of Eden, and Other Wild Guesses: Why Can't Napoleon Chagnon Prove Anything," *Truthout*, September 21, 2013. https://truthout.org/articles/the-emperors-new-suit-in-the-garden-of-eden-and-other-wild-guesses-or-why-cant-napoleon-chagnon-prove-anything/ (accessed September 7, 2025); reprinted by Survival International, www.survivalinternational.org/articles/3438-the-emperors-new-suit-in-the-garden-of-eden-and-other-wild-guesses (accessed September 7, 2025).
29 Steven Pinker, *The Better Angels of Our Nature*, New York: Penguin Books, 2015; and his "Taming the Beast Within Us," *Nature*, no. 478, (2011), pp. 309–11. For detailed refutations of Pinker's selective use of data see, Christopher Ryan and Cacilda Jethá, *Sex at Dawn*, New York: Harper, 2011, pp. 183–87; R. Brian Ferguson, "Pinker's List"; Survival International, "The Myth of the 'Brutal Savage'," n.d. www.survivalinternational.org/articles/3289-brutal-savages (accessed September 7, 2025); and Richard B. Lee, "Hunter-Gatherers and Human Evolution: New Light on Old Debates," libcom.org (February 10, 2019). Another popular author who uncritically accepts the misleading statistics on early human warfare is Yuval Noah Harari, *Homo Deus: A Brief History of Tomorrow*, New York: Harper, 2018, pp.14–19. See also, Margaret MacMillan, *War: How Conflict Shaped Us*, New York: Random House, 2020, pp. 4–5 ("Much of what is known is highly speculative....[T]he evidence seems to be on the side of those who say that human beings, as far back as we can tell, have had a propensity to attack each other in organized ways – in other words, to make war.") See generally, John Halstead and Phil Thomson, "The Prehistoric Psychopath," *Works in Progress*, March 13, 2025, https://worksinprogress.co/issue/the-prehistoric-psychopath/ (accessed September 7, 2025) and their "Violence Before Agriculture: Full Report," November 7, 2022, https://violencetrends.substack.com/p/violence-before-agriculture-full (accessed September 7, 2025). For the argument that violence is more prevalent in the modern era see, Clifton Crais, *The Killing Age: How Violence Made the Modern World*, Chicago: University of Chicago Press, 2025.
30 The characterization of Midgley as a scourge is from Andrew Brown, "Mary, Mary, Quite Contrary," *The Guardian*, January 13, 2001; her remark about Pinker is from Mary Midgley, "It's All in the Mind," *The Guardian*, September 20, 2012.
31 See, Jared Diamond, *The World Until Yesterday*, New York: Viking, 2012. See the review of his book by Ira Bashkow in *The Times Literary Supplement*, April 5, 2013 detailing, e.g., the suit brought by New Guineans charging Diamond with falsifying claims about the prevalence of their warfare, and the article on

that dispute by Edward Helmore, "Jared Diamond in Row Over Claim Tribal Peoples Live In 'State of Constant War'," *The Guardian*, February. 2, 2013. See also, Stephen Corry, "Savaging Primitives: Why Jared Diamond's 'The World Until Yesterday' is Completely Wrong," *Daily Beast*, July 12, 2017.
32 Henry Sumner Maine, *International Law: A Series of Lectures Delivered Before the University of Cambridge*, London: John Murray, 1888, p. 8. See generally, Jorg Kusterman, "Henry Maine and the Modern Invention of Peace," *Journal of the History of International Law*, vol. 20, no. 1 (2018), pp. 57–88.
33 See, Polly Weissner, "Collective Action for War and for Peace," *Current Anthropology*, vol. 60, no. 2 (April 2019), pp. 224–44. David Graeber and David Wengrow, writing in *The Dawn of Everything*, London: Penguin, 2021, p. 207, also note:

> In many of these societies one can observe customs that seem explicitly designed to head off the danger of captive status becoming permanent. Consider, for example, the Yurok requirement for victors in battle to pay compensation for each life taken, at the same rate one would pay if one were guilty of murder. This seems a highly efficient way of making intergroup raiding both fiscally pointless and morally bankrupt. In monetary terms, military advantage became a liability to the winning side. As Kroeber put it, 'The *vae victis* [woe to the vanquished] of civilization might well have been replaced among the Yurok, in a monetary sense at least, by the dictum: "Woe to the victors".'

34 Douglas P. Fry, "Comment," *Current Anthropology*, vol. 60, no. 2 (April 2019), pp. 237–38, at 238. See also, Sahlins, *Tribesmen*, p. 8 ("[P]eacemaking is the wisdom of tribal institutions.")
35 Weissner, "Collective Action for War and Peace," at p. 235.
36 Bernard Bailyn, *The Barbarous Years*, New York: Knopf, 2012, p. 57. M. W. Smith ("American Indian Warfare," *Transactions of the New York Academy of Sciences*, 2nd Series, vol. 13 (1951), pp. 348–65, at 359) makes a similar point when she argues that for the Indians war was a means of reestablishing the validity of violated customs. See generally, Francis Jennings, *The Invasion of America*, New York: W. W. Norton, 1976, pp. 146–70.
37 M. Mirazón Lahr, et al., "Inter-group Violence among Early Holocene Hunter-Gathers in West Turkana, Kenya," *Nature*, no. 529, January 21, 2016, pp. 394–98.
38 Hisashi Nakao, et al., "Violence in the Prehistoric Period of Japan: The Spatio-temporal Pattern of Skeletal Evidence for Violence in the Jomon Period," *Biology Letters*, March 1, 2016, 12: 20160028, http://dx.doi.org/10.1098/rsbl.2016.0028 (accessed September 7, 2025). See generally, Jonathan Haas and Matthew Piscitelli, "The Prehistory of Warfare: Misled by Ethnography,' in Douglas P. Fry, ed., *War, Peace, and Human Nature: The Convergence of Evolutionary and Cultural Views*, New York: Oxford University Press, 2013, pp. 168–90.
39 As one archaeologist notes: "[A]rchaeological explanation does not exist in the best of all possible worlds, it creates scenarios of past worlds based upon limited data and derived interpretations.... Like Alice's Cheshire cat, the archaeological remains of a 'tribal society' sometimes contains the corporeal outline of an entire coherent societal body. Sometimes those remains tease us with only a small component of that body." Michael Adler, "Building Consensus: Tribes, Architecture, and Typology in the American Southwest," in William A. Parkinson, ed., *Archaeology of Tribal Societies*, Ann Arbor: International Monographs in Prehistory, 2002, pp. 155–72, at 169–70.

40 "It is unlikely that there will be any clear archaeological footprint for peacemaking, but supportive evidence can be drawn from several sources." Weissner, "Collective Action for War and for Peace," at p. 235. Some evidence may be found at feasting sites: see, Michael Dietler, *Feasts: Archaeological and Ethnographic Perspectives on Food, Politics, and Power*, Washington, DC: Smithsonian Institution Press, 2001; and Brian Hayden, *The Power of Feasts*, Cambridge: Cambridge University Press, 2014.

41 Marlene Zuk, *Paleofantasy*, New York: W. W. Norton, 2013. See generally, Erika Milam, *Creatures of Cain: The Hunt for Human Nature in Cold War America*, Princeton: Princeton University Press, 2019.

42 See generally, Richard J. Chacon and Rubén G. Mendoza, eds., *North American Indigenous Warfare and Ritual Violence*, Tucson: University of Arizona Press, 2013.

43 For a critique of the stories we tell about human development see, Stefanos Geroulanos, *The Invention of Prehistory: Empire, Violence, and Our Obsession with Human Origins*, New York: Liveright, 2024.

44 Severin Fowles, "From Social Type to Social Process: Placing 'Tribe' in a Historical Framework," in William A. Parkinson, ed., *The Archaeology of Tribal Societies*, pp. 13–33, at 20, citing additional studies showing similar variations and options in a number of other tribal groups.

45 Paul Radin (*The World of Primitive Man*, New York: H. Schuman, 1953, p. 13) states, though without citation, that most tribes have been agricultural since the 1600s: "Roughly speaking, less than five per cent were primarily food gatherers, approximately fifteen per cent were hunters and fishers and ten per cent pastoral-nomads." Radin (p. 31) gives a number of examples of tribes adapting to change:

> The Navajo, originally simple nomadic hunters, adopted a pastoral life without any difficulties shortly after their first contact with the Spaniards; the Central Algonquin passed easily from a hunting economy to an agricultural one, and the food-gathering Yuman tribes of the Lower Colorado too over agriculture eagerly and without any indication of antagonism or fear. Conversely, the eastern Dakota and the Cheyenne abandoned agriculture and adopted hunting without any traces of mystical terror.

For a broad overview of current research on these issues, see Steven Mithen, "Why Did We Start Farming?" *London Review of Books*, November 16, 2017 (reviewing James Scott, *Against the Grain*).

46 See, James C. Scott, *Against the Grain*. Similarly, as Scott notes, for more contemporary hunter-gatherers, their contacts with settled agriculturalists do not necessarily lead them to regard the latter's economy as superior: They maintain many aspects of their traditional background.

47 "The story we have been telling ourselves about our origins is wrong, and perpetuates the idea of inevitable social inequality....Overwhelming evidence from archaeology, anthropology, and kindred disciplines is beginning to give us a fairly clear idea of what the last 40,000 years of human history really looked like, and in almost no way does it resemble the conventional narrative. Our species did not, in fact, spend most of its history in tiny bands; agriculture did not mark an irreversible threshold in social evolution; the first cities were often robustly egalitarian." David Graeber and David Wengrow, "How To Change the Course of Human History (At Least, the Part that's Already Happened)," *Eurozine*, March 2, 2018. www.eurozine.com/change-course-human-history/ (accessed September 7, 2025).

48 *Compare*, e.g., Norman Yoffee, *Myths of the Archaic State: Evolution of the Earliest Cities, States, and Civilizations*, Cambridge: Cambridge University Press, 2005 (arguing that chiefdoms are not a simple antecedent to states) *with* Timothy Earle, *How Chiefs Come to Power: The Political Economy of History*, Stanford: Stanford University Press, 1997 (arguing that chiefdoms are an integral precursor to states).

49 Steward even concluded: "It is difficult to describe an Indian tribe by the affirmative elements of its composition." Quoted in Severin M. Fowles, "From Social Type to Social Process: Placing 'Tribe' in a Historical Framework," in Parkinson, ed., *The Archaeology of Tribal Societies*, pp. 13–33, at 18. See the review of Julian Steward's *Theory of Culture Change: The Methodology of Multilinear Evolution* (Urbana, IL: University of Illinois Press, 1955) by Robert M. Adams (later director of the Smithsonian Institution) in *American Antiquity*, vol. 22, no. 2 (October 1956), pp. 195–96, and Clifford Geertz, *Agricultural Involution*, Berkeley: University of California Press, 1963, pp. 1–11. A more overtly materialistic view, one that concentrates on the acquisition of nourishment, can be found in the work of Marvin Harris, *Cannibals and Kings: The Origin of Cultures*, New York: Random House, 1977. See the exchange between Harris and Marshall Sahlins in the *New York Review of Books*, November 23, 1978 and June 28, 1979.

50 Darwin, upon observing that the Fuegians had divided among themselves in no obvious order the belongings of a group of sailors left behind while he made an exploratory trip, concluded: "The perfect equality of all the inhabitants will for many years prevent their civilization. Until some chief rises, who by his power might be able to keep to himself such presents as animals. &c, &c., there must be an end to all hopes of bettering their condition." [Moreover,] "it is difficult to understand how a chief can arise until there is property of some sort by which he might manifest his superiority and increase his power." Charles Darwin's *Beagle Diary*, Woollya Cove, February 6, 1833.

51 See generally, Charles King, *Gods of the Upper Air: How a Circle of Renegade Anthropologists Reinvented Race, Sex, and Gender in the Twentieth Century*, New York: Knopf, 2019.

52 Leslie A. White, *The Evolution of Culture*, New York: McGraw-Hill Book Co., 1959, p.187.

53 White, *The Evolution of Culture*, p. 20, repeated at 150. On the economic systems of tribal societies as relational and egalitarian, whereas societies like our own (what he calls 'civil society') are "impersonal, nonhuman, and nonmoral… based upon competition and struggle, upon class subjugation and exploitation,' see White, *The Evolution of Culture*, pp. 246 and 307–8. On White's experience of the Soviet model see, William J. Peace, *Leslie A. White: Evolution and Revolution in Anthropology*, Lincoln: University of Nebraska Press, 2004.

54 White, *Evolution of Culture*, pp. 24, 38, and 42 respectively.

55 See, David H. Price, *Threatening Anthropology: McCarthyism and The FBI's Surveillance of Activist Anthropologists*, Durham: Duke University Press, 2004; his *Cold War Anthropology, the CIA, the Pentagon, and the Growth of Dual Use Anthropology*, Durham: Duke University Press, 2016; and my review of the latter, Lawrence Rosen, *Journal of Cold War Studies*, vol. 19, no. 1 (Winter 2016-17), pp. 14–16.

56 Elman R. Service, "The Law of Evolutionary Potential," in Marshall D. Sahlins and Elman R. Service, eds., *Evolution and Culture*, Ann Arbor: University of Michigan Press, 1960, pp. 93–122.

57 Morton H. Fried, *The Notion of Tribe*, Menlo Park, CA: Cummings, 1975. Fried has been critiqued by William C. Sturdevant, "Tribe and State in the Sixteenth and Twentieth Centuries," in Elisabeth Tooker, ed., *The Development of Political Organization in Native North America*, Washington: American Ethnological Society, 1983, pp. 3–16.
58 On a personal note: In the early 1960s, as a senior at Brandeis University, I was hired by David Aberle and David Kaplan on a project aimed at determining the factors leading to the shift from tribes to chiefdoms on the American northwest coast. No publications ever resulted from the project as both principal investigators abandoned the idea of cultural evolution they had accepted while under White's influence at Michigan. Elman Service later dropped both band and tribe as units of analysis in favor of egalitarian and hierarchical societies: See, Elman Service, *Cultural Evolution Theory in Practice*, New York: Holt, Rinehart & Winston, 1972, p. 157; see also, his *Origins of the State and Civilization: The Process of Cultural Evolution*, New York: Norton, 1975. In other instances, as Steven Jay Gould once pointed out, in the field of biology theories are often abandoned simply because they no longer seem able to produce interesting new insights.
59 See, Kevin N. Laland, *Darwin's Unfinished Symphony: How Culture Made the Human Mind*, Princeton: Princeton University Press, 2017. For the view that there exists a distinctive human nature see, Skye C. Cleary and Massimo Pigliucci, "Human Nature Matters," *Aeon*, April 25, 2018.
60 Douglas P. Fry and Anna Szala, "The Evolution of Agonism: The Triumph of Restraint in Nonhuman and Human Primates," in Douglas P. Fry, ed., *War, Peace, and Human Nature: The Convergence of Evolutionary and Cultural Views*, Oxford: Oxford University Press, 2013, pp. 451–74, at 468.
61 Robert Trivers, building on work by W. D. Hamilton and others on non-human species, argues that "reciprocal altruism," in which one is prepared to do something to one's own disadvantage provided that some form of tradeoff is forthcoming at a later time, has characterized human evolution as dependent on such reciprocity. See, R. L. Trivers, "The Evolution of Reciprocal Altruism," *Quarterly Review of Biology*, vol. 46 (1971), pp. 35–57; and W. D. Hamilton, "The Genetical Evolution of Social Behavior II," *Journal of Theoretical Biology*, vol. 7, no. 1 (July 1964), pp. 17–52. That an indefinite number of opportunities need to exist to support such a system, which might seem to be built into tribal forms of reciprocity, is not, however, sufficient in its own right to demonstrate (even when claimed) that tribalism is a necessary means or end to such evolution. See, Christopher Stephens, "Modelling Reciprocal Altruism," *British Journal for the Philosophy of Science*, vol. 47, no. 4 (December 1996), pp. 533–51.
62 See, Daniel C. Dennett, *From Bacteria to Bach and Back: The Evolution of Minds*, New York: Norton, 2018. See also, the review of Dennett's book by Thomas Nagel, "Is Consciousness an Illusion," *New York Review of Books*, March 9, 2017, pp. 32–34. Note the vagueness in the analogies upon which Dennett relies: He cites Richard Dawkins' memes, which the latter defines as "a kind of way of behaving (roughly) that can be copied," while also equating heritability of a trait with copying. But since a successor can accept or reject, alter or make fun of any such copies the whole question of how such features become sufficiently fixed as to constitute real evolution and not simple change or alteration remains unspecified.
63 Robert L. Carneiro, *Evolutionism in Cultural Anthropology*, Boulder, CO: Westview Press, 2003, p. 276. For a much more simplistic version of

this supposed story of human development see, Francis Fukuyama, *The Origins of Political Order: From Prehuman Times to the French Revolution*, New York: Farrar, Strauss and Giroux, 2011.

64 Lewis Henry Morgan, *Systems of Consanguinity and Affinity of the Human Family*, Washington: Smithsonian Institution, 1871.

65 Ernest Gellner's 'kinks' in the system of High Atlas Berbers of Morocco – and by extension to most tribes – being an example of the failure to set aside a rule when the exceptions suggest some other proposition is in fact at work. For a similar instance of an anthropologist trying to make the exceptions fit the existing paradigm see, e.g., Daryll Forde, *Yako Studies*, Oxford: Oxford University Press, 1964.

66 Already in his study of the Nuer E. E. Evans-Pritchard hinted that the idea that primitive peoples simply follow their expressed rules fails to appreciate that many such propositions are rather idealized 'idioms' subject to being manipulated by individual actors. See, Thomas O. Beidelman, 'Nuer Priests and Prophets: Charisma, Authority and Power among the Nuer,' in T. O. Beidelman, ed., *The Translation of Culture: Essays to E .E. Evans-Pritchard*, London: Tavistock, 1971, pp. 375–415.

67 Fredrik Barth, *Political Leadership among Swat Pathans*, London: The Athlone Press, 1959, pp. 2 and 23.

68 Leach's particular findings have been challenged by a number of commentors: see James C. Scott, *The Art of Not Being Governed*, New Haven: Yale University Press, 2010.

69 Robert F. Spencer, *The North Alaskan Eskimo*, Washington, DC: U.S. Government Printing Office, Bureau of Ethnology Bulletin No. 171, 1959. In the UK, too, anthropologists of the Manchester School (Max Gluckman, A. L. Epstein, et al.) were also stressing the role of individuals in tribal societies. It may not be irrelevant that many of these scholars came, both academically and socially, from more marginal parts of British society and saw in individual effort important features of social advancement. The same is perhaps true of many of the anti-evolutionary Boasians in the United States.

70 Mark Nuttal, "Choosing Kin: Sharing and Subsistence in a Greenlander Hunting Community," in Peter P. Schweitzer, ed., *Dividends of Kinship: Meaning and Uses of Social Relatedness*, London: Routledge, 2000, pp. 33–60, at 34 and 45.

71 Ibn Khaldun, *Kitab al-Ibar*, vol. 6, p. 138, cited in Abdelmajid Hannoum, *The Invention of the Maghreb: Between Africa and the Middle East*, Cambridge: Cambridge University Press, 2021.

72 Evans-Pritchard, *The Nuer*, 1940, p. 221; Sahlins, *Tribesmen*, p. 11.

73 Sahlins, *Tribesmen*, p. 55 and 66.

74 Roy Wagner, *The Curse of Souw: Principles of Daribi Clan Definition and Alliance in New Guinea*, Chicago: University of Chicago Press, 1967, p. 191.

75 Roger Keesing, "Statistical Models and Decision Models of Social Structure: A Kwaio Case," *Ethnology*, vol. 6, no. 1 (1967), pp. 1–16, at 2.

76 J. van Velsen, "The Extended-case Method and Situational Analysis," in A. L. Epstein, ed., *The Craft of Social Anthropology*, London: Tavistock Publications, 1967, pp. 129–49, at 146. See also, his *The Politics of Kinship; A Study in Social Manipulation among the Lakeside Tonga of Nyasaland*, Manchester: Manchester University Press, 1964.

77 Clyde Kluckhohn, "The Philosophy of the Navaho Indians," in Morton H. Fried, ed., *Readings in Anthropology, vol. II*, New York: Crowell, 1959, p. 434; and Marshall Sahlins, *Tribesmen*, p. 19.

78 David M. Schneider and John M. Roberts, *Zuni Kin Terms*, Lincoln, NE: University of Nebraska Press, 1956, p. 21. Schneider pursued his revision of kinship theory in *American Kinship: A Cultural Account*, Englewood, NJ: Prentice-Hall, 1968.
79 H. W. Scheffler, "Ancestor Worship in Anthropology: or, Observations on Descent and Descent Groups," *Current Anthropology*, vol. 7, no. 5 (1966), pp. 541–51, at 546.
80 See, e.g., J. Clyde Mitchell, *Cities, Society, and Social Perception: A Central African Perspective*, Oxford: Clarendon Press, 1987.
81 Daniel Gross, "A New Approach to Central Brazilian Social Organization," in Maxine L. Margolis and William E. Carter, eds., *Brazil: Anthropological Perspectives*, New York: Columbia University Press, 1979, pp. 321–42, at 333.
82 Fred Gearing, "The Structural Poses of 18th-century Cherokee Villages," *American Anthropologist*, vol. 60, no. 6 (December 1958), pp. 1148–56, at 1149.
83 See, e.g., J. Van Velsen, "The Extended-case Method and Situational Analysis," in A. L. Epstein, ed., *The Craft of Social Anthropology*, London: Tavistock Publications, 1967, pp. 129–49, at 146 where he argues: "One of the assumptions on which situational analysis rests is that the norms of society do not constitute a consistent and coherent whole. On the contrary, they are often vaguely formulated and discrepant. It is this fact that allows for their manipulation by members of a society in furthering their own aims, without necessarily impairing its apparently enduring structure of social relationships."
84 Dean Snow, "The Dynamics of Ethnicity in Tribal Society: A Penobscot Case Study," in Parkinson, ed., *The Archaeology of Tribal Societies*, pp. 97–108, at 98. For the Comanche example see, Pekka Hämäläinen, *Comanche Empire*, New Haven: Yale University Press, 2008, pp. 255–57.
85 James Woodburn, "Egalitarian Societies," *Man*, New Series, vol. 17, no. 3. (September 1982), pp. 431–451, at 434 (original italics).
86 Gary Witherspoon, *Language and Art in the Navajo Universe*, Ann Arbor: The University of Michigan Press, 1977, pp. 111 and 114.
87 Robert Lowie, *The History of Ethnological Theory*, New York: Rinehart, p. 235; Alfred Kroeber, *Anthropology*, rev. edn., New York: Harcourt Brace, 1948 [1923], p. 261.
88 E. R. Leach, *Political Systems of Highland Burma*, Boston: Beacon Press, 1954, p. 290.
89 Ira Bashkow, "A Neo-Boasian Conception of Cultural Boundaries," *American Anthropologist*, vol. 106, no. 3 (September 2004), pp. 443–58. Bashkow (p. 451) continues: "But as the Boasians knew, a general-purpose compartmentalization of humanity is chimerical. They found no basis for assuming an ideal coincidence of the boundaries of collectivities, cultures, languages, and historical populations or races. Indeed, our knowledge of the possible bases on which human worlds can be segmented has only increased since their time."
90 The nature and extent of physical boundedness undoubtedly varies, and the pressures of colonial intervention – as we will see in Chapter five - has both exploded and created boundaries that were not characteristic of pre-colonial times. For examples, see Issac Schapera, *Government and Politics in Tribal Societies*, New York: Schocken, 1967, p. 14.
91 Francis Jennings, *The Invasion of America*, p. 71.

92 On the Walbiri, see Mervyn Meggitt, *Desert People: A Study of the Walbiri Aborigines of Central Australia*, Sydney: Angus & Robertson, 1962. Interestingly, Meggitt notes (as have others for the Eskimo/Inuit and Bushmen/ !Kung San) that it is in times of greatest scarcity that, even in those cases where territoriality is normally stricter, that one may, with compensation, enter others' territory uninvited. (p. 44). Elman Service (*Primitive Social Organization: An Evolutionary Perspective*, New York: Random House, 1962, pp. 42, 38–39) concludes more generally: "The more primitive the society and the more straightened the circumstances, the greater the emphasis on sharing, and the more scarce or needed the items the greater the sociability engendered."

93 Arthur J. Ray (*Telling It To the Judge: Talking Native History to Court*, Montreal: McGill-Queen's University Press, 2011) describes Canadian First Nation tribes who used an area for sacred purposes that others used for resource purposes.

94 See, generally Bruce Chatwin, *The Songlines*, London: Jonathan Cape, 1987.

95 See, Stanley Walens, *Feasting with Cannibals: An Essay on Kwakiutl Cosmology*, Princeton: Princeton University Press, 1981; and María Nieves Zedeño, "Bundled Worlds: The Roles and Interactions of Complex Objects from the North American Plains," *Journal of Archaeological Method and Theory*, vol. 15 (2008), pp. 362–78.

96 See, e.g., Michael Meeker, *Literature and Violence in North Arabia*, Cambridge: Cambridge University Press, 1979.

97 See, for the official position on the Sahara of the Moroccan government, particularly as it relates to tribes, Government of Morocco, Ministry of Communication, "Historical Foundations of the Moroccanity of the Sahara," 1997. http://web.archive.org/web/20070210082420/http://www.mincom.gov.ma/english/reg_cit/regions/sahara/s_hist.htm (accessed September 7, 2025). See also, the judgment on the dispute by the International Court of Justice, "Western Sahara: Advisory Opinion," October 16, 1975. https://web.archive.org/web/20020211110516/http://www.icj-cij.org/icjwww/idecisions/isummaries/isasummary751016.htm (accessed September 7, 2025).

98 Judith Irvine, "Subjected Words: African Linguistics and the Colonial Encounter," *Language and Communication*, vol. 28, no. 4 (2008), pp. 323–343.

99 Irvine, *Subjected Words*, 2008.

100 See, e.g., the numerous examples for southern Africa in Schapera, *Government and Politics in Tribal Societies*, pp. 19–20.

101 Ira Bashkow, "A Neo-Boasian Conception of Cultural Boundaries," *American Anthropologist*, vol. 106, no. 3 (September 2004), pp. 443–58, at 451.

102 Jared Diamond, *The World Until Yesterday*, New York: Viking, 2012.

103 Gaia Vince, "Why Being Bilingual Helps Keep Your Brain Fit," *Mosaic*, August 6, 2016.

104 E. H. Gombrich, *A Little History of the World*, New Haven: Yale University Press, 2005.

105 Dell Hymes, "Linguistic Problems in Defining the Concept of 'Tribe'," in June Helm, ed., *Essays on the Problem of Tribe*, Seattle: University of Washington Press for the American Ethnological Society, 1968, pp. 23–48, at 44.

106 Bashkow, "A Neo-Boasian Conception of Cultural Boundaries," pp. 453–54.

107 Paul Dresch, "Imams and Tribes: The Writing and Acting of History in Upper Yemen," in Philip S. Khoury and Joseph Kostiner, eds., *Tribes and State Formation in the Middle East*, Berkeley: University of California Press, 1990, pp. 256 and 281; and his "The Significance of the Course Events Take

in Segmentary Systems," *American* Ethnologist, vol. 13, no. 2 (May 1986), pp. 309–24.
108 See, e.g., the case cited by Paul Radin, *Primitive Man as Philosopher*, New York: D. Appleton and Co., 1927, p. 44.
109 Sahlins, *Tribesmen*, p. 55.
110 Dresch, "Imams and Tribes," p. 278.
111 Derek Williams, *Romans and Barbarians*, New York: St. Martin's Press, 1999, p. 206.
112 See, e.g., Richard Fletcher, *The Barbarian Conversion*, New York: Henry Holt, 1997.
113 On the research showing movement of European groups in this period, see the lecture by Patrick Geary, "Barbarian Invasions and Genomic History," Institute for Advanced Study, Princeton, 2013. www.ias.edu/ideas/2013/geary-invasion-video (accessed September 7, 2025).
114 Peter S. Wells (*The Barbarians Speak*, Princeton: Princeton University Press, 1999, pp. 116–19) is, therefore, correct to characterize the Barbarian 'tribes' at the time of Rome as "complex, multilingual, culturally diverse indigenous peoples." But to suggest that the state created the tribes by establishing boundaries and supporting leaders and mediators from the tribes is misleading not because such interactions did not occur but because denominating these entities as tribes and confusing established leadership with the total absence of temporary and purpose-directed leadership misses the key aspects of tribal identity and the tribes' ability to mold themselves around foreign forms. By the time Rome became dominant tribes, in the sense argued here, had already been replaced by paramount chiefdomships, hence the term 'tribe' is poorly applied to the case of the Barbarians of Roman Europe. For an argument similar to that of Wells see, Adrian Goldsworthy, *How Rome Fell*, New Haven: Yale University Press, 2009, p. 107 and citations therein.
115 The terminological confusion may be at the heart of the debate over continuing to use the term tribe to describe African groups. Ass one scholar notes: "Western writers are often squeamish about using the word *tribe*, and some Western and African academics will even tell you the colonialists invented the concept. They are simply playing with words because they are embarrassed that the word *tribe* has, wrongly, for some people become synonymous with 'backwardness.' Nevertheless, tribes exist within many nation-states in Africa and elsewhere – it seems pointless to deny their importance." Tim Marshall, *The Age of Walls*, New York: Scribner, 2018, p. 159 (original italics).
116 "Tribe," *Encyclopaedia Britannica*, 1911, vol. 27, p. 262.
117 H. A. MacMichael, "The Kababish: Some Remarks on the Ethnology of a Sudan Arab Tribe," *The Journal of the Royal Anthropological Institute of Great Britain and Ireland*, vol. 40 (1910), pp. 215–31.
118 E. E. Evans-Pritchard, "The Nuer of the Southern Sudan," in M. Fortes and E. E. Evans-Pritchard, eds., *African Political Systems*, Oxford: Oxford University Press, 1940, p. 278.
119 Alan Bernard and Jonathan Spencer, eds., *Encyclopedia of Social and Cultural Anthropology*, London: Routledge, 1996, p. 626. For these and other definitions see, David Sneath, "Tribe," *The Cambridge Encyclopedia of Anthropology*, September 1, 2016, www.anthroencyclopedia.com/entry/tribe (accessed September 7, 2025).
120 Philip Carl Salzman, ed., *When Nomads Settle: Process of Sedentarization as Adaptation and Response*, New York: Praeger, 1980, p. 4.

121 Thomas S. Kuhn, *The Structure of Scientific Revolutions*, 4th edn., Chicago: University of Chicago Press, 2012 [1962].
122 "We functionalist anthropologists are not really 'antihistorical' by principle; it is simply that we do not know how to fit historical materials into our framework of concepts." Leach, *Political Systems*, p. 282.
123 The internal quotation is from Toshihiko Izutsu, *Ethico-Religious Concepts in the Qur'an*, Montreal: McGill University Press, 1966.
124 See, Lawrence Rosen, *Varieties of Muslim Experience*, Chicago: University of Chicago Press, 2008, pp. 121–30; and Lawrence Rosen, "Ibn Khaldun on the Individual in History," in Houari Touati, ed., *Ibn Khaldun and the Science of Man*, Leiden: E. J. Brill, 2024.
125 Evans-Pritchard, *The Nuer*, 1940, pp. 147–48.
126 Marshall D. Sahlins, "The Segmentary Lineage: An Organization of Predatory Expansion," *American Anthropologist*, vol. 63, (April 1961), pp. 322–45.
127 Sahlins did, however, note: "tribal feelings and intercommunity connections are not always to be trusted in a showdown – Melanesian villages have been known to ally with foreign trading-partners in wars against communities of their own kind – testimony to the spirit of tribalism!" Sahlins, *Tribesmen*, p. 23.
128 Raymond C. Kelly, *The Nuer Conquest*, Ann Arbor: University of Michigan Press, 1985.
129 Patricia Crone, "Tribes and States in the Middle East," in her *From Arabian Tribes to Islamic Empire*, Aldershot, UK: Ashgate Variorum, 2008, p. 361. On the Pashtun word for cousin (*turbur*) – and such proverbs as 'a cousin's tooth breaks on another cousin's teeth' and 'keep a cousin poor – and use him' – see Louis Dupree, "Tribal Warfare in Afghanistan and Pakistan: A Reflection of the Segmentary Lineage System," in Akbar Ahmed and David Hart, eds., *Islam in Tribal Societies*, London: Routledge and Kegan Paul, 1984, pp. 266–86, at 269.
130 See, on the studies of Emrys Peters and others refuting segmentary theory, Dale Eickelman, *The Middle East: An Anthropological Approach*, 2nd edn., Englewood, NJ: Prentice Hall, 1989, pp. 126–50. See also, Lawrence Rosen, *The Culture of Islam*, Chicago: University of Chicago Press, 2002, pp. 39–55.
131 See, e.g., the discussion in this regard at James C. Scott, *The Art of Not Being Governed*, pp. 230ff.
132 Others who echo this view and see tribes as largely a creation of states include Aidan W. Southall, "The Illusion of Tribe," *Journal of Asian and African Studies*, vol. 5, nos. 1-2 (January and April 1970), pp. 28–50; Mahmood Mamdani, *Define and Rule: Native as Political Identity*, Cambridge: Harvard University Press, 2012; and Peter S. Wells, *The Barbarians Speak*, pp. 116–19.
133 For an excellent example of how our view of the Bushmen, for example, is altered when history is taken seriously into account see, Robert Gordon and Stuart Sholto-Douglas, *The Bushman Myth: The Making of a Namibian Underclass*, Boulder: Westview Press, 2nd edn., 2000.
134 David R. Dow, *The Autobiography of an Execution*, New York: Twelve (Hachette), 2010.
135 Donald N. Levine, *The Flight from Ambiguity*, Chicago: University of Chicago Press, 1985.

3
SHIFTING THE PARADIGM

Part I: The Tribal Ethos

> "The heuristic value of scientific analogies is quite like the surprise of metaphor. The difference seems to be that the scientific analogy is more patiently pursued, being employed to inform an entire work or movement, where the poet uses his metaphor for a glimpse only."
>
> Kenneth Burke[1]

> "words...To lure the tribal shoals to epigram / And order."
>
> Seamus Heaney

Kenneth Burke and Seamus Heaney rightly note that any attempt to address the unknown often requires fashioning a metaphor through which what we think we already understand may be linked to whatever we are trying to comprehend. Given the limitations of earlier attempts, how else, then, might we think about tribes? As in so many other ventures in the sciences and humanities we immediately have recourse to metaphors, which are at once comprehensive and inexact, palpable yet imprecise. For if it is true, as the character in a novel once said, that "There are so many ways to go wrong. All we've got are metaphors, and they're never exactly right. You can't ever just Say. The. Thing." – yet it is equally true (to quote another novelist) that "just because something is a metaphor doesn't mean it can't be real" – then perhaps a well-placed metaphor can actually serve as both holistic guide *and* artistic glimpse as one tries to rethink the paradigm of tribe.[2]

Consider the amoeba. If, in approaching the amoeba, you think in terms of its present configuration you may already have missed the point. Biologists use the term amoeba both as a noun that points to a type of cell and in its adjectival form to describe the kind of shape-altering movement that some entities employ as they extend a portion of themselves in various directions. Thus, one of the things that is most distinctive to amoebas is not their momentary shape but their capacity for reconfiguration to fit changing circumstances, the term itself coming from the Greek meaning "change." Amoeboid-like cells do not comprise a restricted taxonomic category: They can be found not only among protozoa but in a variety of plants, fungi, algae, and animals – including human white blood cells – the shared feature being the ability to reach out first in one direction, then another, altering their shape to navigate their environment. Notwithstanding their appearance of structural simplicity amoebas display most of the vital functions of higher animals – reproduction, response to stimuli, metabolism, and growth. When resources are in short supply they may also group together, operating collectively to the advantage of each. Indeed, in potentially toxic environments amoeba can go dormant, forming a protective barrier as they harden into a cyst, remaining in that state until they either die (if unable to outlast a change in circumstance) or re-emerge, disperse, and complete their life cycle. Indeed, just as an amoeba carries a genome 100-200 times larger than that of humans – retaining the accumulated sequences of its exceptionally long history – so, too, perhaps, tribes have sequestered elements of their consolidated past against a time when some obscure part of their repertoire may prove advantageous.[3] Like tribes, amoeba may be viewed simultaneously in terms of the ways they are momentarily configured and the ways in which they mold themselves to their larger surround. And because amoeboid elements may be found in a variety of life forms the notion of a tribal ethos that may be incorporated in a range of social entities makes the analogy all the more appealing.

The danger with any metaphor, of course, is that it may be taken too far, reifying the similarity into a homology or allowing the portion to stand misleadingly for the whole. Yet part of a metaphor's allure no doubt lies in its almost magical quality as "knowledge existing in several states simultaneously and without contradiction," a particularly fitting image when one thinks of tribes as possessing amoeba-like qualities.[4] For like amoebic cells and amoeboid movement tribes are shape-shifters, their essential qualities lying not in their momentary configuration but in the ability to alter their form in order to traverse disparate environs and cope with changing circumstances. Even the image of the amoeboid cyst, hardening itself against an adverse situation and hunkering down – hopefully not to the point of death – while awaiting a more favorable time recalls the situation of many tribes, as we saw in the Mashpee case, whose ability to go dormant is hardly the same as dissolution. If the biologist's task is not just to classify but to analyze the qualities that are distinctive to those entities that display amoeboid capabilities, then the analogy to tribes may be useful in probing its characteristics. So, if we shift the paradigm of tribe away from evolutionary stages and structural forms to concentrate on the features that contribute to the shapeshifting, adaptively ambulatory capacities of tribes several aspects in particular warrant consideration.

Dispersing Power

Let's start with power. After all, even if one does not assume, as did the Michigan cultural evolutionists of the 1960s, that the key to any form of organization is the ability to harness energy – whether for sheer survival, to fuel greater differentiation and specialization, or to propel fellow tribesmen in a desired direction – the means and extent to which control over resources and others' actions is garnered and circumscribed may tell us a good deal about a society's competence and adaptability. In the case of tribes one of the key characteristics has to do with the mechanisms by which power is dispersed. Indeed, if, as the ancient Greek poet Archilochus, said, "The fox knows many things, but the hedgehog knows one big thing," tribes are like the latter, knowing that concentrated power invariably may pose a serious threat to social cohesion. Put most concisely: tribes do not like too much power in too few hands for too long a period of time. That is not to say, as have those who romanticize this feature, that tribes are some form of primal democracy: A generalized distaste for long-term, consolidated control and the elaboration of practices for its implementation do not necessarily incorporate electoral choice or inalienable rights. Nor, as we will see momentarily, does it mean that tribes are characterized by egalitarianism in every situation or circumstance. It also does not mean, as the negative overtones of our use of the term "tribal" too often implies, that tribesmen cannot be trusted to keep their word or show democratic propensities because they are only too ready to alter their attachments as circumstances warrant. And just because power is dispersed does not mean that tribes are necessarily organized around a tacit constitution, whose customary rules, however developed, constrain outcomes, however contested. Rather, the operative class of mechanisms that are characteristic of tribal approaches to power is better thought of as one that slows and diffuses power through a set of behavioral norms and orientations idiosyncratically and contextually applied, many of which are embraced in economic, ritual, and political practices.

One category of such contrivances is often covered under the rubric of "levelling," a feature that embraces a wide range of economic and non-economic manifestations. Economic levelling is common among tribal peoples, but two interconnected stereotypes immediately affect our understanding of such practices. There is, first, the image of everything being produced and possessed collectively, every tribal member being kept at the same common denominator level – so much so that hunter-gatherers have been characterized at times as living in "primitive communism" – and, secondly, an image of tribal groups as suppressing individuality in the name of group survival.[5] Richard B. Lee, who has done extensive studies among the Bushmen (San) of southwest Africa, corrects the first point and summarizes the actual case:

> What is the irreducible core of the communal mode of production? The key to this question lies in the remarkable institution of the levelling device....[V]isualize two horizontal parallel lines. The upper line is a ceiling of accumulation of goods above which an individual cannot rise, and the lower line is a floor of destitution below which one cannot sink. In the communal mode the ceiling and the floor are closely connected; one cannot exist without the other. No one can have too much, and if there is any food in the camp, everybody in the camp is going to get some of it.[6]

In fact, as Lee himself is quick to note, while there are numerous formal and informal mechanisms for redistribution within a given tribe, there are, contrary to the second stereotype, often significant differences in the possession of material goods and personal prestige. And, as we will see later, it is not only in relation to material and status aspects that the individuality of tribal men and women is played up. For now, there are three features concerning property and ownership commonly found among tribal groupings that warrant elaboration.

First, property must be put to good use: In Paul Radin's telling phrase, *"it must serve."*[7] Through constant circulation – whether using gifts to create an expectation of return, engaging in mutual aid tasks for the benefit of all, or fulfilling the obligation to redistribute items to a range of kin and trade partners – keeping goods and services cloistered, hidden, or inert runs contrary to the broad ethos of tribal exchange. This does not mean that cumulation may not occur or that items relating to personal identity may not be exclusive: Even a man's song among the Australian aborigines, the Andaman Islanders, and the natives of Greenland may be a vital individual holding, while a ritual garment among Northwest Coast Indians may remain within one person's control for a lifetime and a bird's nest among the Kai of New Guinea may be the property of whoever first sights it.[8] Among the Iroquois, to take a characteristic example, "ownership of private property certainly existed. Its definition, however, rested on need and use rather than mere possession...[P]roperty belonged to those individuals and kin groups who needed and made active use of them."[9]

> For the Navajo knowledge is power, and the greatest power to transform or restore various conditions comes from the knowledge of various rituals.... Ritual knowledge can be purchased but it cannot be produced; it can be learned but it cannot be discovered; it can be communicated but it cannot be destroyed.... Navajo do not postulate the possibility that language may distort reality or our perception of reality.... *In the Navajo view of the world, language is not a mirror of reality; reality is a mirror of language....* Ritual language does not describe how things are; it determines how they will be. Ritual language is not impotent; it is powerful. It commands, compels, organizes, transforms, and restores. It disperses evil, reverses disorder, neutralizes pain, overcomes fear, eliminates illness, relieves anxiety, and restores order, health, and well-being.
> Gary Witherspoon, *Language and Art in the Navajo Universe*, Ann Arbor: University of Michigan Press, 1977, pp. 33–34 (original italics)

Many forms of property are, in a sense, held in custody, rather than undivided dominion. Thus, the 'owner' of a water source among the Bushmen (San) must allow others access, a special-purpose headman of the Cheyenne must re-equip a miscreant after punishing him with the destruction of his goods, and even such symbolic items as the ceremonial paint bought by a Crow from his mother, the dentalia shells that have circulated to an individual Yurok, and the water allotment of a Middle Eastern tribesman must be put to beneficial use rather than merely cabined in one's control. Indeed, it is here, incidentally, that many explorers and missionaries, when making first contact with indigenous groups, made their fundamental – and sometimes fatal – mistake. For the tribesmen they encountered often appropriated some of the foreigners' goods without permission, the Westerners mistaking as outright theft the native's understanding that items must be circulated or used at all times.

In a sense, too, the seeming antithesis of this concept of beneficial use is actually proof of its applicability. For it is not uncommon in tribal groupings for goods to be destroyed as a way of levelling power and continuing the process of exchange through a new deal, so to speak, of the cards.[10] Destruction of items at the time of burial, conspicuous spoliation as part of a collective rite, or the overproduction of food items for extravagant feasting can, by the elimination of consolidated resources, all serve to revitalize the process of establishing bonds of interdependence and the expression of community values, as well as dispersing potential power based on accumulation of material or symbolic capital.[11] The archaeological record confirms that such practices of burial or destruction of goods upon the holder's death (though found as well in many paramount chiefdoms) has a long history among tribal groupings.[12]

Secondly, it is the relational nature of things that is so central to tribal ideas of territory, property, and space. The findings reported from studies by anthropologist Keith Basso provides a typical example:

> Like many indigenous groups, the Western Apache preserve their knowledge and history by passing them on as stories. If the listeners cannot picture themselves in the physical setting where the events are happening, then the events will be hard to imagine and will appear to 'happen nowhere', a preposterous idea. For them, "placeless events are an impossibility," wrote Basso. "Everything that happens must happen somewhere. The location of an event is an integral aspect of the event itself, and therefore identifying the event's location is essential to properly depicting – and effectively picturing – the event's occurrence. For these reasons ... placeless stories simply do not get told".[13]

Just as beneficial use actualizes relationships so, too, it forms an important basis for identity. As Marilyn Strathern notes: "If in a commodity economy things and persons assume the social form of things, then in a gift economy they assume the social form of persons."[14] This emphasis can, however, produce some notions of ownership that may strike outsiders as rather curious. For example, when Frederick Maning sought to build a house on unoccupied land in New Zealand in the 19th century one claimant said he owned the land because his grandfather had been killed on it, while another claimed it because his grandfather had done the killing![15]

The focus on resources, material and immaterial, as relational also requires a more or less elaborate search for information, whether of another's network of attachments or of the most effective ways to form such bonds. Nick Araho, of the Papua New Guinea National Museum, stresses the importance of a free flow of such information when he writes: "Borrowing information between groups characterizes Papua New Guinea...The sharing of information only requires permission or the exchange of gifts."[16] Such examples underscore two general points about the tribal ethos that will be explored in greater detail shortly. First, a running imbalance of obligation, far from undermining such a system, actually vitalizes it: As many tribesmen demonstrate, in debt there is relationship. And second, while the absence of centralized power and the manipulation of kinship and territory may yield societies that appear loosely organized, if not anarchic, tribal systems may be regarded, like chaotic systems studied by mathematicians and physicists, as rich in information if lacking in settled order even though, in the social if not the physical world, the two are not, in fact, at war with one another.

Perceptions of the person necessarily engage aspects of the concept of things as well. A common stereotype of tribes, for instance, is that their members regard all land as communal and sacred – that no individual has the right to sell the land or otherwise alienate it, and that the land is a source of nurturance whose violation by misuse or misappropriation would be tantamount to sacrilege.[17] In fact, the range of rights and duties, privileges and liabilities is not only vast among the world's tribes but has been the source of serious and consequential argument among observers who have tried to understand it, a point that may, for example, affect the testimony of scholars and the decisions of judges when addressing native land claims cases. Some generalizations may, however, be suggested.

If we think in terms of the interests that various parties have in property we can conceptualize any individual's relationship to a wide variety of objects as involving a person's relationship to that thing or, alternatively, as the relationship he or she has to other people as it concerns that thing. Both forms may receive sanctions, although the latter may tend to be more distinctively jural in nature while the former may also involve a range of intellectual, emotional, and psychological concerns. Analytically, then, I may have an exclusive right to use a fishing site at a given time of the year and all the world (or some portion thereof) may have a duty not to interfere with that exclusive use. Or what I possess is not a right I hold against all the world but a privilege, one that others must respect but which is granted rather than inherent, defeasible, or limited, and may thus imply a continuing interest on the part of the community as a whole. The point is that if we trace out a series of reciprocal relationships toward things and others in these terms the style of tribal approaches to such matters possesses emphases that are somewhat different in distribution and intensity than those that tend to be found in other forms of cultural orientation, particularly as they concern the distinction between rights and privileges. Most Western nations place a great deal of stress on rights and their jural protection, whereas tribal societies tend to emphasize the idea of privilege over that of rights. For example, a single individual may be in charge of a given fishing site or gathering zone, but not only must he or she make continuous use of the resource, but the "owner" may not deny others access if their need is great enough.

Finally, momentary access to a resource may not, in and of itself, be converted into a permanent form of power over others. Robert Denton notes that among the Semai of Malaya (as among many other tribes) there is no word for "thank you" since an expression of gratitude for the meat a hunter must distribute equally, or the performance of an expected service would suggest either an unwarranted degree of calculation or an expression of surprise at the success and generosity of the hunter. Similarly, Richard Lee tells how, as a way of thanking the Bushmen (San) among whom he had worked, he presented a bull for shared feasting only for the tribesmen to belittle the animal – a response he later realized was a way of showing that the donor needs to be reminded that he may not regard himself as superior by virtue of such an act.[18] Indeed, San hunter-gatherers are ritually ridiculed for their prowess: As James Suzman notes, plant foods gathered mainly by women, are "not subject to any strict conventions on sharing," whereas the distribution of hunted meat follows definite lines of relationship. However, "'when a young man kills much meat,' as one Bushman told anthropologist Richard B. Lee, 'he comes to think of himself as a chief or a big man, and he thinks of the rest of us as his servants or inferiors. We can't accept this'." Insulting the hunter is thus intended to "cool his heart and make him gentle." For these hunter-gatherers, Suzman writes, "the sum of individual self-interest and the jealousy that policed it was a fiercely egalitarian society where profitable exchange, hierarchy, and significant material inequality were not tolerated."[19]

Nonetheless, we should not assume simple egalitarianism among tribal peoples: Some inequalities are common, whether symbolic, material, reproductive, or sociological. Unlike ranked chiefdoms, where control of unevenly distributed resources is institutionalized, tribes strive to balance decentralizing and power-accumulating forces. In the process there are both costs and benefits, levelling impulses, and fissiparous tendencies. The result is not necessarily the equalization of all. Thus, among the Arunta of Australia it is the elders – like shamans and medicine men elsewhere – who, reinforcing their position through such rituals as mandatory circumcision of their juniors, are able to require the younger men to supply them with meat for many years, to reserve the best portions for themselves through food taboos imposed on initiands, and to retain access to the tribe's women for themselves.[20] Similarly, Paul Spencer showed how men of the Samburu of East Africa, who move through life in age-graded groups to ever higher levels of power, are under threat of curse by their elders if they should be seen to contemplate marriage to women of their own generation, such women being reserved for the elders.[21] Marshall Sahlins' assertion that egalitarian societies do not project hierarchy onto a supernatural plane is misleading twice over, first because it assumes strict egalitarianism to begin with, and second, because some elements of transcendentalism are present in even those societies that emphasize the presence of the spiritual at every level of existence.[22] Even in the face of levelling devices parents will always have some authority over offspring and leaders will be followed even if for limited times and purposes. Thus, among the Cree, "most power to control others' decisions and behavior was limited to the authority of men and women over their unmarried junior relatives."[23] Equality and hierarchy may be present simultaneously. Among the Iban of Borneo, for example, individuals "compete not only to assert their equality – to prove themselves equal to others – but they also seek, if possible, to excel and so exceed others in material wealth, power and reputation."[24] Moreover, internal conflict is hardly unknown in such societies. Among the Bushmen (San), for example, the image of them as "the harmless people" (to cite the title of Elizabeth Marshall Thomas' well-known book) is replaced by Richard Lee's more detailed studies showing that various levels of violent confrontation are prevalent, together with a variety of mechanisms – from joking to collective responsibility and the adoption of new courts – to cope with disputes.[25] Indeed, one might argue that it is characteristic of tribes that there is a constant – but never entirely successful – struggle against hierarchy, whether confined to a limited domain of kinship relations or evident in those rituals by which the tribesmen approach ancestors and spirits with characteristic ambiguity, being at once submissive and dismissive, deferential and dependent, or haranguing them with obscene joking, suspicion, and fear.[26]

Levelling also operates politically, taking a wide variety and combination of forms. It may involve formal requirements – rotation of position, limitation of terms, division of power by age, gender, or spirituality – features that tribes give priority, notwithstanding their comparable presence in more complex societies. Even in those societies (like Tonga) where significant differences in equality may have developed, periodic "egalitarian rebellions" and the use of multi-generational cycles of leadership often ameliorate the settlement of power in a single social group.[27] Once again, though, what is distinctive among tribes is the pervasive array of mechanisms that disperse power across the entire sociocultural spectrum. Pressures to share are intense, and where someone is regarded as a headman or chief he must persuade rather than command. This often extends to collective decision-making. As Joseph-François Lafitau (1681–1746), a Jesuit missionary and ethnologist who lived among the Iroquois, wrote of the tribesmen's councils:

> In general, we may say they are more patient than we in examining all the consequences and results of a matter. They listen to one another more quietly, show more deference and courtesy that we toward people

who express opinions opposed to theirs, not knowing what it is to cut a speaker off short, still less to dispute heatedly: they have more coolness, less passion, at least to all appearances, and bear themselves with more zeal for the public welfare.[28]

The Iroquois are a matrilineal society, one in which women play important roles in the distribution of governing powers. While not themselves exercising everyday executive power in all matters it was the women, for example, who had to agree to fund wars, and it was they who were deeply involved in the choice or retention of leaders. While there is no known society in which property and formal power are exclusively in the hands of women, the powers that individual females – especially older ones – may exercise can be considerable.[29] Such power may even result from their apparent weakness: Women often hold the good opinion men have of themselves, engage in less visible trade relations that easily rival those of the men, and contribute a more stable and nutritious diet by their gathering and gardening than male hunters may be able to produce – often with men downplaying or ignoring the women's contributions.[30] Indeed, in many tribal settings the women may see matters quite differently than the men. Aram Yengoyan notes how women of the Pitjantjatjara tribe of Australia tease the men about their subincision rites: They "mockingly refer to circumcision rites as 'more meat for the crows'."[31] Berber tribal women used to go out on the battlefield and throw henna, a dye normally associated with women, on any man who acted cowardly or tease the men unmercifully, even by baring their breasts, to egg the men on. We will see more about tribal women's economic roles shortly, but the point here is that gender practices also comport with the many other devices tribes display for the levelling of power across every domain of social life.[32]

Is the tribal version of levelling, then, one in which the demands of reciprocity even out the accumulation of material items and thus supports the preference for other "goods," such as honor, respect, or power over dependents? Mechanisms that would appear to serve this goal abound in tribal groups. We know, for example, that some tribes in the Middle East try to place limitations on power through set bridewealth payments while others effectively force the groom to show his manliness by forging the diverse bonds of obligation needed to gather that payment. At the same time, honor, which may seem intangible to outsiders, may have to be earned and safeguarded far more than any material wealth. In many instances the replacement of wealth with prestige takes place as tribesmen engage in a kind of forced redistribution through the destruction of material goods, the Kwakiutl Indians' potlatch being the most well-known, though atypical, version.[33] Indeed, some anthropologists see in the potlatch not just a transformation of conspicuous consumption into personal prestige but note that it occurs at moments when the alternatives presented by society for succession to influence or choice of marital alliances threaten social chaos. Thus the destruction of surplus may, like many rites of passage, serve to level individual power in the name of group harmony.[34]

Some forms of levelling occur along clear structural lines, others on an irregular and unformalized basis, and still others only at certain ceremonial times and places. There is, for example, ritualized joking behavior, in which certain categories of persons (in-laws, for instance, or even chiefs) are permitted – usually in a rather stylized, if not scatological, fashion – to be addressed by others in a manner that would be regarded as unacceptable under other conditions. Indeed, humor more generally plays a major role in tribal societies. Native American lawyer and writer Vine Deloria, Jr. has written:

> I sometimes wonder how anything is accomplished by Indians because of the apparent overemphasis on humor within the Indian world....For centuries before the white invasion, teasing was a method of control of social situations by Indian people. Rather than embarrass members of the tribe publicly, people used to tease individuals they considered out of step with the consensus of tribal opinion. In this way egos were preserved and disputes within the tribe of a personal nature were held to a minimum. Gradually people learned to anticipate teasing and began to tease themselves as a means of showing humility and at the same time advocating a course of action they deeply believed in. Men would depreciate their feats to show they were not trying to run roughshod over tribal desires. This method of behavior served to highlight their true virtues and gain them a place of influence in tribal policy-making circles.[35]

Elsewhere, tribal humor, institutionalized and ritualized, can be seen to cut people down to size, not letting them convert one form of accomplishment into more generalized power over others. Among the Cuna Indians of the San Blas Islands of Panama, for instance, ambivalence towards the chief's position is accompanied by "often run[ning] down the actual men who are filling it," while the sacred Dakota *heyoka*s, like many other Native American clowns and comic figures, engage in mimicry and outrageous antics that are the reverse of everyday behavior as a way of teasing those who may claim superior power.[36] Levelling may be extended towards religious figures, no less than relatives, leaders, or in-laws. Among southwestern Puebloans, for example, one kind of sacred clown, the *koshare*, drinks urine and bathes in dung as a way of showing how limited even the gods may be. Among the Koyukon of Northern Canada, Dotson'sa, the Great

Raven who fashioned the world, is characterized as "greedy, mannerless, and thoroughly undignified...a magical clown...who first created a world of flawless order and ease, then later transformed it to the imperfect one we know today." Possessing only a limited ability to answer prayers, Raven, while manipulative, may still be tricked: "And so Raven plays his game of wits, his unending frolic through the carnival world of his own creation. The humans in his menagerie – for whom he devised mortality, rivers that flow only downstream, mosquitos, and an assortment of other difficulties – can only look on and shake their heads, return a trick or two, and perhaps sing his mournful song."[37]

In other places it is common to hear native peoples bait the gods – and perhaps by implication those who claim access to them – by noting that if they were not honored by mankind even gods would cease to exist. When humor becomes ridicule it may seriously affect one's credibility and must, therefore, be avoided at all costs.[38] Mathias Guenther notes:

> Of the five mechanisms for keeping persons with power aspirations in check – public opinion, criticism, ridicule, disobedience, extreme sanctions – it is the third at which the Bushmen (and hunter-gathers in general) excel. Laughing at authority figures, or at individuals with authoritarian, arrogant, or boastful airs, is one of the most effective mechanisms for smothering dominance within a small group and for preventing the entrenchment of authority within social relationships.[39]

Indeed, humans are not the only ones who try to avoid ridicule. In Paul Radin's retelling:

> Even the deities are not exempt from this horror of ridicule. Among the Winnebago there exists a delightful story of a man who dared to state that he disbelieved in the powers of the most terrifying and holiest of the Winnebago deities, and who in public expressed his contempt for him. A short time later, the deity in question appeared to the skeptic and pointed his finger at him, an action that was supposed to bring immediate death. The man stood his ground and did not budge and the deity – Disease-Giver was his name – begged the man to die lest the people make fun of him![40]

Other religious figures may be no less susceptible to the levelling power of humor and ridicule. The teasing of shamans, which is common in many tribes of South America and sub-Saharan Africa, may even extend back through the ages to a time when those who painted a falling figure with an erect penis on the walls of Lascaux could have been mocking the power of the local shaman.[41] Humor can be vital in such situations, whether because its claim not to be serious makes a potentially aggressive response unacceptable or because it allows truth to be spoken to power with social approval. Anthropologists who come at such matters from a functionalist perspective usually explain this form of behavior as a device for defusing potential conflict. They point to the similar practice in Western societies where mother-in-law jokes, indicative of potential strain over the wife/daughter between a husband and the woman's mother, are still part of many comedians' repertoire.

But in the tribal situation more may be at stake. As a character in a novel by the Chippewa writer Gerald Vizenor says: "The tricksters and warrior clowns have stopped more evil violence with their wit than have lovers with their lust and fools with their power and rage."[42] Ritualized joking behavior, whether it really dissipates hostility or cagily displaces it, demonstrates that power may lie in words and not only control over material resources, that dominance is not always where or what it may seem to be, and that even a provocative taunt shows that power can be "'blown down with a whisper" and thus cannot be permanently cabined or secured.[43] Joking, as Mary Douglas pointed out, may have a "subversive effect on the dominant structure of ideas" and thus upset the balance of power since it "affords the opportunity for realizing that an accepted pattern has no necessity…that any particular ordering of experience may be arbitrary and subjective."[44] We can, then, understand the frustration of the Jesuit missionary who, upon encountering native peoples in Canada in the 17th century wrote:

> They imagine that by birthright they should enjoy the freedom of wild asses, subjecting themselves to no one, unless they so desire. They reproached me a hundred times that we fear our Chiefs, but they mock and make fun of theirs; all the chief's authority is at the tip of his lips, he is only as powerful as he is eloquent; and when he has killed himself talking and haranguing, he will not be obeyed unless it pleases the savages to do so.[45]

As the example above also suggests, the command of language is vital to both the claim to authority and its challenge. Accounts are rife with influential tribal leaders whose control of rhetorical skills is indispensable to their success. Whether it is the famous speeches of Chief Joseph or the palaver of a New Guinea "big man," capturing the terms of discussion is of the essence of influence within tribal societies. In the Middle Atlas Mountains of Morocco I have watched a poor tribesman shame a wealthy one into aiding in the annual cleaning of the tribal fraction's irrigation canals by reminding all present that it was as much a personal as a collective duty, not something the rich man could hire another to perform. Rhetorical ability is also vital to the settlement of disputes. Among many tribesmen – the Inuit, for example, and the tribes of North Africa – song duels, fraught with humorous barbs at one's opponent, turn on the ability to garner public support through the presentation of one's case.[46] Like the persuasive force of oratory and rhetorical skills, physical contact may also enact the sense of equalization and levelling among tribal peoples of both genders. Kenneth Read describes the "physical possessiveness" that characterizes relationships among highland New Guinea tribals: "Their customary greeting, a standing embrace in which both men and women handled each other's genitals, was an unfailing source of sniggering amusement to Europeans; but even in the villages, among people who saw one another every day, hands were continually reaching out to caress a thigh, arms to embrace a waist, and open, searching mouths hung over a child's lips, nuzzled a baby's penis, or closed with a smack on rounded buttocks."[47]

We see similar forces of levelling at work in the diverse use of trickster figures. Tricksters have been rightly described as possessing a mixture of characteristics – "the selfish rogue, the con man, the not-quite-clever-enough smart alec" who also embodies "touches of [Charlie] Chaplin's little man."[48] Trickster has also been described as "an agile parasite" who exists in "the context of no context," a "technician of appetite and of instinct" whose "hunger devours the ideal," a figure who steals in order to open new worlds and dissimulates to disrupt the accepted categories.[49] Among the tribes of the Northwest coast of America the main trickster figure, Raven, is variously referred to as having "insatiable, restless curiosity" as well as being "greedy, gluttonous, lustful, capricious, and powerful."[50] Among the Azande, the Ture figure may be ambiguously animal or human, doing "the opposite of all that is moral.... He is really ourselves. Behind the image [that] convention bids us present, in desire, in feeling, in imagination, and beneath the layer of consciousness we act as Ture does."[51] The trickster, whose "central – and universal – trait [is] ambiguity," is thus a figure who "enfranchises speculation...[through the] promiscuous intermingling and juxtaposing of categories."[52] Trickster is thus "the one...who embodies the contingent and in doing so lends it the appearance of necessity...[it being] the way of confidence men and tricksters to sell you what you already own."[53] The figure may be male, or female, or both at different times, but as Mary Manybeads Bowers notes generally: "The business of

Shifting the Paradigm, Part I: The Tribal Ethos **85**

FIGURE 3.1A Traditional raven mask from the Northwest Coast.

FIGURE 3.1B "Raven and the First Men" sculpture by Bill Reid.

a trickster is to take her work very seriously. It is to find a way to change the rhythm, to find a way to look at things differently."[54] Trickster figures have thus been invoked as symbols of protest, as, for example, when the Lenni Lenape prophet Neolin, in the 1760s, invoked the giant hare trickster as inspiration for opposing the corrupting influences of white settlers on Native Americans, a movement that further inspired Pontiac's War. Whether it is the coyote figure of the Nez Perce or the Winnebago Wadjunkaga, trickster confutes and exploits ambiguity as he stands on the threshold between a world of order and a world of chaos.[55] In that respect trickster would seem to embrace Henry Adams' notion that "chaos often breeds life, when order breeds habit," while the regularity of his irregular acts supports Terry Pratchett's quip that "chaos always defeats order, because it is better organized."[56]

FIGURE 3.1C Modern businessman portrayed as a raven figure.

That trickster figures provoke humor is also essential to their protean allure: Just as humor may be very serious indeed, so, too, the jesting trickster figures embody – even create – serious ambivalence towards power.[57] Neatly characterized as a "rule-breaking equalizer," the trickster embraces and reinforces ambiguity, thus relativizing power, decentering authority, and ensuring that the ability to manipulate categories does not become so inflexible as to fail in its adaptive potential.[58] Tricksters are also portrayed as culture heroes, credited (over any power-hungry human claimant) as the ones who presented mankind with useful technologies, edible foods, insightful analogies, and identifying myths. But tricksters can, at the same time, be preposterous and irresponsible, thereby suggesting that even the culture hero cannot be trusted with enduring power.

Overall, the rhetoric of power among tribals is commonly one of irony, where something that is said appears contrary to what is meant and (as Kierkegaard noted) a riddle and its solution appear simultaneously. But far from driving out clarity, irony can serve many purposes: It can be a way of countering a superior force without losing one's own sense of integrity; it can mollify one's sense of vulnerability and injury by offering a reaction to power that denies its ultimate force; and when embodied in such figures as a trickster, as Lawrence Sullivan suggests, it reveals that the structure of tribal society lies not in its precise organization but in its modes of attending to the creation of meaning.

> Irony binds widely separated opposites into a single figure so that contraries appear to belong together. In trickster chaos and order, sacred and profane, farce and meaning, silence and song, food and waste, word and event, pretended ignorance and pretended cunning, stone-life and flesh life, male and female, play and reality, compose not only an ironic symbol but a symbol of irony.
> Trickster's character and exploits embody the process of ironic imagination. His dynamism of composition mocks, shatters and re-forms the overly clear structure of the world and the overly-smooth images of the mind...In him the double-sidedness of reality reveals itself...
> What trickster's play reveals [is] how ludicrous is every vision of life constructed of hierarchies without ironic wholeness or formal arrangements without communication between one form and another. He reveals how static is the vision of life built on earthy corporeality without passage to [the] sacred spirit of metamorphosis.
>
> Lawrence Sullivan, "Multiple Levels of Religious Meaning in Culture: A New Look at Winnebago Texts," *Canadian Journal of Native Studies*, vol. 2, no. 2 (1982), pp. 221–47, at 238–39. Quoted in Ryan, *The Trickster Shift*, p. 8.

Here, then, for the first time in this study – but by no means the last – we encounter the power of ambivalence in tribal cultures. For as Paul Radin noted:

> Trickster is at one and the same time creator and destroyer, giver and negator, he who dupes others and who is always duped himself. He wills nothing consciously. At all times he is constrained to behave as he does from impulses over which he has no control. He knows neither good nor evil yet he is responsible for both. He possesses no values, moral or social, is at the mercy of his passions and appetites, yet through his actions all values come into being.[59]

Commenting on Radin's study – and notwithstanding his outdated use of the term "primitive" – Stanley Diamond extends aspects of the trickster as the agent of the ambiguous into the realm of religion more generally: "The principle of ambivalence is incorporated into the myths and rituals of primitive peoples to an extraordinary degree and in a variety of ways....

Even while creating their myths and ceremonials, their meanings and their insights, primitive peoples are aware of the reality they mold."[60] Radin cites the example of a Maori tribesmen who testified at a land claims trial: "'The god of whom I speak is dead.' The court replied, 'Gods do not die.' 'You are mistaken,' continued the witness, 'Gods do die unless there are *tuhungas* ("'priests'; actually, 'skilled practitioners') to keep them alive'."[61] Moreover, as Joseph Henrich reminds us, the gods of many tribal peoples "are typically whimsical. They're immoral. They're not concerned with your sexual behavior or your social behavior. Often you'll make bargains with them."[62] Indeed, while ever more encompassing tribal gods may mimic the levels of genealogical extension of a segmented tribe, frequently the ambivalence that accompanies their reflection of social scope has eluded analysts who may fail to see that the ability to choose the level of inclusion with which one identifies relativizes and limits power.

Trickster figures can serve as a symbolic encapsulation of human nature and the human condition. But they can also be the guide to practical action. Pekka Hämäläinen provides a striking example of the role of trickster in the political history of the Lakota, an example that underscores the themes of ambiguity and shapeshifting that characterize many manifestations of the tribal ethos generally.

> Iktómi, [is] a spider-trickster spirit and an imp of mischief who can speak with every living thing, fool gods with potions, manipulate humans through the strings of his web, and protect them from menace. His temperament, like his form, is supple and ambiguous. It is neither good nor evil.
>
> Iktómi is the mythological hero of the Sioux, a symbolic embodiment of their essential qualities and ideals as a people and, when they act recklessly, a warning of how not to behave. Shapeshifting involves potent spiritual power and it can be at once rewarding and dangerous, unpredictable and uplifting. Mirroring the shapeshifting trickster, Sioux were a pragmatic and adaptable people who considered extreme fluidity, even separation, both natural and necessary. That malleability sprang from the alchemy of kinship. Sioux understanding of the universe and belonging was based on clear categories: the larger Sioux community consisted of *ikčĕ wičháša*, "ordinary people," who formed one kindred community, takúkičhiyapi, beyond which all was danger. But these categories were also dynamic and contained the potential of inclusion. Although people outside the circle of kinship were strangers and enemies, kinship could be extended to them through *wólakȟota,* bonds of peace. The Sioux *were* allies, which was not a static condition but an active

spiritual mandate to embrace others. That embrace can include anyone capable of proper behavior and thoughts. It is theoretically limitless.

By the mid-eighteenth century the Sioux had shifted shape many times over. They had opened their lands and villages for real and potential allies—Sauteurs, Cheyennes, Mesquakies, Frenchmen, and many others—while contending with numerous rivals as they struggled to find a place in the rapidly changing world.

The [tribal] conquest [of the Great Plains] fostered a distinct political and cultural identity. Band by band, Lakotas detached from the main Sioux body, whose interests remained fixed to the east, and made the western grasslands their home. They became the nomads and bison hunters of the prairie; they were re-creating themselves in the West. In Lakota mythology, Iktómi is a helper spirit who can convince people to scatter or come together. Knowing how and when to do that was the basic requirement of successful nomadic hunting: Iktómi was guiding the Lakotas through a precarious metamorphosis, shifting shape with them in the vast new world in the West.[63]

Sexuality, too, may support the tribal emphasis on adaptability through ambiguity. For example, by finding a place for the transexual – like the Native American *berdach*, who cross-dresses and is regarded as possessing certain spiritual powers – the essential negotiability of gendered categories is underscored. Context is often crucial, with (as among the Navajo) ambiguity being played up when the meaning of gender, directions, and colors varies with the situation.[64] In terms of gender, numerous ethnographers – almost always male – had portrayed tribal women as powerless. But when women anthropologists like Phyllis Kaberry, Catherine Berndt, and Jane Goodale studied Australian aboriginal cultures and focused on the context of their actions they found women ran their own secret ceremonies, contracted with future husbands for the bestowal of their daughters, attended to alternative cosmologies, and established complex trade relations that not only paralleled those of men but spread power within the group.[65]

Another device that affects power in many tribes is "avoidance behavior." Here the rules of social interaction may bar certain forms or moments of contact between potential competitors or disputants. Thus, brothers and sisters may avoid one another since the brother's interest in his sister's property or procreative powers – interests that may be opposed to those of her husband – creates the risk of conflict between these two individuals or their respective supporters. In a matrilineal system, for example, the brother has a vital interest in the sister's offspring since it is her children who must service and continue their lineage rather than that of her husband, the respective interests of husband and brother constituting a source of possible tension. Even the idea of how conception takes place may undercut the consolidation of power. In Melanesia and Australia, for example, men may be regarded as irrelevant to procreation. Whether (as Geza Roheim suggests), when coupled with a belief in spirit-entry and reincarnation, this form of repressing images of parental sex allows "the son to represent himself as the agent of his own conception," uncertain claims of fatherhood and debatable theories of conception further diffuse and even randomize the powers that may accompany parenthood.[66]

Like sibling avoidance, mother-in-law avoidance is present in many tribal groups. Such avoidance may be further sanctioned by threats of illness and chaos. Among the aborigines of Australia, for example, a man's mother-in-law

> is a benefactress, his dearest friend because she gave him his wife. In return he must hunt for her and give her meat, yet he must not go near her, look at her, speak to her, or utter her name. She arouses in him feelings of profound shame, as well as fear, and her sexuality must be expunged from his consciousness. She is poison, a source of danger, polluting like a corpse. Yet myths tell of mother-in-law rape and son-in-law seduction, and rituals license forbidden conjunctions.[67]

Once again, ritualized relationships, whether through avoidance, joking, or assumptions about procreation, may contribute to the tribally characteristic diffusion of power.

To what must by now seem a litany of irritants alchemically transformed into functionally beneficial traits should also be added gossip and bloodmoney payments. Max Gluckman famously argued that gossip, far from being a form of divisive backbiting, helps to ascertain group standards, precipitate articulate leaders, establish corporate membership, and indirectly inform individuals of expected behavior.[68] Indeed, mechanisms for addressing disputes may, as Elizabeth Colson argued, give people an opportunity to learn crucial information, such as "the limits of community tolerance for different kinds of behavior under a variety of circumstances, an appreciation of how particular individuals respond to provocation, and some mapping of the changing alliances that form the basis for daily interaction."[69] Similarly, bloodmoney payments, from a functionalist perspective, can be said to limit violence (an eye for an eye – but no more), to spread the responsibility for recompense, to reinclude the offender in society, and to establish the respective value of various relationships and social positions.[70]

In some tribes even witchcraft accusations perform similar power-dispersing functions. For unlike the violent response to witchcraft in the history of Europe and colonial America, in the tribal world witchcraft accusations are often aimed at evening out the power that may be exercised over others. Such accusations may also operate as a kind of social insurance scheme, in which various injuries must be attributed to someone who, in turn, may be responsible for aiding the injured party, thus again distributing burdens (and bolstering interlocking obligations) across a broad and ever-changing social spectrum. Here, too, the usual result is not only a society-wide distribution of burdens but an attribution of blame, usually seen as the result of jealousy or greed beyond conscious control, which may befall anyone who seeks or garners too much power. Thus, even in the case of present-day South and East Africa, where a number of suspected witches have been killed in recent years, it may be better to see these murderous reactions as attempts at addressing a felt imbalance of power rather than as manifestations of boorish superstition and mistaken causality.[71] Similarly, in the American southwest, Pueblo baseball games often involve accusations of witchcraft, whether as a therapeutic way of venting pent-up hostility between families, to remind everyone that ability in one domain should not translate into power in other contexts, or as a way of displacing the greater fear that comes from people gossiping about oneself.[72] Nor is it uncommon, when joking or possible sanctions are voiced, for a spiritual figure to be reminded that his or her powers do not extend to the realm of the secular.[73]

Power-dispersing rituals can be very straightforward or operate indirectly. Indeed, ritual *reversals* are particularly prevalent among tribal groups. In a ritual reversal the normal state of things is turned upside down only for the social norms to be confirmed when everything is set to rights at the end. So, for example, the powerless may briefly take on the role of the powerful, often chiding the latter with vulgarities that would not be allowed to pass under other circumstances. Women and men may cross-dress (or undress) in such rituals, the young may beard the old, and the high-and-mighty may have to perform degrading tasks. Neighboring tribes may even invert one another's rituals thus relativizing their own. Among aborigines of the Kimberleys in Australia, for example, women engage in a ritual whereby they seek to throw off the shackles of their husbands by playing up the otherwise forbidden son-in-law as the ideal lover. Comedy is often integral to such reversals, for if things are funny (as well as being dirty or dangerous) because they are out of category it is imperative that the norms be reset by ritual's end. In the interim, great freedom and creativity receive expression. Similar features are, of course, not limited to tribal cultures. Thus George Meredith, writing in 1877, noted that comedy is woman's great friend, for in comedy the normal bounds are disrupted such that women are free to play roles and exercise powers not usually accorded them. Yet comedy, like other rituals of reversal, is the most conservative of forms, for in the end the social conventions are always reconfirmed: illicit lovers are married, shrewish wives are "tamed," traditional authority is reinstated.[74] In the tribal context, however, there are also certain differences – of emphasis, connection, and import – that synergistically reinforce other levelling devices. Indeed, during the course of ritual reversals in its tribal variants the deeper lesson is often not simply that of reconfirming social norms but reminding everyone that concentrated power is contingent, vulnerable, and susceptible to dissipation.

Moreover, as Victor Turner famously suggested, in ritual the interim between the suspension or dissolution of the norm and its reinstatement may be marked by a liminal period that harbors extreme danger, for not only are the structures of society momentarily suspended but there is no guaranty that matters will not spin out of control and society will not be properly reproduced. In tribal societies various rituals – including those of degradation, renewal, and reversal – are consonant with other cultural practices and beliefs that seek to relativize and even randomize power long enough for shared criteria to be reasserted and the preexisting structure of power, with all its inherent ambivalence, to once again appear dominant. Thus, in many tribal societies rituals of reinclusion are necessary to bring individuals back within the fold of normality after prior engagements – whether military, criminal, or otherwise threatening of the existing order – have rendered them dangerous or unclean. Sebastian Junger may, therefore, suggest that American soldiers are like tribesmen, but he fails to recognize that one of the key mechanisms of tribes, missing in American culture, are such rituals of reinclusion. Columnist David Brooks may rue the absence of such rituals without, however, noting how difficult they would be to incorporate in our society, when he writes: "I wish our culture had many more rites of passage, communal moments when we celebrated a moral transition. There could be a communitywide rite of passage for people coming out of prison, for forgiveness of a personal wrong, for people who felt they had come out the other side of trauma and abuse."[75]

While in some situations the process may be quite individualized, the liminal period may focus on the collective, as in various initiation rituals. In a number of African tribes, for instance, these rituals may transition whole age groups into new positions of authority and responsibility or, as in some New Guinea tribes, move a male through the relatively powerless role of a feminized homosexual partner into the more dominant role of a fully adult heterosexual man.[76] Similarly, in Morocco, the groom is sometimes dressed as a woman and tied up only to be freed and attired as a man at the conclusion of the marriage ritual, thus underscoring the dangers inherent in the transition to manliness. Moreover, in an initiation ritual the infliction of pain or degradation prior to being raised to full social inclusion may emphasize not only the contingent and dispersed nature of power but the foundational similarity and moral equality of all those undergoing the process.[77]

Narrative styles also highlight the relativization of power. Like tricksters, the point is often that multiple narratives are at work simultaneously, and though the world may seem to be violent and disordered a myth or story (like a legal proceeding) can render the multiple voices both comprehensible and resolvable without destroying the vital diversity that they represent and embody. One set of studies even shows that indigenous hunter-gatherers in the Philippines valued individuals' storytelling abilities over hunting or medicinal skills, such abilities leading to the raconteurs' increased receipt of gifts and personal generosity, emphasis on their role as articulators of vital information and group norms, and reinforcement of cooperative efforts among tribal members.[78] Narratives may, of course, vary by gender, no less than by individual experience: Aboriginal women may refer to male foreskins as dead meat, and Arab women may use a vocabulary the men do not understand. In each instance, the way one relates a common experience may be a key indicator of just how much a culture must be shared in order for us to think of it as a single entity.

Leadership

Leadership, too, is commonly partible in tribal groupings. As we will see, the roles of leaders in tribal societies are rarely those conjured by Western stereotypes, in which an individual leader is said to exercise comprehensive power and representation. To the contrary, there may (as among many Native American tribes) be different "chiefs" for different purposes or (as among some African and Middle Eastern tribes) task-specific leaders cast up as the result of contact with a state or town that seeks a person with whom they can deal on a given issue. Wartime leaders, in particular, may be acknowledged, but limits on their powers may take many forms, whether by having to gain assignment from the older women as among the Iroquois, having power rotated regularly as among many Berber tribes of North Africa, or being held responsible for the deaths of followers through poor leadership as among many Native American tribes.

Moreover, if it is necessary in tribal societies to prove that one has the characteristics ideally associated with leadership in order to be acknowledged as a leader than anyone else who shows these qualities may be regarded as ipso facto legitimate. In those instances – where there may also be a basis in descent for potential leadership – a kind of justification by acts is at work as it must constantly be proved that one not only possesses the qualities of leadership but is effective in their deployment. And where inherited tribal power may be part of the equation, as Paul Radin noted: "A clear-cut distinction seems to have been drawn...between the right to inherit authority and the right to exercise it."[79]

Unlike societies where leadership depends on some form of material, spiritual, or biological inheritance, tribes may even depend to some extent on how outsiders view their own leaders. Indeed, it is not uncommon for the leader of a given tribe to have to be acknowledged by the group's enemies, in the certain knowledge that recognition by his own group also requires gaining the enemy's respect. This pattern may be vital since an opponent in one situation or moment is a likely ally in another and thus not to be utterly disrespected, humiliated, or ignored. Moreover, among such groups as the Inuit, one may regard part of another's lineage as an enemy but not another branch of the same lineage. Former Marine Corps General and Secretary of Defense James Mattis could have been describing tribes, therefore, when he famously said, "the enemy gets a vote."[80]

One of the tasks a tribal leader may be expected to perform is that of contact between his own people and other groupings. Later we will see how this has played out in a number of cases when the other entity is a state. Where it is relations of a nomadic tribe to a given town it is often the case that, as Marshall Sahlins notes, "the town's wealth acts upon nomads as a magnet upon iron filings, not merely attracting them but bringing them together in the process."[81] True, many tribes in the Middle East attacked towns on occasion: There is even a Berber saying that "raiding is our agriculture." But in many cases the relation was more complex, trading between tribesmen and townsmen being crucial for both. The Ait Youssi tribesmen of the Middle Atlas Mountains of Morocco, among whom I have worked, call the small city of Sefrou at the edge of the piedmont their "village," and recall that before the colonial period representatives were often chosen to ensure the intertribal peace of the marketplace by keeping the more obstreperous tribesmen in check. Interactions with the town may even have contributed to the inequalities that archaeologists have found suggested by the remains of earlier urban/tribal areas.[82] In other instances we know that the assumption that nomadic tribesmen, in the historical or evolutionary scheme of things, tended to settle down in villages is often the exact opposite of what happened. For it has often been the case that villagers would, for reasons of economic need or security, become nomadic – at least for a period.

Indeed, tribesmen, in the past and even now, have often moved back and forth in their identities and associations. They may belong to both urban and rural groupings, seeing no contradiction between the two. As Edmund Leach, James Scott, and others have shown for mainland Southeast Asia, tribesmen have formed and reformed coalitions as they have interacted with one another. Leach, for example, writes more generally: "In reality all social boundaries are conventional. Real social groups are always fuzzy at the edges. When groups interact, any particular individual can, without much difficulty, move across the social boundary."[83] The proposition (attributed to Sir Arthur Keith, a proponent of 'scientific racism') that "no tribe unites with another of its own free will" is largely false. Anthropologists have shown that "dynamic group membership turnover is typical of tribal societies...[M]igration by individuals, families, or larger subsets of the tribe is a common occurrence. Outsiders are allowed in by adoption or might be actively recruited. At other times – as when warfare or disease decimated Native American tribes – adoption might follow capture.[84] Current members might drift away or even be expelled for various reasons. Two tribal groups might merge into one, or one might split into two or more independent groups."[85] Inclusion of outsiders is extremely common in tribal societies: Many tribes are reported to have fewer than ten percent of their members related by blood, and outsider rates as high as eighty percent have been reported for a tribe in the High Atlas Mountains of Morocco.[86] Indeed, tribal people frequently have more ties with outsiders than with close kin.[87] Even a form of religious conversion may be quite seamless: In native North America an "Indian captive accepting adoption into an Indian tribe simply exchanged his tribal god for that of his adopted tribe and was brought in under the latter's protection."[88] Writing about what Lafitau called the "requickening" (*resusiter*) of a tribe that has lost members, the early American novelist Washington Irving noted:

> [Prisoners of the Indians who were not killed] are adopted into their families in the place of the slain, and are treated with the confidence and affection of relatives and friends, nay, so hospitable and tender is their entertainment, that while the alternative is offered them, they will often prefer to remain with their adopted brethren, rather than return to the home and the friends of their youth."[89]

The moment that [the captive] enters the lodge to which he is given...his bonds are untied....He is washed with warm water to efface the colors with which his face was painted and he is dressed properly. Then he receives visits of relatives and friends of the family into which he is entering. A short time afterwards a feast is made for all the village to give him the name of the

> person whom he is resurrecting…and from that moment, he enters upon all his rights.
>
> Joseph François Lafitau, *Customs of the American Indians Compared with the Customs of Primitive Times*, William N. Fenton and Elizabeth L. Moore, eds., 2 vols., Toronto: Champlain Society, 1974

Tribal membership may reinforce the ambiguities of identity. Among the Maori, it has been shown that tribal and sub-tribal groups rely on more than one principle for group inclusion, historical circumstance and the sheer ambiguity of each principle affecting momentary outcomes. Raymond Firth could therefore state: "I think it possible that further empirical investigation may show that in the concept of 'membership' of a descent group there may be a considerable degree of permitted ambiguity."[90] A group may (as Firth puts it) slough off members and acquire replacements as it responds to unpredictable patterns of migration, conflict, environmental shifts, and encounters with the other.[91] The very identity of tribes has thus varied a good deal over time: As a number of archaeological sites suggest, "it appears that tribal societies emerged and then faded away in many areas and times."[92]

Violence, too, can be a vehicle for dispersing power. In the previous chapter we saw the debate over whether tribes are inherently violent or whether their violence tends to be more ritualistic. There is no doubt that violence has been present in many tribal societies, whether in the form of outright combat or as self-help retribution. Yet, as we have also seen, it is commonly constrained, often having more in common with pugilistic games than with warfare. As Anton Vaino, Vladimir Putin's chief of staff, notes: "In war, there is us and them, friends and enemies, front and rear. A war has an end and a beginning. Victory and Defeat. In a game, everything is different. A game is …in a different space than that of war, with a different degree of foresight of the convergent processes of interaction between adversaries. In a game, time flows differently and interaction, too, is different. One of us can be theirs, and one of them can be ours."[93] If, in many instances, violence is channeled by shifting alliances then even contained aggression may have the effect of further dispersing power within a given tribe insofar as it means that punches must be pulled and one may not be able to consolidate power through the utter defeat of enemies.

Even here, of course, a wide range of practices is noted in the literature. Horatio Hale, the chief ethnologist on an expedition in New South Wales, Australia in 1839, reported that inter-tribal battles were conducted with formality, in accordance with agreed principles and an established code of honour. The two sides assembled after an exchange of messages, and the tournament began with the hurling of insults by senior women. A warrior from one side then advanced and launched several spears. A warrior from the other did the same, and soon. Such combats, according to the report, seldom resulted in loss of life and often became reduced to a duel between the most determined rivals.[94]

By contrast, cruelty to a defeated enemy among many American Indian tribes could be extreme. In each instance, however, restrained leadership and dispersed power made personally unbridled aggression less likely to threaten collective wellbeing.

In tribes, as opposed to those hierarchical (or paramount) chiefdoms in which a position may be inherited and validated by clear religious and/or legal rules, there may be no single, all-purpose leader. Instead, various individuals may be put forward for a particular purpose or period of time. Even tribal "chiefs" who enjoy certain privileges and duties because of their recognized (and often temporary or limited-purpose) position may be seen as occupying multiple roles, thus multiplying the ways in which others may have to relate to them. Max Gluckman's concept of multiplex roles is particularly apt in this regard. By virtue of being connected to others in a diversity of groupings – residential, kin-based, religious, etc. – any individual will have to consider the repercussions of his or her actions for relationships beyond a specific context. Gluckman gives the example of a Barotse man who could legally refuse to give the wife he was divorcing more than the prescribed household goods, rejecting entreaties by the judges who wanted him to be more generous. During a brief adjournment in the proceedings, however, the husband was apparently reminded that although the court could not force him to act like a good husband the judge, who was also an important figure in their religious group and neighborhood association, would appreciate it if he did so. The husband, no doubt realizing he had to deal with these individuals in more than one role, grudgingly acquiesced.[95] Social placements may, therefore, not only intersect; they may appear to Westerners as discreet roles when it is actually the totality of crosscutting attachments that may more truly define any tribesman's position. The mistake made by many Westerners confronting tribesmen in colonial, military, and treaty-making contexts has often been to assume that when one demands "take me to your leader" such a singular role-player already exists, an error that, as we will see in more detail in chapter five, has been carried forth in recent approaches to the tribes of Iraq and Afghanistan.

Ranked societies with more permanent and specialized leadership notwithstanding, the common pattern among tribal peoples is for a leader to have to take on the characteristics ideally associated with his position in order to be acknowledged as possessing that status. This "big man" pattern means that legitimacy is gained through knowledge and acts rather than being limited to spiritual or genealogical inheritance. Interstitial figures, like shamans and other ritual specialists, may reinforce this pattern by underscoring the criteria by which leadership is reckoned. Public opinion is crucial. While acknowledgment of leadership may not be unanimous, the process of articulating its criteria reinforces that the chosen leader embodies the standards of the group, is capable of conveying its values, and may therefore serve as custodian for its collective interests. It is not therefore surprising (as we shall see when discussing the economic aspects of tribal societies) that a leader may be regarded as the trustee of collective assets or the one who ensures their appropriate redistribution. What may appear as exclusive 'ownership' of resources is commonly so hedged by requirements of stewardship that the leader can neither deny access to others nor fail to share any largesse that comes his way. "The chief owns everything," says one African proverb, "the chief owns nothing." Among the Cheyenne, to take another example, if a warrior disrupted the buffalo hunt by acting on his own, thereby risking the dispersion of the entire herd to the detriment of everyone, the appropriate chief may have all the offender's goods destroyed but then had to give him new equipment from his own possessions. In doing so the chief simultaneously reinforces the group standards and is kept from amassing physical assets that might otherwise be convertible to pervasive or long-lasting power. That is why, in his description of the Tuareg, an individual known as the Amnenokal, who is said to be "the owner of the land," is described by one anthropologist as "essentially a chief executive and not a true king or autocrat chieftain in the commonly accepted sense of those terms."[96] So, too, destruction of a man's goods upon death – as among many Native American and Nordic tribes – may seem economically insupportable until one appreciates that it is politically vital to the dispersal of power and the legitimization of individual effort. Indeed, instances exist of tribes in which, if a leader fails to share with others what is expected of him, he may actually be killed.

Tribal leaders may even play different roles at different levels of organization. In the mid-19th century, for example, the Comanche developed into a highly organized empire, one in which leaders served primarily at the local level but might also at times be seconded to lead larger agglomerations.[97] Trying to be both tribal and state-like may, however, have constituted an inherent weakness, for when the plains suffered a long-term drought – in which the drying of the grasses harmed the horses on whom the tribesmen depended for hunting the buffalo and exercising power over others – the strain between being simultaneously tribes and empire-builders broke their organization suddenly and quite completely. The resilience of tribal ways may, therefore, collapse under the pressure of maintaining the levels of power built into tribal institutions and creating a durable structure for the exercise of power over a wide range of subordinate groups.

Tribal Law-ways

Law, too, can be constructed as a brake on the consolidation of power, but it may not be accomplished only by balancing one institution against another. In fashioning the constraint of law on power, tribes, like all others, must consider three interrelated factors: how best to handle uncertainty, what role to assign custom, and how to balance the interests of the individual with those of the community. Each aspect warrants close consideration.

Legal philosopher H. L. A. Hart once said that any legal system must confront two key problems: the uncertainty of fact and the indeterminacy of aim. But the first, uncertainty, relates not only to ascertaining the facts in a case: In small-scale societies, where people live in very close proximity, what happened is often treated as common knowledge. Uncertainty also concerns the consequences for any given decision, the choice among competing concepts, and the effectiveness of any sanction or inducement. Moreover, law is not only about addressing disputes; it is also about articulating a sense of the orderliness of everyday life – what anthropologists mean when they speak about cosmology.[98] And since everything does not necessarily fit easily into preconceived categories, a delicate line may have to be trod between forcing every event or relationship into a set of existing molds and leaving room for contested concepts and new adaptations. An emphasis on procedure rather than substantive rules may constitute part of the solution; not fully theorizing judgments in the interest of maintaining a sense of cosmological harmony may be another. Whatever the emphasis, we once again face issues of theme and variation, rather than utter uniformity, when we consider how tribes address each of these problems.

Anthropologists have tangled with the challenge of uncertainty since they first began looking at the law of non-literate cultures. Bronislaw Malinowski had noted that rules in "primitive" societies were not just obligatory and enforced but "far from being rigid...are maintained by social forces, understood as rational and necessary, elastic and capable of adjustment."[99] For him, therefore, the issue of certainty was not solved by tribesmen through "automatic submission to custom." To the contrary, as many later scholars were to note, custom and its application actually incorporate a range of variation. Edmund Leach, for example, noted that "very different types of practical behaviour can be covered by the same customary norms.... Custom purports to be precise and to specify how things ought to be; yet in practice most custom is ambiguous and open to varied interpretation."[100] We can see this where variant customs may yield more than one answer as to whether a given marriage was actually formed or terminated, whether a horse was "stolen" or "borrowed," whether one is entitled to use a fishing site or tribal symbol without seeking permission. Whereas legal systems with more formalized institutions may seek to reduce ambiguity, tribesmen – as we have seen in so many other domains – have a high degree of tolerance for ambiguity, using it to expand and contract the bounds of civility and inclusion as they balance potentially disruptive initiative with the need for predictable order. The result is a more nuanced approach to justice and the role of the individual.

For many tribal groups justice lies not in the abolition or suppression of ambivalence, as is common in many non-tribal societies, but in its very celebration.[101] By stressing context over abstract rules and opening the "bounds of relevance" wide enough to embrace both personality and subsidiary relationships, tribal systems of justice commonly place emphasis on repairing social ties rather than asserting impersonal directives. To outsiders tribal laws may, therefore, appear to lack consistency, whereas to those who entwine their lives with this perspective the failure of individuation and contextualization would mark a freezing of principles for which the price may be both the unwanted centralization of power and the loss of adaptive potential. A few examples may help illustrate the point.

Consider, once again, the Cheyenne in the pre-contact era. Karl Llewellyn, after reviewing numerous cases, concludes that theirs is a system of "flexible adaptability...attuned to the net dynamic need of the people. This the Cheyenne had, rather than a regime of letter or of rule or of form."[102] Following a review of numerous cases and the broader cultural postulates that inform them, he and his co-author E. A. Hoebel concluded more generally "that neither ritualization of procedure nor fixed wording of legal rules is needed to produce much of predictability."[103] Similarly, among the Tiruray of the Philippines, an individual respected for his self-control and knowledge of local ways must attend simultaneously to an individual's felt sense of injury (which could lead to the offended party becoming violent) and shared community sentiments as to what is or is not justifiably regarded as injurious.[104] The result is neither a wholly subjective nor objective approach to law but one that recognizes that where law and justice are involved one size does not fit all. It could, then, be said of many other tribes whose characteristic focus is on persons and situations rather than abstract rules, as John Comaroff and Simon Roberts have said of a group of Bantu-speakers of South Africa, that their legal system is a "loosely constructed repertoire rather than an internally consistent code, that Tswana were not unduly concerned if these rules sometimes contradicted one another, and that almost any conduct or relationship was potentially susceptible to competing normative constructions."[105] Indeed, by emphasizing the norms of proper behavior over rigidified rules the Tswana provide the basis for "the legitimization of competing constructions of reality, in terms of which situational conflict is expressed."[106]

An equally telling example is provided by the Inuit song duels to which we referred earlier. In their striking essay on the subject, Penelope Eckert and Russell Newmark argue that the power of these encounters lies in no small part in the ambiguous nature of the songs and the ritual itself. Participants must behave as if their utterances were ironic, rather than overtly aggressive, so that the loser "is guilty of simply having performed less well than his opponent in a song contest, and any accusations levelled against him in the contest were only ironic." Because the ritual embraces – indeed demands – an ironic tone the substance of what is said remains ambiguous: No insult can be said to have been intended, and the ambiguity of the potentially damaging message is left intact. "Failure to behave as if all insults are ironic amounts to three transgressions: (1) acknowledging the possible truth of the insult, (2) bringing the event into the real world and thus precipitating overt conflict and (3) not performing properly in the speech event and thus declaring oneself a poor participant and an outsider to the community."[107] That support for one or another of the participants establishes where community sentiment lies may render some form of resolution to the precipitating dispute. But it also delegitimizes further violence while dispersing power, now through irony and ambiguity, consistent with the tribal ethos that is present in so many other domains of Inuit culture.

If, in tribal societies, custom and legal outcome can have recourse to propositions that are as amoeboid as other elements of the tribal ethos then it should come as no surprise – Western stereotypes notwithstanding – that a stress on the individual is also characteristic of the ways in which tribes contend with potential disruption. As Robert Lowie noted a century ago: "It cannot be too often explained that the extreme individualism often found in primitive communities is very far from favoring universal anarchy or anything approaching it."[108] Such stress on the individual means that a single vision of truth is not indispensable to social order. Canadian First Nations lawyer, judge, and senator Murray Sinclair thus notes that if one asks an indigenous person to swear to tell the whole truth and nothing but the truth he will think that such a standard "is illogical and meaningless.... The Aboriginal viewpoint would require the individual to speak the truth 'as you know it' and not to disrupt the validity of another viewpoint of the same event or issue."[109] Indeed, application of a clear rule may take second place to an assessment of the person involved, as was the case, for example, when a Chippewa charged with improperly using a fishing net in the off-season successfully argued that he was upholding the larger tradition of insuring that no fish is to be wasted if people are to survive: "By virtue of the defendant's integrity as a community member, tribal law was effectively suspended in this case as unduly impersonal in favor of communitarian recompense motivated in traditional law or custom."[110]

Song duels, settlement-wide palavers, ordeals that conduce recognition of one's own bad behavior – all of these and many other mechanisms may appear the very antithesis of the rule of law as Westerners conceive it, that is, as a system in which, among other features, rules must be relatively stable, may not contradict one another, and must be administered as set forth.[111] But ambiguity and rule-avoidance may serve in tribal societies (a) to address any one person's felt sense of injury, (b) to maintain flexibility in the face of changing circumstances, and (c) to focus on process over prescriptions as a means of bringing at least momentary order to the actual as well as the desirable ambivalence of human relationships. The point is brought home quite strikingly in the telling phrase of Max Gluckman, building on his own study of tribal societies, when he says: "The 'certainty' of law resides in the 'uncertainty' of its basic concepts."

* * *

Two features stand out, then, as one reconsiders aspects of the tribal ethos: a deep ambivalence to power and a remarkable degree of social and cultural flexibility. As to the former, whether through ritualized gossip and scandal, ceremonial reversals or avoidance behavior, numerous mechanisms are constantly at work to limit the consolidation of power. Indeed, ambivalence to power is part of a larger quality of playing up ambiguities in social life without a loss of either individual or collective identity. Thus, we have seen that while common orientations are essential if one is not to mistake another's meaning, that does not mean that rigid rules are indispensable to social order. As Edmund Leach notes, members of a society must "share more or less compatible ideas about how things ought to be…but in fact the boundaries of consensus are much less extensive than most of us like to imagine."[112] However, while passing acquaintance and acting 'as if' we understood others perfectly may characterize elements of any human construct, it is quite another matter to observe how particular cultural forms address the relation of certainty and creativity. And in the tribal world that balance is integral to the institutionalized mechanisms for dispersing power, more than resultant structures, that comprise the tribal ethos.

David Bromwich introduces a useful distinction when he argues that "diplomacy can allow for 'strategic ambiguity,' well understood by all parties, where too much specification would hamper an agreement." This, he suggests, contrasts with "'literary ambiguity" which involves a "suspension between two states of mind" in a situation where "someone confined to either state could not know the reality of the other" and "turns on a hidden complexity that the reader is prompted to notice in a single word."[113] Both forms are vital to the tribal ethos – strategic ambiguity for both dispersing power and not becoming the captive of a primal instance governing all subsequent events, and literary ambiguity for insuring that axial symbols, like the trickster or the shamanic ceremony, focus each individual's attention on vitalizing shared meanings with the individual resonances and relationships formed through them. Flexibility is therefore key. Archaeologists have shown that "societies organized as tribes, or as autonomous villages within a tribal confederation often exhibit changing patterns of spatial organization" whether through seasonal moves or long-term reorganization and relocation. Perhaps more significantly "it is precisely [the] ability of tribal societies to shift through organizational forms with ease that makes them adaptive over the long term."[114] Robert Lowie concluded his own study of small-scale societies by saying: "Instead of dull uniformity, there is mottled diversity; instead of the single sib [clan] pattern multiplied in fulsome profusion we detect a variety of social units, now associated with the sib, now taking its place."[115] In the case of tribes, then, the sheer ambiguity inherent in many situations – that ever-present amoeboid adaptability – is itself played up, whereas in other societies (through law, politics, and parental upbringing) it may be overtly played down. In an intriguing passage from a novel by *Washington Post* columnist David Ignatius one character is heard to say of another:

> [He] wasn't a zero or a one. He occupied a space where things were ambiguous, where people are simultaneously friend and foe, loyal and disloyal, impossible to define until the moment when events intervene and force each particle, each heart to one side or the other. A binary separation between black and white might be the human condition, but it wasn't the natural order of things.

Tribesmen, too, may have come to intuit that binary choices are perforce the human condition but not the natural one, and they strive, however painfully, however gainfully, to conform to the demands of the natural while remaining susceptible to the ambiguities of the human.

For tribesmen, then, advantage may lie in the retention of a degree of individual freedom of action, but the disadvantage may be that power is too easily diffused when cooperation could be advantageous. Either way – and contrary to popular stereotype – this open-textured, shapeshifting form of human vision that characterizes tribes yields a cultural cluster whose sheer plasticity has been vital to their survival. Regularity, therefore, may lie in process and repertoire, rather than in resultant structures, culminating not in the proposition that form follows function, but that order follows meaning. However, before we can more fully address this possibility we need to flesh out 'the tribal ethos' by considering its indispensable accompaniment, 'the spirit of reciprocity.'

Notes

1 Kenneth Burke, *Permanence and Change: An Anatomy of Purpose*, 3rd ed., Berkeley: University of California Press, 1984.
2 The references are, respectively, from Jennifer Egan, *A Visit from the Goon Squad*, New York: Knopf, 2010; and Terry Pratchett, *Reaper Man*, New York: Harper, 1991.
3 See, Nicholas P. Money, *The Amoeba in the Room: Lives of the Microbes*, Oxford: Oxford University Press, 2014, p. 12–14.
4 The internal quote is from G. Willow Wilson, *Alif the Unseen*, New York: Grove Press, 2013, p. 228. An alternative analogy is offered by a student of the archaeology of tribes: "In a way, the search for particular tribal characteristics is akin to asking 'what color is a chameleon?' – it simply poses the wrong question. One must instead investigate the variability of colors over time and space and from there ask how and why these colors change." Severin M. Fowles, "From Social Type to Social Process: Placing 'Tribe' in a Historical Framework," in William A. Parkinson, ed., *The Archaeology of Tribal Societies*, Ann Arbor: International Monographs in Prehistory, Archaeological Series 15, 2002, pp. 13–33, at 19. Others have described tribes as being like jellyfish (James Scott, *The Art of Not Being Governed*, p. 210, citing Malcolm Yapp, *Tribes and States in the Kyber, 1838-1842*, Oxford: Clarendon Press, 1980). Scott also refers to the groups in the Southeast Asian massif as 'shape-shifters.' In this "migrant shatter zone," where hill peoples may have had to reconfigure themselves as a result of interaction with states, consistent with Leach,

> [s]uch populations do not so much change identities as emphasize one aspect of a cultural and linguistic portfolio that encompasses several potential identities. The vagueness, plurality, and fungibility of identities and social units have certain political advantages; they represent a repertoire of engagement and disengagement with states and with other peoples.
> (Scott, *The Art of Not Being Governed*, p. 212)

This is quite different, though, from tribes that are not created by or in reaction to states. Indeed, the ability of the peasant groups who are the focus of Scott's work may be carrying over some aspects of an earlier tribal ethos but are themselves clearly not, despite his occasional use of the term, tribes in the sense described here.

5 For a discussion of 'primitive communism' and examples from the ethnographic literature, see Richard B. Lee, "Primitive Communism and the Origin of Inequality," in Steadman Upham, ed., *Evolution of Political Systems: Sociopolitics*

in Small-scale Sedentary Communities, New York: Cambridge University Press, 1990, pp. 225–46. As Lee notes, it was Lewis Henry Morgan, in his 1881 publication *Houses and House-Life of the American Aborigines*, who first discussed the concept, which he called "communism in living." However, Robert Lowie, a century ago, made clear, through numerous examples, that such primitive communism "is demonstrably false."
Robert Lowie, *Primitive Society*, New York: Harper & Brothers, 1947 [1920], p. 206.

6 Lee, "Primitive Communism," p. 244. Paul Radin (*The World of Primitive Man*, p. 106) called this "the principle of an irreducible minimum," to which each member of the group bears entitlement. E. E. Evans-Pritchard writes:

> Nuer seldom have a surplus of food and at the beginning of the rains it is often insufficient for their needs. Indeed, it may be said that they are generally on the verge of want and that every few years they face more or less severe famine. In these conditions, it is understandable that there is much sharing of food in the same village, especially among members of adjacent homesteads and hamlets. Though at any time some members may have more cattle and grain than others, and these are their private possessions, people eat in one another's homesteads at feasts and at daily meals, and food is in other ways shared, to such an extent that one may speak of a common stock.

E. E. Evans-Pritchard, "The Nuer of the Southern Sudan," in M. Fortes and E. E. Evans- Pritchard, eds., *African Political Systems*, Oxford: Oxford University Press, 1940, p. 273. He concludes: "In general it may be said that no one in a Nuer village starves unless all are starving." E. E. Evans-Pritchard, *Kinship and Marriage among the Nuer*, Oxford: Clarendon Press, 1951, p. 132.

7 Radin, *The World of Primitive Man*, p. 118 (original italics).
8 For numerous such examples see, Lowie, *Primitive Society*, pp. 205–56.
9 Daniel K. Richter, *The Ordeal of the Longhouse*, Chapel Hill, NC: University of North Carolina Press, 1992, pp. 21–22.
10 Among the Quechan (Yuma) Indians, for example, not only were the deceased's belongings burnt but so was the person's house.
11 See also, Judith Scheele, "The Values of 'Anarchy': Moral Autonomy among the Tubu-Speakers of Northern Chad," *Journal of the Royal Anthropological Institute*, vol. 21, N.S. (2014), pp. 32–48, at 44.
12 See, e.g., Peter Bogucki, "A Neolithic Tribal Society in Northern Poland," in Parkinson, ed., *The Archaeology of Tribal Societies*, pp. 372–83.
13 Michael Bond, *From Here to There*, p. 76, citing Keith H. Basso (1988), "Speaking with Names: Language and Landscape among the Western Apache," *Cultural Anthropology*, vol. 3, no. 2 (1988), pp. 99–130.
14 Marilyn Strathern, *The Gender of the Gift*, Berkeley: University of California Press, 1988, p. 134.
15 Frederick Edward Maning, *Old New Zealand and Other Writings*, London: Leicester University Press, 2001 [1863].
16 Nick Araho, presenter, "Appendix: Summaries of Small Group Discussions," in Kathy Whimp and Mark Busse, eds., *Protection of Intellectual, Biological, and Cultural Property in Papua, New Guinea*, Canberra: Australian National University E Press, 2013, p. 186.
17 Thus it is often said that Native Americans did not think they were selling the land to colonists because Mother Earth is not subject to sale. And it is probably true that when Manhattan Island was 'sold' for $26 worth of beads the inhabitants thought they were granting certain use rights rather than outright alienation. But

it is a mistake to imagine that native peoples did not quickly come to understand that the transactions were, in fact, full disposition of any claim. As Francis Jennings (*The Invasion of America*, New York: W. W. Norton, 1975, p. 137) states: "Some students have doubted that Indians understood how they were dispossessing themselves by sale of land to Europeans. Perhaps that was so in the earliest transactions, but Indian sophistication grew rapidly. European power soon drove home the lesson that a land sale involved full and final alienation of right."

18 Richard Lee, *The Dobe Ju/'hoansi*, 2nd edn., New York: Harcourt Brace, 1993, pp. 183–88.
19 James Suzman, *Affluence Without Abundance*, New York: Bloomsbury, 2017. Christopher Boehm (*Moral Origins*, New York: Basic Books, 2012) gives a comparable example from among the Bushman: "Say that a man has been hunting. He must not come home and announce like a braggart, 'I have killed a big one in the bush!' He must first sit down in silence until someone else comes up to his fire and asks, 'What did you see today?' He replies quietly, 'Ah, I'm no good for hunting. I saw nothing at all . . . maybe just a tiny one.' Then I smile to myself because I know he has killed something big." See also, Mathias Guenther, *Tricksters and Trancers: Bushman Religion and Society*, Bloomington: Indiana University Press, 1999, and Richard B. Lee and Irven DeVore, eds., *Man the Hunter*, Chicago: Aldine, 1968. See generally, John Lanchester, "The Case against Civilization," *The New Yorker*, September 18, 2017.
20 As even the archaeological record indicates, vehicles have long existed for institutionalizing the dispersal of goods and powers in tribal societies. See generally, Severin M. Fowles, "From Social Type to Social Process: Placing 'Tribe' in a Historical Framework," in Parkinson, ed., *The Archaeology of Tribal Societies*, pp. 13–33.
21 Paul Spencer, *The Samburu: A Study of Gerontocracy in a Nomadic Tribe*, London: Routledge, 2004. The mock denunciation by younger men at an elder's wedding to one of the much younger women may, however, be seen as a ritual reversal that confirms the status quo or as a prelude to the elderly being later pushed into oblivion. The killing of the very old, as among some Inuit, is the ultimate vehicle for chasing the elderly out of the community altogether.
22 See, Marshall Sahlins, *The New Science of the Enchanted Universe*, Princeton: Princeton University Press, 2022.
23 Robert Brightman, *Grateful Prey: Rock Cree Human-Animal Relationships*, Berkeley: University of California Press, 1973, p. 11.
24 Clifford Sather, "'All Threads Are White': Iban Egalitarianism Reconsidered," in James J. Fox and Clifford Sather, eds., *Origins, Ancestry and Alliance: Explorations in Austronesian Ethnography*, Canberra: Australian National University E Press, 1996, pp. 70–110, at 74.
25 See, e.g., Richard B. Lee, *The Dobe Ju/'hoansi*, pp. 93–107. Elizabeth Marshall Thomas, *The Harmless People*, New York: Knopf, 1959.
26 See, e.g., the examples given in Sahlins, *The New Science*, pp. 100–101. Leveling mechanisms may also serve to avoid or at least ameliorate the sense that one has been humiliated, itself described as the "the nuclear bomb of emotions." L. M. Hartling, E. Lindner, U. Spalthoff, and M. Britton, "Humiliation: A Nuclear Bomb of Emotions?" *Psicología Política*, vol. 46 (2013), pp. 55–67. As Vivian Gornick notes: ("'Put on the Diamonds': Notes on Humiliation," *Harper's Magazine*, October 2021, pp. 59–65):

> Anton Chekhov once observed that the worst thing life can do to human beings is to inflict humiliation. Nothing, nothing, nothing in the world can

destroy the soul as much as outright humiliation. Every other infliction can eventually be withstood or overcome, but not humiliation. Humiliation lingers in the mind, the heart, the veins, the arteries forever. It allows people to brood for decades on end, often deforming their inner lives .... There are many things we can live without. Self-respect is not one of them.

By ritualizing those contexts that might otherwise lead to a felt sense of personal humiliation tribes can level out those emotions that threaten the solidarity of the group and the individual's own sense of self-worth.

27 See, Severin Fowles, "Inequality and Egalitarian Rebellion, a Tribal Dialectic in Tonga History," in William A. Parkinson, ed., *The Archaeology of Tribal Societies*, pp. 74–96.
28 Quoted in Robert Launay, *Savages, Romans, and Despots: Thinking about Others from Montaigne to Herder*, Chicago: University of Chicago Press, 2018, p. 103.
29 On the absence of formal matriarchy see, David M. Schneider and Kathleen Gough, eds., *Matrilineal Kinship*, Berkeley: University of California Press, 1961. There is, however, continuing controversy over the centrality of women in certain tribal societies. Recent findings in biology and archaeology suggest that some of the Celtic cultures of ancient Europe practiced matrilocality, i.e., men moved to live in the wife's area of residence. See, Cassidy, L. M., Russell, M., Smith, M., et al., "Continental Influx and Pervasive Matrilocality in Iron Age Britain," *Nature* (January 15, 2025). https://doi.org/10.1038/s41586-024-08409-6 (accessed May 31, 2025). DNA and burials are not, however, dispositive on the import of such findings. Not only do studies of living matrilocal societies indicate (a) that matrilocality does not necessarily correlate with other factors, such as matrilineal descent, and (b) that the key relationship may nevertheless be between the husband and the wife's brother, who is the trustee for matrilineage interests even though his own children are not members of his matrilineage, but they also show (c) that there is no known matrilineal or matrifocal society in which formal power lies predominantly in the hands of women. Moreover, burial sites of women containing alleged status items may only represent the practice of many tribal peoples of levelling power at death through the destruction of goods that might otherwise be used by a successor to lord power over others, a power not earned by individual effort and interpersonal relationships. In short, these recent findings risk bringing a story we wish to tell ourselves about ourselves to facts that do not carry an unambiguous message about the actual roles of ancient women.
30 On women's economic roles in Papua New Guinea, see, e.g., Rena Lederman, *What Gifts Engender: Social Relations and Politics in Mendi, Highland Papua New Guinea*, New York: Cambridge University Press, 1986; and Annette Weiner, *Women of Value, Men of Renown*, Austin: University of Texas Press, 1983.
31 Aram A. Yengoyan, "Copulation, Conception and Deception in Aboriginal Australia," *Reviews in Anthropology*, vol. 5, no. 1 (1978), pp. 107–15, at 114.
32 See, e.g., Bruce G. Trigger, "Maintaining Economic Equality in Opposition to Complexity: An Iroquoian Study," in Steadman Upham, ed., *The Evolution of Political Systems*, Cambridge: Cambridge University Press, 1990.
33 "Even in the context of the rivalry and individual prowess favored in various Amerindian cultures, the big Kwakiutl potlatch is (in contrast to the ordinary smaller celebrations) a case of abortive exaggeration. Vying in generosity, the contestants mix the more friendly feelings expressed in their gift-giving

with so much hostility and rivalry that the giving loses its unifying effect and degenerates into an instrument of civic destruction. At a certain stage, the contest in gift-giving changes into a contest in the destruction of valuables. The gift disappears from the scene and a form of controlled warfare by means of calculated destruction takes it place." J. van Baal, *Reciprocity and the Position of Women*, Assen/Amsterdam: Van Gorcum, 1975, p. 45.
34 See, Abraham Rosman and Paula G. Rubel, "Potlatch: A Structural Analysis," *American Anthropologist*, vol. 74 (1972), pp. 658–69.
35 Vine Deloria, "Indian Humor," *Custer Died for Your Sins*, New York: Macmillan, 1969, pp. 146–67. See also, Frank Miller, "Humor in a Chippewa Tribal Council," *Ethnology*, vol. 6, no. 3 (July 1967), pp. 263–71. Humor may also act as a vehicle for preserving a culture in the face of external threat: Dell Hymes thus speaks of the "power of patterns of verbal humor, against difficult and even desperate circumstances, a power still evident in Indian country." Dell Hymes, "A Theory of Irony and a Chinookan Pattern of Verbal Exchange," in Jef Verschueren and Marcella Bertucelli-Papi, eds., *The Pragmatic Perspective*, Amsterdam: John Benjamins Pub., 1987, p. 293–337, at 329.
36 James Howe, "How the Cuna Keep Their Chiefs in Line," *Man*, New Series, vol. 13, no. 4 (December 1978), pp. 537–53, at 540.
37 Robert K. Nelson, *Make Prayers to the Raven: A Koyukon View of the Northern Forest*, Chicago, University of Chicago Press, 1983, pp. 79–80, 84.
38 For a similar example of the power of ridicule, see Scheele, "The Values of 'Anarchy,' p. 40. Self-ridicule is also expected and deflects ridicule by others while verbal abuse hurled by opposing groups, like song duels, provokes hilarity among onlookers: see, Guenther, *Tricksters and Trancers*, pp. 34–36 and his references to other tribes cited therein.
39 Mathias Guenther, *Tricksters and Trancers: Bushman Religion and Society*, Bloomington: Indiana University Press, 1999, p. 34, also citing Pierre Clastres, *Society against the State*, New York: Urizen Books, 1977, p. 121.
40 Paul Radin, *Primitive Man as Philosopher*, pp. 50–51. Also retold at p. 376.
41 For the Lascaux interpretation, see Barbara Ehrenreich, "The Humanoid Stain," *The Baffler*, no. 48, November 2019.
42 Gerald Vizenor, *Bearheart: The Heirship Chronicles*, quoted in Allan J. Ryan, *The Trickster Shift: Humor and Irony in Contemporary Native Art*, Vancouver: UBC Press, 1999, p. 12.
43 As R. H. Tawney (*Equality*, London: G. Allen & Unwin, 1931) noted: "[Power] is thus both awful and fragile, and can dominate a continent only in the end to be blown down by a whisper. To destroy it, nothing more is required than to be indifferent to its threats, and to prefer other goods to those it promises. Nothing less, however, is required also."
44 Mary Douglas, "The Social Control of Cognition: Some Factors in Joke Perception," *Man* (NS), vol. 3 (1968), pp. 361–76, at 364–65.
45 Robert Launay, *Savages, Roman, and Despots*, p. 94. Jesuit Father Gabriel Lallemant, writing of the Wendat Iroquois, says that each individual "considers himself of as much consequence as the others; and they submit to their chiefs only in so far as it pleases them." *The Jesuit Relations and Allied Documents: Travels and Explorations of the Jesuit Missionaries in New France 1610–1791*, Reuben Gold Thwaites, ed., 33:49, quoted in Graeber and Wengrow, *Dawn of Everything*, p. 140.
46 For an example of an Inuit song duel, see *The Fast Runner*, a film directed by Canadian Inuit Zacarias Kunuk. Similar song duels take place among tribesmen in North Africa. Indeed, shaming through singing may be quite

widespread among tribal groups: see, Jean-Luc Chodkiewicz, "Song Contests in New Guinea," *APLA: Newsletter of the Association for Political and Legal Anthropology*, vol. 6, no. 1 (1982), pp. 5–9.
47 Kenneth E. Read, *The High Valley*, New York: Charles Scribner's Sons, 1965, p. 19.
48 E. Wright, review of E. E. Evans-Pritchard's "The Zande Trickster," *Journal of Asian and African Studies*, vol. 5, no. 1 (January 1970), p. 128–29. William J. Hyne and William G. Doty (*Mythical Trickster Figures*, Tuscaloosa: The University of Alabama Press, 1993, pp. 34–42) state that every trickster has several of the following traits: sacred and lewd bricoleur, fundamentally ambiguous and anomalous, deceiver and trick-player, shape-shifter or master of disguise, situation-inverter, messenger and imitator of the gods.
49 Lewis Hyde, *Trickster Makes the World*, New York: Farrar, Strauss and Giroux, 1998, pp. 43, 39, 19, 28, and 13 respectively.
50 These phrases appear in a video presentation of raven at the Royal Museum of Victoria, BC.
51 E. E. Evans-Pritchard, *The Zande Trickster*, Oxford: Clarendon Press, 1967, p. 30.
52 Guenther, *Tricksters and Trancers*, p. 101; Victor Turner, quoted in Guenther, *Tricksters and Trancers*, p. 238.
53 Michael Chabon, "Foreword," to Lewis Hyde, *Trickster Makes the World*, New York: Farrar, Strauss and Giroux, 2010 edition, p. xi.
54 Sharon Manybeads Bowers, "Louise Erdich at Nanapush," in Regina Barrena, ed., *New Perspectives on Women and Comedy*, New York: Gordon and Breach, 1992, pp. 135–41.
55 Ritual clowns, as among the Puebloans of the American southwest, similarly represent an ability to interact simultaneously with chaos and the unknown. "If clowns survive the encounter with nonorder, then so too may all humans." Arden King, "North American Clowns and Creativity," quoted in Ryan, *The Trickster Shift*, p. 11.
56 Henry Adams, *The Education of Henry Adams*, Boston: Houghton Mifflin, 1918, ch. 16.; Terry Pratchett, *Discworld Series*.
57 "Many native traditions held clowns and tricksters as essential to any contact with the sacred. People could not pray until they had laughed, because laughter opens and frees from rigid preconception. Humans had to have tricksters within the most sacred ceremonies for fear that they forget the sacred comes through upset, reversal, surprise. The trickster in most native traditions is essential to creation, to birth." Byrd Gibbens, quoted as an epigraph in George Carlin, *Napalm and Silly Putty*, New York: Hyperion, 2001.
58 The 'rule-breaking equalizer' phrase is found in Martti Missinen, *Ancient Prophecy*, Oxford: Oxford University Press, 2017, p. 3.
59 Paul Radin, *The Trickster*, New York: Schoken 1972, p. xxiii.
60 Radin, *The Trickster*, p. xxiii. Stanley Diamond writes: "Radin was fascinated by human ambiguity, and social ambivalence....[He] saw in the trickster myth...a different mode of expression of ambiguity – its confrontation, its cultural history, so to speak, its transcendence....The trickster, of course, is giver and destroyer, creator and negator. He is the burlesque of the sacred; at the same time he *is* sacred. The world is the result of the trickster's energies, almost by accident; at the same time the trickster can obliterate. He is the messenger of the gods, and he *is* God." Stanley Diamond, "Paul Radin," in Sydel Silverman, ed., *Totems and Teachers: Perspectives on the History of Anthropology*, New York: Columbia University Press, 1981, pp. 67–97, at 79.

61 Radin, *Primitive Man as Philosopher*, p. 244, quoting J. Gudgeon, "The Tipua-Kura and Other Manifestations of the Spirit World," *Journal of the Polynesian Society*, vol. 15, no. 1 (1906), pp. 27–57, at 27.
62 Joseph Henrich, "How Culture Drove Human Evolution," *Edge*, September 4, 2012.
63 Pekka Hämäläinen, *Lakota America: A New History of Indigenous Power*, New Haven: Yale University Press, 2020, pp. 83–84 (original italics).
64 Gary Witherspoon, *Language and Art in the Navajo Universe*, pp. 140–49.
65 On these women anthropologists' contributions, see L. R. Hiatt, *Arguments about Aborigines*, Cambridge: Cambridge University Press, 1996, pp. 64–68.
66 The *locus classicus* of this issue is Bronislaw Malinowski, *The Father in Primitive Psychology*, New York: Norton, 1927. The quote from Roheim, and further analysis of this issue, may be found in Hiatt, *Arguments about Aborigines*, pp. 120–41, especially 124.
67 Hiatt, *Arguments about Aborigines*, p. 151.
68 Max Gluckman, "Gossip and Scandal," *Current Anthropology*, vol. 4, no. 3 (1963), pp. 307–16. On the debates in anthropology about gossip see generally, Sally Engle Merry, "Rethinking Gossip and Scandal," in Donald Black, ed., *Toward a General Theory of Social Control, Volume 1: Fundamentals*, New York: Academic Press, 1984, pp. 271–302.
69 Elizabeth Colson, "The Contentiousness of Disputes," in Pat Caplan, ed., *Understanding Disputes: The Politics of Arguments*, Oxford: Berg, 1995, pp. 65–82, at 80.
70 For a contemporary study of bloodmoney payments in Iran, see Arzoo Osanloo, *Forgiveness Work: Mercy, Law, and Victims' Rights in Iran*, Princeton: Princeton University Press, 2020.
71 See, e.g., Adam Ashforth, *Witchcraft, Violence, and Democracy in South Africa*, Chicago: University of Chicago Press, 2005, and "Witchcraft, Justice, and Human Rights in Africa: Cases from Malawi," *African Studies Review*, vol. 58, no. 1 (2015) at 5-38, at 7: "[T]here is no sign that the plausibility of witchcraft narratives is diminishing in contemporary Africa."
72 Robin Fox, "Pueblo Baseball: A New Use for Old Witchcraft," *Journal of American Folklore*, vol. 74, no. 291 (January-March 1961), pp. 9–16. Fox writes: "Baseball in the Pueblos is a competitive intrusion into essentially non-competitive social systems. While competition is between villages, no untoward events occur, as this is in line with tradition, but within villages, it is, as we have seen, potentially destructive. Pueblo institutions act as a counter to aggressive tendencies in the Puebloans and are so constructed as to eliminate and nullify aggressive conflict between people by placing them in automatically determined overlapping role situations." Fox, *Pueblo Baseball*, p. 15. For an update see, Patrick T. Readon, "Deep as Blood," *Chicago Tribune*, August 15, 2006.
73 For example, among Australian aborigines "men of eminence in the realm of the sacred were accorded no special powers or privileges in secular domains." Hiatt, *Arguments about Aborigines*, p. 93.
74 George Meredith, *Comedy: An Essay on Comedy*, New York: Doubleday Anchor, 1956.
75 Sebastian Junger, *Tribe: On Homecoming and Belonging*, New York: Twelve, 2016. David Brooks, "Fighting the Spiritual Void," *New York Times*, November 20, 2018, and his "There Should Be More Rituals!" *New York Times*, April 22, 2019.

76 See, e.g., Gilbert Herdt, *The Sambia: Ritual, Sexuality, and Change in Papua New Guinea*, 2nd edn., Belmont, CA: Wadsworth Cengage, 2005.
77 Pierre Clastres ("Of Torture in Primitive Societies," *L'Homme*, vol. 13, no. 3, 1973, original italics) argued that torture in rites of passage had the function of prohibiting inequality: "The law they come to know in pain is the law of primitive society, which says to everyone: *You are worth no more than anyone else; you are worth no less than anyone else.* The law, inscribed on bodies, expresses primitive society's refusal to run the risk of division, the risk of a power separate from society itself, *a power that would escape its control.* Primitive law, cruelly taught, is a prohibition of inequality that each person will remember." One is reminded, in this regard, of the similarity to fraternity/sorority hazing and many military academies and fighting units. See also the critique of Clastre's book, *Chronicle of the Guayaki Indians*, by Clifford Geertz, "Deep Hanging Out," *New York Review of Books*, October 22, 1998.
78 Daniel Smith, et al., "Cooperation and the Evolution of Hunter-Gatherer Storytelling," *Nature Communications*, December 5, 2017. The trials of animals in western Europe may do similar work: See, Paul Berman, "Rats, Pigs, and Statues on Trial," *New York University Law Review*, vol. 69 (1994), pp. 288–326.
79 Paul Radin, *The World of Primitive Man*, p. 225.
80 The full quote reads: "No war is over until the enemy says it's over. We may think it over, we may declare it over, but in fact, the enemy gets a vote."
81 Sahlins, *Tribesmen*, p. 38.
82 See generally, Kent Flannery and Joyce Marcus, *The Creation of Inequality*, Cambridge: Harvard University Press, 2012.
83 Edmund Leach, *Custom, Law, and Terrorist Violence*, Edinburgh: Edinburgh University Press, 1977, pp. 9–10.
84 As noted for the Iroquois by Pekka Hämäläinen (*Indigenous Continent: The Epic Contest for North America*, New York: Liveright Publishing Co., 2022, p. 101): "The Iroquois League, having lost nearly half of its members, went to war to repopulate itself by making Iroquois out of others." These so-called 'mourning wars,' occasioned largely by the decimating diseases brought by Europeans, involved the ritual slaying of some enemy captives and the full inclusion of others as members of Iroquois kin groups. So extensive was the practice that Jesuit missionaries reported Iroquois villages in which captive adoptees constituted between sixty and eighty percent of the population. Elsewhere, among the Nuer and Dinka tribes of Sudan, mutual raiding also led to very high rates of adoptive inclusion (E. E. Evans-Pritchard, *The Nuer*, Oxford: Clarendon Press, 1940). So, too, Jacques Berque, in his, 'Qu'est-ce qu'une tribu nord-africaine?" (in *Éventail de l'histoire vivante, Hommage à Lucien Febvre*, Paris, Armand Colin, 1954, pp. 261–71) argues that straight line descent does not describe Berber kinship groupings, where adoption and genealogical manipulation are widespread.
85 Dean Snow, "The Dynamics of Ethnicity in Tribal Society," in Parkinson, ed., *The Archaeology of Tribal Societies*, p. 98. "The practice of adopting entire tribes was also common in the lower Mississippi." Gordon M. Sayre, *Les Sauvages Americains: Representations of Native Americans in French and English Colonial Literature*, Chapel Hill: University of North Carolina Press, 1997, p. 286.
86 See, Jacques Berque, *Structure Sociales du Haut Atlas*, Paris: Presses Universitaires de France, 1955.

87 See, Douglas W. Bird, et al., "Variability in the Organization and Size of Hunter-Gatherer Groups: Foragers Do Not Live in Small-Scale Societies," *Journal of Human Evolution*, vol. 131 (2019), pp. 96–108; Kim Hill, et al., "Co-Residence Patterns in Hunter-Gatherer Societies Show Unique Human Social Structure," *Science*, vol. 331 (2011), pp. 1286–89; and Andrea Migliano, et al., 2017, "Characterization of Hunter-Gatherer Networks and Implications for Cumulative Culture," *Nature Human Behaviour*, vol. 1, no 2 (2017), p. 43.

88 The Moroccan reference is from Jacques Berque, *Structures Sociales du Haut-Atlas*, Paris: Presses Universitaires de France, 1955; the Americanist reference is from Richard Slotkin, *Regeneration through Violence: The Mythology of the American Frontier, 1600-1860*, Middletown, CT: Wesleyan University Press, 1973, p. 54. Warfare and epidemics might also prompt wholesale adoptions, as among the Iroquois in the 17th century as indicated in the sources cited above at note 82. More generally, "dynamic group membership turnover is typical of tribal societies. While some tribes might successfully maintain strict rules of endogamy, most do not...Outsiders are allowed in by adoption, or might even be actively recruited." Dean Snow, "The Dynamics of Ethnicity in Tribal Society," in Parkinson, ed., *The Archaeology of Tribal Societies*, p. 98. For data on the tribes of southern Africa see, Schapera, *Government and Politics in Tribal Societies*, pp. 17–18.

89 "Traits of Indian Character," *Selected Writings of Washington Irving*, New York: The Modern Library, [1820] 1945, p. 95. On the level of the individual or that individual's role: "The Jesuit Barthelemy Vimont, in the *Relation of 1642*, [22: 288–89] told how 'Mothers or other relatives who love a son, or a daughter, or any of their kindred, cause such persons to be resuscitated, through a desire to see them close by them, transferring the affection that they felt for the deceased to the persons who take their names'." Quoted in Sayre, *Les Sauvages Americains*, p. 288.

90 Raymond Firth, "Bilateral Descent Groups: An Operational Viewpoint," in I. Schapera, ed., *Studies in Kinship and Marriage*, Royal Anthropological Institute Occasional Papers No. 16, London: Royal Anthropological Institute, 1963, pp. 22–37, at 36.

91 See, Eric Schwimmer, "The Maori Hapu: A Generative Model," *Journal of the Polynesian Society*, vol. 99, no. 3 (1990), pp. 297–317.

92 David G. Anderson, "The Evolution of Tribal Social Organization in the Southeastern United States," in Parkinson, ed., *The Archaeology of Tribal Societies*, p. 248.

93 Quoted in Leonid Bershidsky, "To Deal with Putin, First Know His Goals," *Bloomberg News*, January 6, 2017.

94 Hiatt, *Arguments about Aborigines*, pp. 83–84.

95 See, e.g., "The Case of the Ungenerous Husband," in Max Gluckman, *The Judicial Process among the Barotse of Northern Rhodesia*, Manchester: Manchester University Press, 2nd edn., 1967, pp. 172–74.

96 Lloyd Cabot Briggs, *Tribes of the Sahara*, Cambridge: Harvard University Press, 1960, p. 136.

97 See, Pekka Hämäläinen, *The Comanche Empire*, New Haven: Yale University Press, 2009, pp. 346–61.

98 See generally, Lawrence Rosen, *Law as Culture*, Princeton: Princeton University Press, 2006.

99 Bronislaw Malinowski, *Crime and Custom in Savage Society*, London: Kegan Paul, Trench, Trubner, 1926, p. 74.

100 Leach, *Custom, Law, and Terrorist Violence*, pp. 12, 20.

101 The contrast to many Western thinkers on the subject is striking: "In both Plato and Job, it needs to be noted, the abolition of injustice depends on the obliteration of ambivalence, and the obliteration of ambivalence is the death of tragedy." Stanley Diamond, "Introductory Essay" to Paul Radin, *The Trickster*, p. xxi.
102 K. N. Llewellyn and E. Adamson Hoebel, *The Cheyenne Way*, Norman: University of Oklahoma Press, 1941, p. 323.
103 Guenther, *Tricksters and Trancers*, p. 334.
104 Stuart Schlegel, *Tiruray Justice*, Berkeley: University of California Press, 1970.
105 John Comaroff and Simon Roberts, *Rules and Processes*, Chicago: University of Chicago Press, 1981, p. 18.
106 Comaroff and Roberts, *Rules and Processes*, p. 78. One is reminded, in this regard, of the rules for vessels in international waters, one of which says you must always follow the rules and another that you may not use your rule-given rights to stand on into an accident.
107 Penelope Eckert and Russell Newmark, "Central Eskimo Song Duels: A Contextual Analysis of Ritual Ambiguity," *Ethnology*, vol. 19, no. 2 (April 1980), pp. 191–211, at 203, 204.
108 Lowie, *Primitive Society*, New York: Boni and Liveright, 1920, p. 398.
109 Murray Sinclair, "Aboriginal Peoples. Justice and the Law," in Richard Gosse, et al., eds, *Continuing Poundmaker's and Riel's Quest*, Saskatoon: Purich Publishing, 1994, p. 180.
110 Larry Nesper, "The Sovereign Tribal State's Reach into Seasonal Family Praxis," paper delivered at Law and Society Association Meetings, 2002, pp. 15–16.
111 In *The Morality of Law* (New Haven: Yale University Press, 1969) Lon Fuller argued that for the rule of law to exist rules must be general, public, prospective, coherent, clear, stable, and practicable.
112 Edmund Leach, *Custom, Law, and Terrorist Violence*, p. 27.
113 David Bromwich, "In Praise of Ambiguity," *New York Review of Books*, October 26, 2017.
114 The first quote is from John M. O'Shea and Claire McHale Milner, "Material Indicators of Territory, Identity, and Interaction in a Prehistoric Tribal System," in Parkinson, ed., *The Archaeology of Tribal Societies*, pp. 200–26, at 200. The latter quote comes from Fowles, "From Social Type to Social Process," in Parkinson, ed., *Archaeology of Tribal Societies*, pp. 19–20, at 26.
115 Lowie, *Primitive Society*, 1920, p. 427.

4
SHIFTING THE PARADIGM
Part II: The Spirit of Reciprocity

> "...one lives and analyses data within a frame,
> unaware that the solution is most often just outside of that frame."
>
> Darrell Calkins

Calkins' admonition that one must at times step outside of the usual bounds of analysis has particular relevance to the intersection of economics and social life within tribal groups. As an analytic approach it resonates with the connections underscored in the seminal work of Max Weber. When Max Weber wrote *The Protestant Ethic and the Spirit of Capitalism* he distinguished between a culture's *ethos* – the underlying commitments and self-conceptions fostered by a set of assumptions, values, and actions – and the institutions that may embody them. Moreover, while ethos and organization are connected, they may, at times, move independently of one another, thus suffusing particular structures – including those affecting leadership, rituals, and markets – with variable significance and importance. Similarly, the *spirit* of institutionalized forms suggests that the rationale for engagement in certain practices – the way people orient their actions towards one another so as to impart a meaningful order to their lives – may also change even when the structures within which that process takes place do not. Weber did not, therefore, argue that capitalism was produced by Protestantism but that the meaning of constantly marshaling means to ends had been loosed from its earlier implications of demonstrating religious salvation and became incorporated in the belief that rational calculation was a source of legitimacy in its own right, even if, in his native Germany, that had resulted in an "iron cage" of bureaucracy.

Weber's application to capitalism aside, we have seen that to speak of the tribal *ethos* is to suggest that the meaning of actions – and not just their institutionalization – is central to tribal life. Dispersing and levelling power, for example, expresses an ethic of egalitarianism without displacing individual initiative; being able to reconfigure genealogies and negotiate kinship categories in culturally recognizable ways infuses particular modes of relationship with a sense of orderliness that transcends idealized structures. And to connect the ethos of decentralization with the spirit of reciprocity focuses attention on the ways in which constant exchange suffuses particular practices, rendering them both possible and coherent. Since anthropologists assume that all parts of a culture have some bearing on one another we therefore need, in connecting the tribal ethos with the spirit of reciprocity, to consider how that ethos suffuses multiple domains, its effects on various elements of tribal exchange, the approach it entails for the treatment of others as moral equals, the characteristic concepts of the person it occasions, and the effects it has on the tenor of tribal religions.

Exchange and Expectation

"To take to give is all, return what is hungrily given…"
Dylan Thomas[1]

"You see, we don't trade with things. We trade with people."
!Kung Bushman[2]

Anthropologists have a weakness for gifts. Not that they are more generous or acquisitive than others: They simply have a good deal of experience with societies in which the exchange of "gifts," as Marcel Mauss and others indicated, creates relationships of debt that are crucial to the maintenance of both social ties and the conventions that give them meaning. The lines along which gifts move may also represent – indeed, create – the boundaries of inclusion and separation: As historian Peter Brown notes, "gifts have the quality of connecting antithetical groups while maintaining a distance between them."[3] Gifts are not usually just freewill offerings. As Mauss himself noted: "Mostly they are already return-gifts or services performed not only to pay for services and objects but also with a view to maintaining a profitable relationship."[4] Or, in the much more succinct formulation of my grandmother: "a gift is just a loan."

The emotional expectation of reciprocation may be particularly felt if, for example, you have given a birthday present to another and received nothing on the occasion of your birthday. The unfulfilled obligation may also be experienced as a great weight: As an Egyptian woman once told anthropologist Unni Wikan, "an unreciprocated gift is a terrible burden to bear," while the pressure to reciprocate a gift among the Maori explains their saying that the person who clings to things discovers that "property is knitted brows," it "drains the giver's life." Or, as the Inuit say, "gifts make slaves." At times, therefore, obligations are avoided, sometimes by demanding a bridewealth payment so extravagant that the relationship calling for later reciprocation is avoided, sometimes by belittling the food offered to downplay an indebting feast.[5] Hospitality, too, places burdens for which reciprocity in some convertible form may, in an ongoing process of one-upmanship, later be sought. Equivalence may not always be achieved: As Patricia Crone notes for the ancient Middle East, "pre-Islamic poetry is full of complaints of kinsmen who fail to fulfill their end of the bargain."[6] Indeed, as Marshall Sahlins points out, balanced reciprocity may be unstable and tend towards self-liquidation, features that may account for balanced reciprocity "not [being] the prevalent form of exchange in primitive societies."[7] Thus we must keep in mind, as elsewhere in our analysis of tribal societies, two cardinal considerations: that even acts that are more-or-less balanced are not simply disinterested, and, notwithstanding that tribal peoples do not always follow their own professed rules, that fact is neither a negation of their mechanisms for controlling power nor grounds for lessening our respect for their orderliness.

> Once I was in Victoria, and I saw a very large house. They told me it was a bank and that the white men place their money there to be taken care of, and that by and by they got it back with interest. We are Indians and we have no such bank, but when we have plenty of money or blankets, we give them away to other chiefs and people, and by and by they return them with interest, and our hearts feel good. Our way of giving is our bank.
>
> (Chief Maquinna)

It is the multiple forms and sometimes contradictory implications of reciprocity in general, not gift-giving alone, with which we have to grapple. For although reciprocity is common throughout human societies and is hardly unique to tribal cultures we need to attend to some of the distinctive modes of reciprocation and their connection with other characteristics when analyzing tribal life.[8]

FIGURE 4.1 Maquinna was the chief of the Nuu-chah-nulth people (Nootka) in the 1780s–1790s.

The usual way of thinking about tribal economics is as a function of social structure – indeed as supporting the social structure. If one assumes that tribes are layered like Russian dolls or onions – each unit being replicated at ever more encompassing, if sometimes more porous or vulnerable, levels – then the economic structure can be said to mirror and invigorate that form of organization. Accordingly, the dealings at each level may vary with the genealogical (and often ecologically interdependent) distance involved. Close kin, therefore, are said to engage in rather generalized sharing, free from constant calculation. As characterized by Elman Service and Marshall Sahlins, such 'generalized reciprocity' conveys the sense of the relatively altruistic gift, a process they describe as one in which "the expectation of reciprocity is left indefinite…not only conditional on what the donor gave, but also on what he needs and when, … [an obligation that is] diffuse." Indeed, especially as it concerns the weak, "Failure to reciprocate, or to give just as much as was received, does not cause the original giver of things to stop: the goods move one way, in favor of the have-not, for a long time." By comparison, they argue, more distantly connected parties are said to focus on "balanced reciprocity," in which expected returns may be immediate or delayed. However effected – whether through barter of goods or the ostensible "sale" of a bride – "balanced reciprocity is less 'personal' than generalized reciprocity," and hence the economic and social aspects appear to be more separated. Finally, at the further limits of relationship, so-called "negative" exchanges are commonly of greater benefit, if not overt detriment, to one or another party, each individual being engaged in "mustering enough countervailing pressure or guile to serve, or better, enhance one's own interests."[9]

> [Among the Eskimo (Inuit):] It was absolutely necessary for the seal to be shared throughout the camp. This was done according to a set of precise rules involving a system of partnership. During childhood a mother will select for her small son about a dozen sharing partners, all non-relatives. The partnership endured for life…Whenever a hunter killed a seal each one of his sharing partners was given his specific part [of the seal] and only that part to which he was entitled. Meat sharing partners called each other not by their personal names but by the corresponding seal cuts they exchanged.
>
> Asen Balikci, "A Comparative Study in Subsistence Ecology and Social Systems: The!Kung Bushmen and Netsilik Eskimos," *Proceedings of the VIIIth International Congress of Anthropological and Ethnological Sciences,* Tokyo, vol. 3 (1968), pp. 261–62, at 262.

Most anthropological accounts of tribal economics thus begin with propositions best regarded as idealizations that may or may not describe relationships at all moments but do, like any such model, serve as both guide and brake on actual liaisons. Dispersing power and requiring beneficial use play key roles. So, Paul Radin, for example, characterizes tribesmen as engaging in what he calls "the principle of an irreducible minimum."[10] Surplus, he says, is to be distributed in a non-profit manner: For possession to vest, any resource must be used – though not to the exclusion of those whose basic needs must be met. Dispersal of power through destruction of a person's possessions at death is also a common practice among tribal groups: Like redistributions at initiation or transition ceremonies, such destruction serves, in part, to level individual control of valued resources. The Western stereotype that nothing is personally "owned" in tribal societies is also misleading, particularly if "ownership" is understood to mean not simply one's control over a given object but the nature of one's relationships with others as concerns that object.

As an idealized model the taxonomy of reciprocation put forth by Sahlins, Service, and others can help ferret out certain connections in any of these social systems. But the types are not pure. Who has not calculated the precisely correct gift to one's friend or lover only to have seriously missed the mark? Who has not engaged in a professed relationship of balanced reciprocity only to be hurt when the form of reciprocation fails to meet expectation? The transaction may involve the collectivity – as in regularized marital exchange among descent groups – or it may contravene group attachments. Among the Inuit, for example, one might trade with some members of a lineage while being at war with other members, so individualistic are the ties and so reluctant the community to interfere.[11] The Inuit who "gives" his wife to another for the night has even been interpreted as facilitating cooperative relations among male hunting and trading partners, creating fictive sibling bonds among resultant offspring, and ending feuds (since the children of such liaisons were forbidden to engage in further bloodshed).[12] As in so much of social and emotional life, we deal here in ranges, blurrings, and ideals, all of which it is necessary for any successful society to address realistically. But if we start with some of the positive aspects we can see that building on the typology of exchange anthropologists have suggested may reveal linkages that might otherwise escape notice. Such connections are nicely set forth by Bernard Bailyn in his discussion of the Native Americans in the British colonial period.

> In such a world, reciprocity was the key to stability, to happiness, in the end to survival. Injuries had to be requited, insults repaid, losses recovered. Raids were launched, wars were fought, over the failure

FIGURE 4.2 Picture of Inuit men sharing a wife.

of reciprocal trade....[R]eciprocity, the maintenance of equilibrium, the restoration of balance – among people, between people and their environment, and among the elemental forces of life – was a complex process, full of mysteries that people struggled to comprehend.[13]

But how is such balancing exchange actually managed? Reciprocity is often portrayed as following along the pathways set out in reasonably strict form by the terms of tribal kinship relationships. However, as we saw when discussing segmentary organization in the preceding chapter, there is a problem that often crops up in this kind of analysis, namely that if one charts actual relationships tribesmen frequently have stronger ties with more distant relatives or non-kinsmen than with some of those more closely related. Tribes may indeed be segmented. But that is quite different from being segmentary (recombining mechanically at ever higher levels of genealogical inclusion). Indeed, segmentarity may actually be the enemy, the very antithesis, of segmentation, for it theoretically calls for recombination that seldom takes place automatically and thus undermines the flexibility of segmentation itself. If, however, the way to make segmentarity work is not to stand back and let the structure govern itself but for individuals to invoke it as further support for personally constructed alliances, then segmentarity, far from being self-governing, casts up the very personalism that might seem to be its antithesis. Indeed, when truly successful as a mechanism that is triggered by preset obligations irrespective of those who have formed them, segmentarity may very well yield entrenched hierarchy, which is death to tribalism.

Genealogy, then, may under these circumstances be less a rule of relationship than a tool of highly differential utility, a template for encouraging or justifying a resultant network, or a vocabulary of relational possibilities maintained by common discourse. Considering, as even Sahlins is quick to note, "the general propensity of tribal peoples to cloak alliances of convenience in kinship garb," we should not be surprised by the range of variation of motives and categorizations that pervade tribesmen's economic life.[14] Given the bias of functionalist thinking to assume that all features contribute to the continuing operation of the whole, insufficient attention may, therefore, have been paid to the negotiable and disputatious arrangements common at any level in a tribal society. The focus on structure often leads anthropologists either to ignore telling exceptions or to be torn between the particularism of individual cases and the claimed universality of socio-economic forces.

Moreover, it would be a mistake to assume that reciprocity among fellow tribesmen implies that everyone gives and receives equally. To make such an assumption would not only romanticize tribes as utterly egalitarian but imply that, the balance always being righted, tribal societies are essentially stagnant. Studies, however, show that not infrequently one party may indeed benefit in a seemingly equal exchange.[15] Changes in technology or ecological adaptation may also severely alter prior patterns. Among the equine cultures of the plains of North America, for example, the introduction of the horse disrupted exchange relations because the animals were kept outside of the pool of items to be exchanged through reciprocity and, as limited prestige items, played an important role in the formation of an indigenous elite.[16] Sahlins' notion of unbalanced reciprocity is not, however, in and of itself contrary to the central features that characterize tribes. It is important to consider imbalances just as one needs to follow exchanges longitudinally in order to see if countervailing pressures for levelling are present. Moreover, as Karl Polanyi argued, it may rather be the social than the material implications of exchange that drive the system. What seems to be noteworthy about tribes is simply that numerous pressures exist to keep exchange relatively balanced, though not static, and hence the system of exchange is deeply implicated in those other devices by which power is dispersed without destroying individual effort and identity.

In sum, reciprocity emphasizes the relation of exchange to other social ties and underscores the flexibility that may be lacking in other forms of exchange. Reciprocity has, therefore, almost always been used by anthropologists in conjunction with accounts that focus on the social structural aspects of a given tribe – how the rotation of mates among a circle of lineages creates return exchanges of goods from their interdependent ecological zones, how exchanges associated with an initiation ceremony reinforce roles based on gender or age, or how goods thrust on a sister's husband demonstrate the brother's interest in his sibling's progeny for the continuation of their own matrilineage. Valuable as understanding these connections are, however, a concentration on reciprocity as such tends to gloss over a feature that may be more central to the distinctive form of exchange found in tribal groups. Thus, instead of idealizing different forms of reciprocity as constructed like a series of concentric circles it might be more accurate to focus on what may be thought of as the power of convertibility. For neither generalized nor balanced reciprocity sufficiently underscores that in tribal societies something given in one form may be rendered back in any of a very wide range of alternative forms, a process that may be true regardless of genealogical or residential proximity. If, for example, I help someone with food on one occasion I may seek or expect help, say, in arranging a dependent's marriage or support in a question of leadership; if I lend another the wherewithal to prepare goods for a trading venture or building a new home I may use whatever cultural tools are available – social pressure, shame, gossip, joking, genealogical manipulation – to conduce a return in the form, say, of assistance in a hunting party or access to pastureland. The point is that a cultural expectation of negotiable return suffuses – and in many instances utterly negates – the sense of layered segmentation that an orientation towards tribe as structure conveys even in so seemingly cultural a concept as reciprocity.

Other forms of reciprocation may also serve the broader goal of keeping power dispersed. For example, the relative lack of privacy in tribal societies is not simply a matter of size but renders information more accessible and less easily cumulated by one individual or group. Keeping the cost of determining, say, whether another would be a reliable hunting partner or in-law requires constant interpersonal contact and spreads risk against times of scarcity or insecurity.[17] The relative absence of privacy also can reinforce individualism as each tribesman seeks to find out – and make strategic use of – arrangements every other person has organized.

Seen from the perspective of convertibility a number of apparent contradictions in the analysis of particular forms of tribal organization might also be reconciled. It is very common in anthropological accounts of tribes, for example, to find terms given for what appear to be distinct tribal segments correlating with ever more distant kinship affiliation. So, to take the example of some tribes in North Africa, terms are used that refer to various branching parts of the body while in other groups the terminology may refer metaphorically to larger and smaller canals in the local irrigation system.[18] But just when the investigator thinks that he or she has grasped "the system" informants will also be found using the terms for the more inclusive level to refer to a less embracing unit, and vice versa.[19] As one begins to trace actual relationships and terminological usages it becomes obvious that these levels of segmentation are subject to varied application, particularly as one tries to elicit or ratify the behavior or exchange expectation ideally associated with the term applied to a given level of relatedness. Just as one might say "we are cousins" when the genealogical distance is quite great, yet one is trying to conduce behavior ideally associated with closer proximity, so too one may speak to a close kinsman using the term for the more distant connection of "tribe" rather than the closer one of "lineage" to avoid an undesired entanglement. Nor is relatedness a guarantee of ideal behavior: Among tribesmen of Southwest Asia, for example, "In-group tensions usually relate to the inheritance of property and sex. Islamic law and local customs carefully delineate inheritance patterns, but wily brothers and uncles sometimes out-snooker less wily brothers and nephews."[20] Now, what had appeared as glitches in the system become the system, in the sense of a repertoire of relational possibilities that may well serve as a potential template and legitimizer of resultant relationships. Convertibility thus services these flexible modes of relationship – indeed is integral to them. More than one theory may be helpful in this regard. From a functionalist perspective one might claim that such malleability contributes to relative peacefulness;[21] from an evolutionary view, that the convertibility of reciprocation creates greater flexibility in adapting to changing social needs.[22]

Moreover, it cannot be too strongly emphasized that trade and barter between and among various tribes is entirely consistent with the modes of exchange within any tribe. Of course, different commodities may be involved, different ties (of marriage or alliance) generated than from intratribal reciprocity, but the styles, while variant, may simply underscore the key role played by exchange in tribal life. All of this is hardly new: For example, we now have evidence of beads having been traded over vast distances as long as 150,000 years ago.[23] But then, as an historian of the Roman period wryly notes: "Wherever unlike people meet, money is to be made."[24]

From multiple perspectives, then, negotiable reciprocity fits well with its tribal spirit. In such systems we are faced not with a fixed set of categories and attendant social expectations that a structural analysis of tribal life would have us acknowledge: That repetitive use of a particular component of the repertoire may link individuals in habitual ties in no way means that they are ruled by structural requirements lacking in personal choice. Indeed, it is the very open texture of the terms of relatedness that renders this possibility conventional. Even E.E. Evans-Pritchard, who described the Nuer and Sanusi of the Sudan in segmentary terms, acknowledges, upon close reading, that kinship is an "idiom," and the use of a sliding scale of actual and fictive kin terms is so common among tribesmen that one would really have to call it the norm. When we add to this the common practice of assimilating one's enemies by adoption, marriage, manipulated or fictional histories – or sloughing off members through revised membership rules, out-marriage, or idiosyncratic fission – there is support for the idea that it is the conceptual toolbox and the regularized ways of engaging others within a particular group or set of groups, rather than structural constraints, that is the key to understanding the actual, rather than academically idealized, range of tribal relationships. And just as each element of the tribal spirit of reciprocity is connected to every other aspect of tribal life, so too the concepts of morality and personhood also have a direct bearing on the meaning of interpersonal exchange.

Moral Equality

We all make judgments of others. But we do so within the framework of a set of cultural assumptions and orientations. We may regard each person as autonomous or as the building block of a larger assemblage; we may believe it is possible to access another's intent or regard inner states as available only to God or the Devil. Whatever the case, the cultural lenses through which we view others are based on categories that traverse and unite multiple domains to the point where they seem both obvious and natural. Moral formulations, too, must cohere if the world is to make sense. Moreover, whole societies may share particular ways of viewing morality and persons notwithstanding major differences of detail. Dictatorial states may, therefore, seek to cancel or impute individual intent in the interest of those ruling the collectivity, or religious cults may share an orientation towards emotion as worthy of support only when rendered in a publicly controllable fashion.[25] Tribes, to return to the subject at hand, vary greatly in their appraisal of morality and the person, but just as in the ways they disperse power or stress reciprocity there is a family resemblance that justifies discussing tribal ways of viewing one another as a distinct phenomenon.

Particularly noteworthy is the tendency of tribesmen to regard one another as moral equals. That is, no segment of the tribe – no individual – can claim to be the inherent embodiment of morally correct behavior all others must follow. Indeed, there is no single standard by which everyone, regardless of context, can be judged. In the absence of a universal and persistent standard for such baseline ranking both moral standing and person appraisal are, therefore, infinitely divisible. Paul Dresch's characterization thus applies to a wider range of tribes than those among whom he has worked in northern Yemen when he writes: "The morality all tribesmen recognize is indefinitely fragmented into separate spaces. [Theirs is] a kind of moral particularism or pluralism."[26] This does not necessarily mean that different moral standards apply to those who are close versus those more distant. Rather, it often implies that (a) just as in kin relations the bounds of moral expectation are themselves variable and subject to contextual negotiation, and (b) there are no absolute moral precepts that apply even within the group, chaos being avoided by the regularized ways in which one assesses and distributes power away from any individual who might do the group harm.

> [I]n primitive communities free scope is allowed for every conceivable outlet. No moral judgment is passed on any aspect of human personality as such. Human nature is what it is and each act, emotion, belief, unexpressed or expressed, must be allowed to make or mar a man. It is each man's inalienable right – he would indeed be unfair to himself if he did not make use of it – to seek the approbation and respect of other individuals and of the community, even if this right be abused and exaggerated. No false modesty should be allowed to deter him. But there is an important corollary. If by the exaggeration of this craving a man comes into conflict with the world and with social realities, he will personally suffer and, what is far more reprehensible and dangerous, he may involve others in the consequences of his personally initiated self-seeking.
>
> Paul Radin, *Primitive Man as Philosopher*, p. 32

Gender, of course, may complicate these propositions, inasmuch as some tribes certainly differentiate the roles played by men or women with overtones of morality. For the most part, however, it appears that the division of labor – including ritual and religious labor – does not simply correlate with inferior or superior moral virtue in such societies. Rather, it is commonly a question of moral equivalence, rather than equality. That is, the tasks or places of each gender are not so much ranked as they are segregated but placed on an equivalent plane, each being necessary to the operation of the whole. Seen in that fashion, the principle of moral stature that is characteristic of tribes generally is consistent with the idea that roles may differ without undercutting the emphasis on moral behavior seen more in terms of personal behavior than category restriction. This perspective is replicated in other domains as well.

Earlier, we saw both Marshall Sahlins and Clyde Kluckhohn arguing that tribes were characterized by "situational norms," "sectoral morality," "temporary versions," "rule variation," and even "spiritual indeterminacy." These qualities thus have a bearing on one of the key stereotypes of tribes found in Western commentary, namely that adhering to a moral code applies only within a tightly defined group, tribesmen being perfectly willing to apply quite a different standard when encountering those who lie outside the tribal boundary. Recall that Thomas L. Friedman has said that "[i]n a tribal world it's rule or die, compromise is a sin, enemies must be crushed and power must be held at all costs," while Edward Banfield famously characterized southern Italians as practicing "amoral familism," where theft and even murder may be acceptable beyond the bounds of family but would never be regarded as moral within that confine.[27] So, tribes pose for the social scientist and the moral philosopher alike a key question: How is moral particularism possible if it applies down to the level of every individual? Indeed, how is total anarchy avoided if no principles of moral behavior have general application? For some guidance in addressing these questions we need to consider matters from both an anthropological and a philosophical perspective. For where culture is the answer, philosophy helps us understand the question that culture will have to confront.

Western philosophers have long contended with the question of universal versus particular moral precepts. Aristotle, most notably, had argued that general principles could be misleading and that specific circumstances, informed by individual intentions, are indispensable to equitable judgment. For him, in the phrasing of Edith Hall: "Each dilemma requires detailed engagement with the nuts and bolts of its particulars. When it comes to ethics, the devil really can be in the detail."[28] Put simply, moral particularism suggests that no two cases are necessarily alike and therefore general principles – to the extent that they can be articulated at all – must come up against actual instances where one size does not fit all. Thus while there may be procedural regularities for eliciting the relevant information in any given situation – procedures that partake of cultural norms that indicate what *is* relevant information – each situation must be understood and judged for its own consequences and the preservation of individual freedom. When thus posed as an issue of treating everyone equally and being personally able to do as one chooses, Isaiah Berlin could characterize the opposition between equality and freedom as an "intrinsic, irremovable element in human life."[29] Those who favor universal moral principles versus those who see each instance as essentially unique have some difficulties with this position and, as Jonathan Dancy says in his review of the subject, one must then ask:

> what relevance other cases do have to a new case, if not the sort of relevance that the generalist supposes. The answer to this is that experience of similar cases can tell us what sort of thing to look out for, and the sort of relevance that a certain feature can have; in this way our judgement in a new case can be informed, though it is not forced or constrained, by our experience of similar cases in the past. There is no need to suppose that the way in which this works is by the extraction of principles from the earlier cases, which we then impose on the new case.

Similarly, there is concern with the risk that without some regularity to moral precepts another's actions will be unpredictable. As Dancy further notes:

> [The concern] here is that a particularist morality is a lax morality: without principles, anything goes. But there are various ways in which this thought can be built up. The first is just to say that morality is in the business of imposing constraints on our choices. For there to be constraints, there needs to be regulation, and regulation means rules, and rules mean principles. This, however, is just wrong. There can be fully particular constraints on action, and the judgement that this action would be wrong is surely just such a thing. Constraints do not need to be general constraints, any more than reasons need to be general reasons.[30]

Clearly there are strong overtones of moral particularism in tribal cultures. We see it in numerous domains. Trickster figures, as we have noted, possess no "moral fanaticism": They may even seem immoral given their pragmatic and individualistic approach to particular problems.[31] So, too, we see connections between this form of pragmatic moralizing and reciprocity. A striking example is provided in an incident that occurred to Jean Cabot Briggs when she was living among the Eskimo. Some white sport fishermen wanted to borrow a canoe that Briggs knew the Eskimo needed but might feel obliged to lend. After she intervened to tell the sportsmen they were taking advantage of the natives she learned that the Eskimo were shunning her and telling others that she did not understand that one was expected to help any person in need and that in this particular case the right thing to do was to agree to the loan.[32] From the Eskimo perspective whatever actions were to be taken did not depend on a view of the other as someone to be treated as unworthy of the same moral valence accorded the assessment of all others.

It is from the Eskimo, too, that we can draw an example of an issue that arises, at least in Western perceptions, for many tribes. For if there are no firmly regulating, and generally applicable moral principles it may seem that anyone can do whatever the traffic will bear. Indeed, Arthur E. Hippler and Stephen Conn, discussing the Eskimo, put it bluntly:

> Simply stated, most Eskimo behavioral norms derived from an attitude that predisposed the Eskimo to believe that one should never interfere in the life of another. This attitude stemmed from a strong feeling of individuality and the fear that interfering with someone else's individuality would lead to retaliatory violence. Flowing from this all-encompassing attitude were such normative beliefs as: one should not kill, steal, commit adultery, tell lies, or in any way intervene in another's life. Running counter to these beliefs, however, was the implicit statement: one should not do these things unless he can get away with it.

This latter point might indeed suggest an extreme version of moral particularism. Moreover, such amoral behavior is a theme that recurs in descriptions of many tribes – at least by Western observers. An example worth pursuing in some detail is that of several tribal groups in Chad where, according to Judith Scheele, "trust, even among close family members, is a sign of gullibility."[33] She continues:

> This, however, does not mean that there are no moral judgements. People mostly agree on what it means to be a good person, or rather a 'proper' Teda or Dazagada [tribesman]: one ought to be strong, assertive, independent, fearless, versatile, have many social connections, be rich, generous, clever, and not be interrupted when one talks (it is rather

common for people to talk all at once). One ought to be different and memorable, and one way of doing this is precisely to break rather than follow any social 'rule' that one might abstract from the general gossip. Where laughter is the strongest social sanction, this means that people tread a thin line: outrageous actions might spark admiration, but they might also be simply defined as ludicrous.

In this society, Scheele notes, reciprocity is, moreover, limited: Individually negotiated ties – especially marital alliances and monetary exchanges – might seem to replace regularized norms of social organization. But as Scheele indicates: "The local emphasis on money rather than, say, gift exchange is symptomatic of a more general worldview, where social relations are seen as inherently fluid, unstable, and unpredictable." Indeed, "status is increased not by accumulating social ties and potential clients, but by showing in grandiose fashion that one can do without."[34] With property viewed not as a source for security but for conflict – and with ridicule one of the few mechanisms cited as constraining behavior – the stage would appear to be set for testing whether in this and similar tribal cases we are confronted with a case of descending from moral particularism into outright anarchy.

Scheele herself does not resolve the problem. She notes that in the face of colonial pressures the Tubu-speakers' seeming anarchy may keep them adaptable to an impersonal money economy and reconfigured political power. She even suggests that "where disorder itself emerges as a key value, imaginations of a larger whole are crucial," though she is unclear as to what that larger whole is.[35] Even assuming this is a case of willful disordering there is, however, reason to suggest that the interpretation on offer is not the most fitting for the situation. There is, of course, no way of knowing whether Scheele's example from Chad is characteristic or aberrant among tribal examples, nor if it is a reaction to acts by the state and dominant populations or a pattern of long duration.[36] An alternative possibility might, however, be derived from the work of moral philosopher Elizabeth Anderson.[37] She suggests that where people broaden the range of respected tasks and where, through involvement in diverse roles, they adapt the values of one domain into others what may appear as a contradiction between freedom and equality can be reconciled. As one shifts from using distribution as a way to resolve inequality to valuing each person's contributions in the light of shared criteria a cascade into utter moral relativism can be largely assuaged. Thus, among the Bushmen, for example, attributing the right to distribute the product of a hunt not to the hunter but the person – quite possibly elderly – who fashioned the hunter's arrow equalizes to some extent each person's contribution to society. Or, by treating each individual as a moral equal while still pressing advantage to the limit of ridicule, levelling prevents particularism from descending into mere anarchy. In no case is perfect balance achieved: As Isaiah Berlin suggested, one must continue to haggle over the terms and applications on a case-by-case basis. But by creating systems of cross-cutting ties, by seeing similarities in individual behavior without presupposing uniformity as a value, by retaining a focus on the situated individual and not applying different moralities to different levels of attachment (themselves highly mobile), and by carrying these themes across multiple social and cultural domains tribal peoples may find a way of muddling through that no society given over to moral certainties and their rigorous enforcement can match for long-term survival in a world of constant change. "Morality and expediency coincide more than the cynics allow," noted British Labour politician Roy Hattersley, and the form of pragmatic wisdom of tribes may lie, as Paul Radin phrased it, in their "realistic and unsentimental perception of life and of the nature of human contact...[where] every ethical precept must be submitted to the touchstone of conduct."[38] Nevertheless, conduct is only one of several interrelated aspects of the person that tribes elaborate, so it is necessary to consider several additional features that bear on tribal constructions of the person.

The Construction of Persons

When social scientists talk about the construction of the person they are referring to the conceptual vehicles through which the appraisal of one's own and another's qualities are formed. While generalizations about the processes through which this perception and evaluation occurs in tribal societies must again be approached cautiously there is reason to suggest that, in a theme and variation sense, some common features may be discerned. We can group our approach to these factors under four categories: how one assesses others' believability and the meaning of their actions; how the individual is perceived in terms of multiple roles or as an indivisible personality; how much the differences among individuals are elaborated or muted; and how concepts of time and context reveal information vital to orienting one's actions towards another.

Throughout this study we have seen the notable strain of pragmatism that characterizes tribal societies – the testing of concepts against the practicalities of daily life. What seemed to earlier investigators to be examples of the very opposite – magical thinking, attributions of witchcraft or spirit worship – have come to be seen predominantly as vehicles for creating a sense of the orderliness of the cosmos and corresponding to its course. As Sahlins notes: "rather than 'superstitious,' 'deluded,' or otherwise taken in by wishful fantasies, [for those whose worlds are populated by 'spirits'] their enchantments are effects of a sustained and radical empiricism."[39] So, too, in the domain of person perception the focus is on conduct, the effects that one's actions have on the well-being of oneself and others. Intent is read out of actions, not as a separate state that is accessible to another. Character is also read out of conduct, but conduct that includes a wide range of manifestations, not least among them one's rhetorical capacities (for speech is itself an act and not a mere verbalization). Credibility arises from the observation of actions as well, such that believing or following another – or indeed attending to his or her felt sense of injury – flows from appraising the consequences of such emotions on an individual's peacefulness or recourse to violence. The cost of seeking such information about another may be more time-consuming than in a culture that depends on literacy for the conveyance of intelligence. But that reliance on the observable and the word of those who have had access to such observations intensifies social ties and spreads one's acceptance of the credible across multiple persons thereby dispersing the power that comes with any one person controlling the narrative.[40]

Reading another's intentions is also culturally dependent. In the West, at least since the 12th century, it has been assumed, in religious thought and daily life, that people have inner lives separate and distinct from their overt acts and utterances.[41] Accessing these inner states requires assessments, in law or common encounters, that often are proxies for observable acts, but which nonetheless assume a certain fractionation of the self. This has been coupled with the belief that one can act within discreet roles, such that, for example, a judge can set aside her personal beliefs about abortion or the death penalty and apply the established law without suffering either personal dissonance or loss of public legitimacy. But in tribal societies it would appear that this fractionation of the self into discreet and potentially conflicting roles is either absent or muted. Harm to another may emanate from uncontrollable jealousy, the resultant witchcraft accusation resulting not in punishment but aid to the injured. In tribal law (as in Europe before the 12th century renaissance) strict liability may be applied, another's intention being regarded as beyond human availability. Once again, this should not be taken as some pre-modern mentality or as a failure to apprehend some scientific claim. Rather, the unfractionated self of the tribesmen is of a piece with viewing the other as a person with whom one has multiple and cross-cutting interactions – as kinsman, ally, age mate, leader – each component of which reinforces and spreads the power associated with any one role.[42] The relative lack of total privacy, the flexibility of kin and associational attachments, the respect for individual difference, the legal focus on the situated person rather than absolutes – all cohere into a pattern for which maintaining an image of the person as an integrated whole who cannot (as in paramount chieftainships and other structures) be segregated into independent role behaviors serves to support the levelling of power and the capacity for shapeshifting vital to tribal integrity.

Indeed, it is the recognition of difference at the individual level that is also central to tribal concepts of the person. This is true not just for physical abilities but for emotional qualities. Paul Radin thus writes: "Primitive people accept the expression of all human emotions as normal. But they go much farther; they frankly accept the fact that this expression is specifically different in different individuals. Each man, woman and child stands by himself," and it is these features that account, among tribesmen, "for seeing human relations and understanding human conduct so objectively."[43] Indeed, this stress on the individual – contrary to most Western images – is vital to tribal peoples, notwithstanding the great variation in its connections with other features of their societies. Thus, in the case of the Navajo, James F. Downs can argue: "Despite close and absolutely essential familial ties, the Navajo remain highly individualistic people. Their primary social premise might be said to be that no person has the right to speak for or to direct the actions of another."[44] Some version of this proposition could well be cited for any number of other tribal groups.

In tribes, as in any human community, distinctive cultural features cluster to reinforce one another. Consider the absence of personalized portraiture from almost all tribal art. For societies that place so great a stress on individuality this might seem surprising. But the question arises: What does a portrait actually show? In the West we have come to think that we can tell something about a person's character from their features or expression: We acquire information we need about them from their appearance and extend it to an overall assessment. But in tribal societies the vital information is relational, not something that can be read out of a static image. Moreover, individuality may lie not in total distinctiveness but by enacting an idealized form. In the West this may be achieved by performing a ballet or sonata in as close to the archetypal ideal as possible, a performance that would seem to obliterate individuality but is conceived as one means of its perfect achievement. So, too, the distinctive in tribal settings may be achieved through idiosyncratic acts or (without contradiction) realizing a settled form – through the flawless performance of a ritual or retelling of a tale. Portraiture is not absent, then, because of a lack of individuality or immersion in the collective: It is absent (in the Western sense of such representations) because individuality resides in live interaction and personal accomplishment may be embedded in, rather than separated from, the realization of an ideal form. Or, to take another example, it is also misleading to think there is evidence of the tribal lack of individual difference from our reading of Native American captive accounts. David Brooks, following Sebastian Junger, thus gets it exactly backwards when he says that captive whites often remained with their Indian captors by choice but that Indian captives did not remain with whites because of communal benefits as opposed to intense individualism. Brooks is wrong because he starts with a stereotype of collectivist natives rather than appreciating the open texture of tribal societies, where multilingualism is common, inclusion of outsiders is frequent, and communality does not necessarily come at the cost of individualism.[45] Return to one's tribe is a return to individual personhood, not a retreat from it.

Movement, too, is a domain where tribal distinctiveness may be played up. Norman Mailer once said that "in motion a man has a chance."[46] There is an understandable tendency for Westerners to equate the tribal with the nomadic, and the nomadic with freedom. But not only are most tribes not nomadic, in the sense of being constantly on the move, but movement itself carries a range of implications and representations, whether in myth, religion, art, or social perception. The meaning of mobility can be seen in the origin myths and songs of the tribes of North America, the Berber ideograph of a man as one engaged in exaggerated movement, or in the Dreamtime quest of an Australian aborigine across many miles. It can imply choosing to abide by group demands or it can mean being able to avail oneself of the options regarded as permissible. In the case of tribes, as we have seen, movement may be associated with means more than ends: In his sensitive account of Navajo cosmology, Gary Witherspoon notes that the Navajo emphasis on the verb "to go" rather than "to be" as it "seems to indicate a cosmos composed of processes and events, as opposed to a cosmos composed of facts and things."[47] And by its implication that "in intragroup relations no individual, regardless of position or status, has the right to impose his will on the group" the Navajo example could represent the concept of the person in many other tribes as well.[48]

> Movement dominates and pervades the Navajo view and classification of the world. The Navajo world is a world of motion – a world of action in which all beings and entities are either acting or being acted upon; a world of change in which both individual entities and systems are constantly going through phased cycles and processes of deformation and restoration; a world of things in motion and things at rest, but one in

> which even things at rest are defined by the withdrawal of motion and are classified according to their ability or potential to move or to be moved.
> Gary Witherspoon, *Language and Art in the Navajo Universe*, p. 140.

Concepts of time also play into the view of the person in tribal groups. Again, a comparison to the West may highlight the contrast. There, it may be said, time reveals the truth of persons. Not only is time seen as directional – indeed, usually suggestive of progress – but when a person's story is told it is commonly done so chronologically. By comparison, in tribal societies it is contexts of actions and relationships that reveal who a person is. Stories, too, often feature time as largely irrelevant, the unfolding of the truth of a myth or tale coming through an array of instances in which different aspects of the person, spirit, or creature involved is made evident. In such a situation historical precision and reduction to writing are not especially valuable: It is more important to focus on *who* is telling the tale, who augments its believability through their own attachments and accomplishments, and that the story is related in a narrative style that imports truthfulness. It is not the progress of the group that is usually manifested in such tales but particular persons moving through diverse relationships. Indeed, in some cases – as, for example, among the tribes of Yemen – there may be "no unified story to tell, only the indefinitely fragmented body of heroic tradition...no theory of progress or decline...[C]ollective identities are not constructed in such a way that the story of a single tribe would have the slightest coherence. There are only the *akhbar*, or self-contained tales, which come in no particular sequence, and the moral equality of tribe against tribe, from which the tales derive their significance."[49] Where mythic figures are involved they are often shapeshifters who, like the amoeboid motions of the tribe they validate, can insert themselves into different contexts, dwelling in one place, then another, the totality of which can alone serve to define their momentary form. And it is in the finality of a person's life and the question of what lies beyond that we can also discern still more features of the tribal ethos and its characteristic spirit.

Tribal Religion

The stereotypes of tribal religions usually involve images of bodies raucously painted and plumed, or shamans and sorcerers frightening the children. For the academic descendants of Emile Durkheim, by contrast, expressions of religiosity are said to mimic the social order – indeed to reinforce it – by projecting it onto a supernatural screen. Yet even this functionalist view may slide over some key aspects of the role religion plays in tribal societies. While the generalizations made here, like those in every other domain of our analysis, must be taken in a theme and variation sense, some connections to other aspects of the tribal ethos and its attendant spirit warrant closer consideration.

We have stressed that in tribes power is dispersed, and that would appear to be the case for many religious and ritual features as well. Not only is there commonly a plurality of gods and supernatural agents who mirror any levels of segmentation in the tribe but where an overarching god is posited that entity is usually a rather vague initiator rather than a factor in daily actions. Robert Lowie's exclamation about the Crow Supreme Being – "what chaos is Crow theology concerning the most elementary definition of his identity!" – leads Marshall Sahlins to conclude generally for tribes: "But then, the Supreme Being often doesn't do much – or at least what has he done lately?"[50] Such vagueness may, however, be unsurprising inasmuch as the invocation of greater segmental inclusiveness is, as we have seen, decidedly manipulable, and hence casting a high god in terms that are too specific, rather than allowing units of various points of genealogical inclusiveness to claim attachment through a superordinate deity, might undermine the ability to maneuver among the alternative levels of common identity.[51] Such an interpretation might have special appeal to cultural evolutionists who, following the work of Peter Turchen and his colleagues, have argued that gods with specific moralizing agendas only arise in complex societies, where coordination among disparate elements is facilitated by an overarching deity supplying clear direction and sanctions.[52] To the extent that tribal gods may reflect tribal structures it is not, however, a simple hierarchy of those gods one encounters but, like the manipulation of social segments, gods who are fungible, adaptable, available, amoeboid, contingent, not immune to derision, and often quite distant.

Indeed, one may speculate that tribal gods are actually less the guarantors of tribal space than of tribal time, their invocation being tied predominantly to natural and calendrical events more than title to property. This is not to deny the importance many tribesmen attribute to the place they and their ancestors occupy. Rather, it is to suggest that tribal movement and the preservation of an ideology of potential movement is very common and that gods who are the guarantors of time – the gathering of a season, the memorializing of a drought – have the advantage of aiding in the "situationally activated", whereas attachment to place alone might leave the tribe immobilized and unaccommodating. Indeed, the higher and more universal the god the more transportable. Claiming that "the people" have been located in a given place since time immemorial may aid in a time-bound assertion of territorial rights, just as the present-day denial of the laws of Darwinian evolution may suit claims of inviolable attachment to a given place.[53] But for both the gods and the tribe portability is not without its merits: As Gertrude Stein said, "What use are roots if you can't take them with you?"

Ambiguity and uncertainty, so pervasive in other domains, also make their appearance in tribal religions, including the magic and tactics of the hunt or trading expedition and what might be called the ritual division of labor by gender. So, for example, hunters in northern regions, knowing that deer and other game become familiar with human patterns of movement, may use the markings on an animal bone or other oracles to randomize the direction of their hunt. Magic may not conduce a specific result so much as focus attention on the actions necessary to take advantage of a chanced opportunity. And, in a world whose imagined balance is essential to survival, engagement in rituals of reaffirmation or renewal bring together the participants and the revelation of collective wisdom without which the practical work of maintaining order may be jeopardized. The relation of such rituals to gender relations and economic wellbeing are only another instance of how cultural domains are interconnected. Thus, in Australia:

> The popular notion that the Pitjantjatjara man gains his status as a man through being a hunter and provider needs reconsideration. As a food gatherer, he was unreliable: the women, with their forging and capture of small animals, were reliable in this respect and were thus the main providers in Western Desert society....The women gathered the main supplies of food, but men's rituals ensured that it was there for the gathering. Rituals and discussions of rituals once occupied the greater part of men's lives: from this sprang their reason for being.[54]

Consistent with the image of tribal peoples as the slaves of custom and groupthink is the idea that they are not riven by doubt in the same way Westerners may exemplify. Here, as in so many other ways, we are hobbled by the lack of written records from most tribesmen and, indeed, from an absence of questioning along these lines by many investigators. But there is no reason to suppose that doubt is not part of tribal ways of encountering their world. Paul Radin and Jack Goody are two scholars who have raised this issue. In *Primitive Man as Philosopher* and in his detailed studies of the Winnebago, Radin emphasized that tribal societies are characterized by "respect for the individual," including any of those who are (in his phrase) "non-religious or intermittently religious," such a person being "primarily a man of action and a pragmatist for whom an effect precedes a cause."[55] Given his psychological orientation Radin attributed religiosity primarily to an individual's felt sense of psychic imbalance, but he also recognized that unbelief, or at least skepticism, was not unknown in tribal groups and that such attitudes could play an important role in whether to acknowledge a particular man's claim to supernatural connection. Goody, by comparison, asserts that skepticism is "intrinsic to the nature of religious belief itself," that there is always a "kernel of doubt" prompted by "contradictions involved in the conceptualization of supernatural beings whose presence can only be deduced from their possible effects."[56] Tribesmen may also have a special appreciation that in being overly strict, whether in the postulates of social relations or religious concepts, the cost to useful ambiguity may not be worth the ostensible gain in predictability. As Mary Douglas notes: "Purity is the enemy of change, of ambiguity and compromise." Indeed, she argues: "The final paradox of the search for purity is that it is an attempt to force experience into logical categories of non-contradiction. But experience is not amenable and those who make the attempt find themselves led into contradiction."[57]

Earlier scholars had faulted "primitive man" for his supposed inability to separate cause and effect. But at least since the 1940s anthropologists have shown that neither sympathetic magic nor irrationality is at the heart of many tribesmen's notions of causality. Rather, the entire thought process and accompanying rituals have come to be seen as ways of connecting the disparate elements of the cosmos – indeed as ways of supporting and sustaining one's own sense of orderliness. Such ritual activity, as Clifford Geertz explains, "is not conceived as instrumental.... It is considered as expressive or representational.... It's seen, by those involved, not necessarily explicitly of course, as an attempt to display to themselves and to reinforce in themselves the fact that the world is the way they think it is."[58] Indeed, to approach objects as infused with sentience is to be able to treat things rather like persons, that is, to engage them in a form of reciprocity. Thus, a New Guinean tribe can be described as engaging in the "humanization of the conceived elements of the world...[projecting] notions of human identity and agency upon animals, plants, ritual objects, and all the rest: they share kinship with human beings, have names, belong to subclans, marry and so forth."[59] To do so, however, is not to assume everyone sees matters equally and unquestioningly: As Sahlins notes, "some have been known to disavow the ancestral powers, to purposely neglect them, or even smash their skulls – and find someone else to reverence."[60] Whatever the merits of Goody's claim to the universality of skepticism there is clear evidence that potential doubt and a vision of the world of ordinary sense is no less common among tribal peoples than any others.

Finally, one must consider the role of fear. Franz Boas spoke of the Eskimo's belief at moments of peril that "he hears the voices of spirits which inhabit the mischief laden air;" a Chukchee told a visitor that "we are surrounded by enemies. 'Spirits' always walk about invisibly with gaping mouths. We are always cringing, and distributing gifts on all sides, asking protection of one, giving ransom to another, and unable to obtain anything whatsoever gratuitously;" and an Iglulik shaman told Knud Rasmussen, "We do not believe, we fear. We fear the souls of dead human beings and of the animals we have killed."[61] It would, however, be as great an error to reduce tribal religions – or any others, for that matter – to a response to premonitory and pervasive fear as it would be to ignore that the entities and events that tribal peoples may at times fear are distinctive to their forms of organization and their ways of attending to the world.

Arguably, too, there is no religion that does not offer humankind some form of personal life after death. In the tribal universe that promise may take the form of becoming a ghost or ancestor capable of affecting events in the world of the living, sometimes beneficially, sometimes malevolently, an animating power that achieves immortality by being endlessly transmuted into another form. No less important, at least for men, is the way in which one is remembered after one's death: In a sense, one lives on in the memory of others rather than being certain of reincarnation in one's familiar form. Indeed, life is often thought to continue through each creature being recycled in the natural world, often shapeshifting into a different form. Rather than a sharp break between life and death, therefore, many tribes see life's end as a natural transition, such that even the corpse of the deceased may, as among the Plains Indians, be exposed to the elements and the creatures of the wild or, as among even the royalty of Arabia, consigned to the ground without the need for a localized marker. In each instance, an elaborate eschatology is not vital since the ease of movement between life and afterlife is not one involving an unbridgeable gap.

Many of the features noted here come together quite strikingly in an example that is worth exploring in some depth. Once again it involves the Bushmen of southwest Africa. In his study of Bushman religion Mathias Guenther says: "The hallmark traits of Bushman religion are fluidity, flexibility, and variability, each manifested to a striking degree."[62] Given that one finds the San (Bushmen) coalescing at times as bands, at others under paramount chiefs – and (when large numbers of warriors have gathered) even as being "state-like" – Guenther argues that "the fluidity of Bushman religion is an ideological counterpart to the fluidity of Bushman society," one that he and others have noted for its "amorphousness, ambivalence, and ambiguity."[63] These features are replicated in numerous domains of San (Bushman) life – in kinship, where principles of joking relations and idealized expectations from relatives may be at loggerheads as one goes "foraging for relatives"; in the division of labor, where women may engage in some forms of hunting and men in some types of gathering; in marriage and divorce, where the choice of a mate can follow contradictory paths and where (as in most tribes) divorce is easy and an actual state of marriage not always clear.[64] So, too, in the realm of religion. Focusing on two key figures in their religion, Guenther notes that we can see "the trickster figure as the embodiment of the ambiguity that pervades Bushman mythology and cosmology, much the same as the trance dancer embodies this state with respect to ritual."[65] Both figures are constantly fluctuating and transforming themselves, enacting and exacerbating their ambiguous characteristics. Both conjoin the elements that can be regarded "as an ideology consistent with the mobility, openness, fluidity, flexibility, adaptability, and unpredictability of the foragers' life."[66]

It is not only true that "religion rings true for the Bushmen because of its texts and subtexts of ambiguity":[67] That is probably true for most tribes as well. But as Guenther points out, anthropologists – who above all should possess a high degree of tolerance for ambiguity – have historically been tone-deaf to its role in society and have thus given it little place in their theories.[68] Whether it has been the functionalists or the structuralists, most anthropologists have favored structure over ambiguity. Even those who have approached religion as incorporating rituals and beliefs that stand in clear opposition to normative principles of the society in question tend to revert to a foundational structure to which the society is said to return after its flirtation with the chaotic. In part this has been a healthy reaction to the Durkheimian idea that religion mirrors directly the structure of its society. Nevertheless Guenther, like many others studying tribal religions, may go too far. That is, by rejecting the one-to-one correlation that Durkheim emphasized between structure and idiom we may have also been blinded to the ambiguities in social structure that emanate from the ambiguity of key religious concepts. For just as religious elements often contain amorphous and fluid elements – whether in a high god whose qualities and actions remain vague or a ritual that does not end in certainty – so, too, we have seen that, in the diverse aspects of the tribal ethos and the spirit of reciprocity, much remains open-ended in the actual relationships of people on the ground. If that texture is present in the features of tribesmen's actions – their indeterminate exercise of personal choices, their mobility and assiduous maintenance of recognizable options – it is not surprising that such features should be integral to religious concepts and practices as well. It is not only the San who "cherish the interpersonal idiosyncrasies of ideas" but tribal peoples more widely.[69] And it is the great strength of tribal organization that they should be able to live more comfortably with ambiguity than are many of those who have studied them, and that tribal peoples have found in such openness a basis for both survival and happiness.

* * * *

Social and cultural forms bleed into one another: There are no pure types. Indeed, it is the essence of our species that we are constantly creating and recreating our collective lifeways, and we do so not primarily by cancelling each other out but by interleaving our visions of the world. "Bad poets borrow and good poets steal," it is said, and humankind, in its own poetic way, adopts to endure, appropriates to thrive, and mimics to feel. In the process, elements may be rearranged kaleidoscopically, the configuration of one set of features taking on quite a different design as the pieces fall momentarily into place. This is particularly evident in the domain of the tribal not because it constitutes some primordial aspect of our nature but because its qualities are, as we have seen throughout this study, so flexible and robust as to penetrate and integrate a wide range of structures and ideologies.

All of the mechanisms we have discussed here could be seen as elements of social structure or as generative cultural conceptualizations which, in every instance, must take on some specific content and relationship to other structural features. The issue, however, is not whether structure dominates and culture is merely superficial, or vice versa. Rather, it is that each contributes to the genesis and perpetuation, the inherent limitations, and unexplored potentialities, of the other, and that, in the case of tribes, too great a focus on momentary structural forms may obscure an appreciation of the underlying goals and orientations vital to tribal success.

At several points we have, therefore, alluded to what (with apologies to Max Weber) we have called "the tribal ethos and the spirit of reciprocity". Tribal ways of taking on reality, while clustering around particular structures of kinship and segmentation, marriage alliance and power diffusion, may be carried into quite different organizational forms, like the DNA of a distant kinsman, transformed yet familiar, resonant not simply of an earlier human stage but of enabling possibilities. The tribal ethos may, therefore, be found, loosed from its more common structures, in a polity, for example, where the sultan may be viewed as vulnerable to the dispersal of his power through rituals of reversal – as when the Moroccan king had to submit to the annual demand of a student chosen as sultan for the day. Or a tyrant who leads his people into chaos may find his opponent has built a more effective network of indebtedness that legitimizes the latter's no less vulnerable grasp of authority. Getting our thoughts in order and getting our lives in order, to recall Lloyd Fallers' wise aphorism, are not the same thing, the logic of the one not necessarily mapping directly onto the other. Tribesmen, like those into whose other polities aspects of their orientation may have drifted, have created a logic of meaning and a set of mechanisms that preserve the ability to adapt even as, at any given moment, they shift their shape and angle around impediments.

In approaching the study of the tribal ethos it may, therefore, also be helpful to think in terms of what is sometimes called "emergence," the idea that co-operation among things of unlike kind that do not "normally" go together may produce novel forms, and that, where this capacity is particularly prevalent, concentration on any given moment's resultant forms may be misplaced. Alternatively, one might draw an analogy between the way tribal structures are manifested and the expression of particles in physics, where, as Nobel Prize Laureate Frank Wilczek says, "particles are avatars of fields," each known particle being an excitation within its own domain, in much the same way that a photon is an excitation of the electromagnetic field.[70] Or, by focusing our attention on the self-organization of these complex systems, we may want to think of tribal interactions as somewhat akin to a game of chess. For just as the players of chess see no need to add more pieces or expand the board simply because they have been playing within a structure that has remained unchanged for centuries, so, too, tribesmen can see endless variety in the moves they make and the notable achievements of memorable players. Indeed, tribesmen's conceptions of time belie any claim that they live in some eternal present. In the words of one Bushman: "As long as we keep changing we feed life and are replenished. We dance and shake to help transform everything.... To heal, we must enter the changing."[71] Change – the impulse to seek variation, never knowing what form adaptation may demand – is, then, ever-present among tribesmen, though to an outsider it may not seem so. Thinking about tribes not as momentary structures but as generating varied encounters shifts our vision of tribesmen no less than it might affect our ways of interacting with them.

The merit of this more cultural approach is threefold: (1) It is consonant with the importance of cultural categorization as central to both human development and the flexibility of tribal forms – and thus is not at war with theories of biological evolution or the recognition that societies do manifest themselves as quite variant in terms of complexity and specialization; (2) it emphasizes emergence over manifestation, and thus concentrates the analysis at a point where history and variation can be taken into account rather than having to imagine sudden and inexplicable leaps of form, something that has characterized many accounts drawn in evolutionary or structural-functional terms; and (3) such a dynamic approach allows for a theory of what it is that must survive – i.e., the contextual and equilibrating nature of morality, the negotiability of social ties, the perception of persons not in settled roles so much as in cross-cutting sets of relationships, etc. – if the structural form into which these features have for a time been poured is itself to remain viable. Such an approach would allow us to rethink how the *qualities* of the tribal, rather than the *forms*, suffuse multiple domains, whether legal, kin-based, religious, or economic. This is not to deny the importance of resultant structures: In Clifford Geertz's phrasing, we do not want to make the mistake of isolating "the meaning form aspects…from the practical contexts that give them life."[72] Shifting the paradigm to focus on the tribal as a repertoire turns the analytic concept of tribes inside out – from being structures of relationship to carriers of a family of relational possibilities – and with it to offer a solution to what must be maintained at the cultural level if the forms of organization we have encountered are to survive in any recognizable mode. To see just how adaptive tribal ways may be – and how the perception and treatment of tribes form the contexts within which these adaptations must take place – we need, therefore, in the next chapter, to consider how they have reacted to pressures from colonizing forces, military encounters, and corporate intrusion.

Notes

1 Dylan Thomas, "On No Work of Words," *Collected Poems*.
2 The quote by a Bushman informant is in Richard Lee, *The Dobe Ju/'Hoansi*, 2nd edn., New York: Harcourt Brace, 1993, p. 104.
3 Peter Brown, "No Barbarians Necessary," *New York Review of Books*, September 24, 2020, pp. 61–62, at 62.
4 Marcel Mauss, "Essai sur le don," *Année Sociologique*, New Series, vol. 1 (1924), pp. 30–186. Mauss also notes that in German the etymology of the word for gift also connotes 'poison'.
5 See, e.g., Scheele, "The Values of 'Anarchy': Moral Autonomy among the Tubu-Speakers of Northern Chad," *Journal of the Royal Anthropological Institute*, N.S., vol. 21 (2014), pp. 32–48, at 43.
6 Patricia Crone, "Tribes and States in the Middle East," in her *From Arabian Tribes to Islamic Empire*, Aldershot, UK: Ashgate Variorum, 2008, p. 361.
7 Marshall Sahlins, *Stone Age Economics*, New York: Aldine, 1972, p. 223.
8 Reciprocal exchange can be an instrument of power as well as miscommunication. Early European explorers and colonists, for example, took quite different approaches to the use and meaning of gift exchanges in their contact with indigenous populations. In general, the British preferred to treat such engagements as straightforward business transactions, something given for something received, and balked when more than what was bargained for was expected. The French, particularly in Canada, saw such exchanges as relational, one element in an ongoing series of relationships that might include not only the exchange of goods but intermarriage and political alignment. The Spanish, by contrast, regarded their 'gifts' as forming dependency on the part of the recipient, an act of *lèse-majesté* for which unquestioning loyalty was the demanded response. Each of these assumptions often led to grave misunderstandings that not infrequently ended in distorted relationships, an imbalance of power, and outright violence.

9 Quotes are from Sahlins, *Tribesmen*, at p. 83.
10 Paul Radin, *The World of Primitive Man*, New York: E. P. Dutton & Co., 1971, p. 106 ff.
11 "An individual might have a positive trading relationship with a man who was the mortal enemy of another friend without having one of these relationships necessarily disrupt the other. All relationships were strictly on the personal, individual level. In fact, men from one community could be at war with men from another community while others of the two communities peacefully traded. At the same time, some residents of either community might be feuding with others in their own community." Arthur E. Hippler and Stephen Conn, *Northern Eskimo Law Ways and Their Relationship to Contemporary Problems of 'Bush Justice'*, Fairbanks: Institute of Social, Economic and Government Research, Occasional Papers No. 10 (July 1973), p. 23. Similarly, among the Iroquois: "Yet another linkage involved 'particular friends' (as visitors usually put it). This 'very ancient' feature of Iroquoian culture tied pairs of men (not women) together on a lifelong basis. As a result, wrote [Jesuit priest Joseph-Francois] Lafitau [1681–1746], 'the two become companions in hunting, warfare, and good or bad fortune'; moreover, 'they are entitled to food and shelter in each other's lodging'." John Demos, *The Unredeemed Captive*, New York: Vintage Books, 1994, p. 163.
12 See, Robert F. Spencer, *The North Alaskan Eskimo*, Washington: U.S. Government Printing Office, Bureau of American Ethnology Bulletin No. 171, 1959. On the strict rules that relate to Inuit wife-sharing see, Lawrence Hennigh, "Functions and Limitations of Alaskan Eskimo Wife Trading," *Arctic*, vol. 23, no. 1 (March 1970), pp. 1–63. https://doi.org/10.14430/arctic3151
13 Bernard Bailyn, *The Barbarous Years*, New York: Alfred A. Knopf, 2012, pp. 5–6.
14 Quoting Sahlins, *Tribesmen*, p. 11. On segmentary theory and the writings of Ernest Gellner, see the chapter entitled "What Is a Tribe and Why Does It Matter?" in Lawrence Rosen, *The Culture of Islam*, Chicago: University of Chicago Press, 2002, pp. 39–55.
15 See, e.g., the examples given in Laura Betzig, "Redistribution: Equity or Exploitation?" in Laura Betzig, et al., eds., *Human Reproductive Behaviour: A Darwinian Perspective*, Cambridge: Cambridge University Press, 1988, pp. 49–63.
16 Pekka Hämäläinen, "The Rise and Fall of Plains Indian Horse Cultures," *The Journal of American History*, vol. 90, no. 3 (December 2003), pp. 833–62.
17 Some of these points are elaborated in Richard A, Posner, *The Economics of Justice*, Cambridge: Harvard University Press, 1981, ch. 6.
18 On the irrigation metaphor see, Stephania Pandolfo, *Impasse of the Angels: Scenes from a Moroccan Space of Memory*, Chicago: University of Chicago Press, 1998, pp. 87–88.
19 See, for more detail, Lawrence Rosen, *Bargaining For Reality: The Construction of Social Relations in a Muslim Community*, Chicago: University of Chicago Press, 1984, pp. 70–73; and Lawrence Rosen, *The Culture of Islam*, Chicago: University of Chicago Press, 2002, pp. 39–55.
20 Louis Dupree, "Tribal Warfare in Afghanistan and Pakistan: A Reflection of the Segmentary Lineage System," in Akbar Ahmed and David Hart, eds., *Islam in Tribal Societies*, London: Routledge and Kegan Paul, 1984, pp. 266–86, at 269.
21 Sahlins, *Tribesmen*, pp. 8 ("peacemaking is the wisdom of tribal institutions.... Primitive society is at war with [Hobbesian] Warre."), and 12–13.
22 See, e.g., Robert L. Trivers, "The Evolution of Reciprocal Altruism," *The Quarterly Review of Biology*, vol. 46, no. 1 (March 1971), pp. 35–57.

23 Sarah Cascone, "Archaeologists Just Discovered the World's Oldest Jewelry: This Set of 150,000-Year-Old Snail Beads in Morocco," *Peabody Essex Museum*, November 19, 2021, https://news.artnet.com/art-world/worlds-olest-jewelry-morocco-2037635 (accessed September 8, 2025). See also, Jennifer M. Miller and Yiming V. Wang, "Ostrich Eggshell Beads Reveal 50,000-Year-Old Social Network in Africa," *Nature*, vol. 601 (2022), pp. 234–39.
24 Derek Williams, *Romans and Barbarians*, New York: St. Martin's Press, 1999, p. 30.
25 For an example of the state imputing motives to its people, see Kay B. Warren, "Each Mind Is a World: Dilemmas of Feeling and Intention in a Kaqchikel Maya Community," in Lawrence Rosen, ed., *Other Intentions: Cultural Contexts and the Attribution of Inner States*, Santa Fe: School of American Research Press, 1995, pp. 46–67.
26 Paul Dresch, "Imams and Tribes: The Writing and Acting of History in Upper Yemen," in Philip S. Khoury and Joseph Kostiner, eds., *Tribes and State Formation in the Middle East*, Berkeley: University of California Press, 1990, pp. 252–87, at 255.
27 Thomas J. Friedman, "The American Civil War, Part II," *New York Times*, October 2, 2018; Edward Banfield, *The Moral Basis of a Backward Society*, New York: Free Press, 1958. The argument that tribes have no concept of universal morals (propounded with a certain air of noblesse oblige) is contained in the following passage by political philosopher George Kateb:

> I grant that in many cultures, especially tribal ones, and others, in the past, the idea of universal morality and the idea of the unqualified search for truth and right understanding did not exist. These concepts were unavailable to people in such societies. I agree that they cannot be blamed for what they could not know or understand, but that should not prevent us from holding that such societies, though not guilty, were still deficient, and that we should not place them on the same level as cultures that possess universal standards, even though cultures acquainted with universal standards have done inconceivably more evil than cultures without them. Universalist societies have also done a greater amount of good, which of course does not excuse or balance the evil but only palliates it.

George Kateb, "Can Cultures Be Judged? Two Defenses of Cultural Pluralism in Isaiah Berlin's Work," *Social Research*, vol. 66, no. 4 (Winter 1999), pp. 1009–38, at 1031.
28 Edith Hall, "Why Read Aristotle Today?" *Aeon* (May 2018). https://aeon.co/essays/what-can-aristotle-teach-us-about-the-routes-to-happiness (accessed September 8, 2025).
29 Isaiah Berlin, *Liberty*, Oxford: Oxford University Press, 2002, p. 213.
30 Jonathan Dancy, "Moral Particularism," *Stanford Encyclopedia of Philosophy*, https://plato.stanford.edu
31 "Good and evil, creation and destruction – the dual image of the deity, as expressed in the trickster – are fused in the network of actions that define primitive society. Therefore, moral fanaticism, based as it is on abstract notions of pure good, pure evil, and the exclusive moral possibility or fate of any particular individual – what may be called moral exceptionalism – is absent among primitive people. In primitive perspective, human beings are assumed to be capable of any excess. But every step of the way, the person is held to account for those actions that seriously threaten the balance of society and nature." Stanley Diamond, "Introductory Essay: Job and the

Trickster," in Paul Radin, *The Trickster*, New York: Schocken Books, 1972, p. xxi.
32 Jean Briggs, *Never in Anger: Portraits of an Eskimo Family*, Cambridge: Harvard University Press, 1971, pp. 283–90.
33 Judith Scheele, "The Values of 'Anarchy'," p. 38.
34 Scheele, *The Values of 'Anarchy'*, p. 44.
35 Scheele, *The Values of 'Anarchy'*, p. 46.
36 Dresch, speaking of Yemen, writes: "The ideal in many cases would seem to be of moral autonomy in the face of ... practical dependence on others ... Social philosophers claim no one ever prospered in isolation. The ambition to do so recurs widely." Paul Dresch, "Mutual Deception: Totality, Exchange and Islam in the Middle East," in Nick J. Allen and Wendy James, eds., *Marcel Mauss: A Centenary Tribute*, Oxford: Berghahn, 1998, pp. 111–33, at 112, 127.
37 See, Elizabeth Anderson, "What Is the Point of Equality?" *Ethics*, vol. 109, no. 2 (January 1999), pp. 287–337. See generally, Nathan Heller, "The Philosopher Redefining Equality," *The New Yorker*, January 7, 2009.
38 Roy Hattersley, *The Guardian*, September 30, 1988; Paul Radin, *Primitive Man as Philosopher*, pp. 38–39, 72. On moral philosophy and muddling through see, Julian Baggini, "Time to Abandon Grand Ethical Theories," *Times Literary Supplement*, May 25, 2018.
39 Sahlins, *The New Science*, p. 39.
40 Compare the interpretation offered here with that suggested by Posner, *The Economics of Justice*, chapter 6, e.g., that in primitive communities character is a proxy for credibility and that the costs of obtaining information are higher in such societies.
41 See generally, Colin Morris, *The Discovery of the Individual: 1050-1200*, New York: Harper & Row, 1972; and Lawrence Rosen, "Intentionality and the Concept of the Person," in J. Roland Pennock and John W. Chapman, eds., *Criminal Justice (NOMOS XXVII)*, New York: New York University Press, 1985, pp. 52–77.
42 In this respect I disagree with elements of Michael Walzer's generalization ("The New Tribalism," *Dissent*, Spring 1992, pp. 164—71, at 171): "The self is more naturally divided; at least it is capable of division and even thrives on it."
43 Paul Radin, *Primitive Man as Philosopher*, pp. 78–79.
44 James F. Downs, *Animal Husbandry in Navajo Society and Culture*, Berkeley: University of California Press, 1964, p. 69.
45 David Brooks. "The Great Affluence Fallacy," *New York Times*, August 9, 2016, Section A, p. 23, citing Sebastian Junger, *Tribe: On Homecoming and Belonging*, New York: Twelve, 2016.
46 Norman Mailer, "The White Negro," *Dissent*, Fall 1957.
47 Witherspoon, *Language and Art in the Navajo Universe*, p. 49.
48 Witherspoon, *Language and Art in the Navajo Universe*, p. 83.
49 Paul Dresch, "Imams and Tribes," pp. 258, 272. See also, Michael Meeker, *Literature and Violence in Norther Arabia*, Cambridge: Cambridge University Press, 1979.
50 Sahlins, *Tribesmen*, p. 104, quoting Robert H. Lowie, *Primitive Religion*, New York: Liveright, 1948, p. 21. Sahlins (*The New Science*, p. 110) also notes: "The rule in immanentist cultures [i.e., those that envision gods and spirits at work in the mundane world] is that the high gods are at once the most remote and the most powerful of beings." See also, Mathias Guenther, *Tricksters and Trancers: Bushman Religion and Society*, Bloomington: Indiana University Press, 1999, p. 63 ("Generally, [Bushman] ideas about the creator

god tend to be clouded in vagueness, probably because this divinity, unlike his trickster-adversary, is fairly remote from the affairs of people.")
51 Treating a high god as a distant initiator may also account for tribesmen accepting another's god with some ease. Thus, a number of Berber tribes of North Africa converted to Judaism prior to the Muslim invasions, though just what place the Yahweh of Israel occupied in the rituals of the tribes may be obscured by their placing him at such a generalized level as to have limited impact on the preexisting substrate of beliefs. See generally, H. Z. Hirschberg, "The Problem of the Judaized Berbers," *Journal of African History*, vol. 4 (1963), pp. 313–39; and Abdelmajid Hannoum, *Colonial Histories, Postcolonial Memories: The Legend of the Kahina, A North African Heroine*, London: Heinemann, 2001.
52 See, Turchin, P, et al., "Explaining the Rise of Moralizing Religions: A Test of Competing Hypotheses Using the Seshat Databank," *Religion, Brain & Behavior*, vol. 13, no. 2 (2022), pp. 167–94.
53 Many Native Americans, for example, are creationists, their fear being that if they have not been in the same place forever their title to the land they now occupy may be challenged. As we will see in Chapter Five, this may, however, be more a reaction to encounters with colonial states than an instance of territorial immobility than long predates such encounters.
54 Noel M. Wallace, "Change in Spiritual and Ritual Life in Pitjantjatjara (Bidjandjadjara) Society, 1966 to 1973," in Ronald M. Berndt, ed., *Aborigines and Change*, Atlantic Highlands, NJ: Humanities Press, 1977, pp. 74–89, at 87–88.
55 Radin, *The World of Primitive Man*, p. 102.
56 Jack Goody, "A Kernel of Doubt," *Journal of the Royal Anthropological Institute*, New Series, vol. 2, no. 4 (1996), pp. 667–81, at 678–79.
57 Mary Douglas, *Purity and Danger*, London: Routledge & Kegan Paul, 1966, p. 162.
58 Jonathan Miller, "Dialogue with Clifford Geertz: Notions of Primitive Thought," *States of Mind*, New York: Pantheon, 1983, p. 204.
59 Simon Harrison, *Stealing People's Names: History and Politics in a Sepik River Cosmology*, Cambridge: Cambridge University Press, 1996, p. 58.
60 Sahlins, *The New Science*, p. 97.
61 Franz Boas, *The Central Eskimo*, Lincoln: The University of Nebraska Press, 1964 [1888], pp. 195–96; Waldemar Bogoras, "The Chukchee," *Memoirs of the American Museum of Natural History*, vol. 11, New York: G. E. Strechert, 1904–9, p. 295; Knud Rasmussen, *Intellectual Culture of the Iglulik Eskimos*, Report of the Fifth Thule Expedition, 1921–24, vol. 7, no. 1, Copenhagen: Gyldendalske Boghandel, Nordisk Forlag, 1929, pp. 54–56.
62 Guenther, *Tricksters and Trancers*, p. 4.
63 Guenther, *Tricksters and Trancers*, pp. 5, 13. He also refers to Bushman gatherings in the past as at times forming "mini-states." (pp. 14, 18). Mostly, though, he characterizes the Bushmen as a "small-scale tribal society." (p. 40).
64 *Tricksters and Trancers*, pp. 29–31. The phrase "foraging for relatives" is from Alan Barnard, "Primitive Communism and Mutual Aid: Kropotkin Visits the Bushmen," in C. M. Hann, ed., *Socialism*, London: Routledge, 1993, pp. 27–42, at 33. See also, George B. Silberbauer, *Hunter and Habitat in the Central Kalahari Desert*, Cambridge: Cambridge University Press, 1981.
65 Guenther, *Tricksters and Trancers*, p. 4.
66 Guenther, *Tricksters and Trancers*, p. 246.
67 Guenther, *Tricksters and Trancers*, p. 57.

68 Guenther, *Tricksters and Trancers*, pp. 228–37. Guenther gives as a counter-example this statement from Thomas O. Beidelman's study of tricksters among the Kaguru of East Africa: "We should remain suspicious of approaches that allocate ambiguity, contradiction and conflict to the periphery of society. Contrary to being indications of change, dysfunction, or 'cognitive dissonance', these phenomena under scrutiny represent the essence of social life." "The Moral Imagination of the Kaguru," in W. J. Hynes and W. C. Doty, eds., *Mythical Trickster Figures*, Tuscaloosa: University of Alabama Press, 1993, pp. 174–92, at 191. See generally, Donald N. Levine, *The Flight from Ambiguity*, Chicago: University of Chicago Press, 1985.
69 Guenther, *Tricksters and Trancers*, p. 227.
70 Frank Wilczek, *Fundamentals: Ten Keys to Reality*, New York: Penguin, 2020.
71 Bradford Keeney and Hillary Keeney, "N!o'an-Kal'ae: The Changing," *Parabola*, vol. 50, no. 1 (Spring 2025), pp. 38–45, at 43.
72 Clifford Geertz, *Local Knowledge*, New York: Basic Books, 1983, p. 48.

Interlude
Is Judaism a Tribal Religion?

> "We were a tribe – on one hand, invented, and on the other, no less real."
> Ta-Nehisi Coates, *Between the World and Me*

Coates' striking assertion that tribes are at once real and the product of the human imagination – like Clifford Geertz's general assertion that "the real is as imagined as the imaginary" – underscores that a tribal ethos, and not just a given instance of tribal organization, may be at the heart of many social forms that have developed out of this seminal paradigm. This is no less true when we look at the relation of the tribal ethos to certain world religions. Consider, for example, Judaism.

We have all heard the comments: If someone is Jewish he or she is "a member of the tribe"; if once there were "twelve tribes of Israel" somehow ten of them got lost along the way; if someone marries a non-Jew there is concern whether "the tribe" will survive. But equating Jews with tribes only underscores that it is the tribal part of the equation that has been misapplied. If, instead, we start with a better understanding of what tribes are actually like perhaps we can not only get past the misguided references to humans as having a "tribal instinct" and our current politics as simply "tribal." The result may be a more realistic sense of whether, in certain essentials, Judaism, for example, really is a tribal religion – and why, if it is, that would not be such a bad thing.

Tribes, it has been noted, are commonly seen as truculent and exclusionary, a throwback to an earlier evolutionary form to which even the most "advanced" may retreat under stress. Whether cast in terms of that human temperament implanted in our species' youth or as an adaptation to the constraints of our mutual dependence, tribes have been curated as artifacts of a simpler time and/or condemned as inconstant allies in the pursuit of progress. In each instance the key features of tribal life are more often distorted than grasped. This is especially true as it relates to tribal religions.

The easy way to approach this subject is also the least helpful. When thinking of the "tribal" elements of Judaism, for example, reference is frequently had to circumcision as a form of sublimated sacrifice, food taboos as spiritual purification, or in-group marriage as a way to keep both identity and property within bounds. Such explanations, while intermittently insightful, are easy because they operate through analogies with groups thought to be at a more basic evolutionary stage or because they constitute a residue the rest of us have outgrown.

By contrast, the more difficult approach starts with an understanding of some of the distinctive features that commonly escape notice about tribes and then asks how they may suffuse a religion even while its socio-political surround has changed vastly over the course of time. Such features, then, can be seen not merely as survivals of by-gone eras or a drag on social advancement but as part of a collective ethos that continues to have meaningful effect.

Previously, it was indicated that there are three main ways that tribes may be analyzed – as a stage in human social evolution, as a distinct class of structural forms, or as cultural entities with characteristic modes of dispersing power and altering their shape to fit changing circumstance. Although a few writers remain attached to the notion that humankind progressed along a uniform path from band to tribe to chiefdom to state, ethnography and archaeology have demonstrated there was no such unwavering course and that the criteria for 'advancement' – organizational complexity, energy capture, population dynamics – simply do not correlate with a fixed array of social and political forms: Indians of Ohio gave up large towns in favor of tribal life, thousands of years passed before some tribesmen who engaged in part-time agriculture settled down to it regularly, and diverse tribes often formed into confederations without affecting the decentralization of power.

So, too, the idea that our brains developed at an early stage of hominin evolution and continue to exhibit some type of "tribal instinct" is, at the very least, impossible to correlate with any specific form of social or cultural organization. Moreover, as field studies have added a broader array of examples, anthropologists have learned that tribes cannot be understood simply as a rigidified set of structural forms based largely on kinship and residence. To the contrary, not only are tribes widely variant in their organizational forms but, far from being settled to the point of being inert, tribes have histories no less than other human arrangements.

That leaves a more cultural approach to tribes as the best candidate for comprehending their distinctive qualities. Here, the two principles and one analogy to which we have earlier alluded remain useful.

The first principle is that tribes do not trust too much power in too few hands for too long a period of time. This, as we have seen, is manifested in many ways: rituals of reversal, regulated joking, rotation of authority, multicentric decision-making, recourse to ambiguity, and limitations even on the Divine. The second principle is that reciprocity is crucial to the maintenance of both order and flexibility. Here, too, ritually inflected gift-giving, ceremonial demonstrations of emotional support, and recognition that human differences actually facilitate mutual aid all place restraints on individual gain and undercut the formation of a hierarchy of moral worth justifying inequality. The result is a highly flexible and adaptable set of orientations such that, to reprise our analogy, tribes look more like amoeba than crystals, their essential features being not those of settled structure but of shape-shifting capability. Seen from such a dynamic perspective, we can avoid the pitfalls of romanticizing tribes while challenging the image of them as simply pugnacious, territorial, and obsolete.

How, then, does Judaism fit here? While the mapping is certainly not exact the resonances are striking. Bearing in mind that one does not have to be a Protestant to possess the Protestant Work Ethic, so, too, what might be called 'the tribal ethos' that informs Judaism owes much to the features associated with its tribal backdrop without being bound to its more common organizational forms.

Consider, in this particular context, the importance of levelling. Limitations on power occur frequently in Jewish texts and practices. Whether it is kings whose personal imperfections limit their legitimacy or Moses, whose failure to follow divine instruction precluded his entry to the Holy Land, Jewish leaders are often brought low not by a tragic flaw but by the expectation that their powers must be curbed to be legitimate. Prophets, sages, saintly figures, and righteous *lamadvavniks* all serve, in different Judaic traditions, as checks on the power of rulers and one another. Jewish humor, too, often works as a levelling device, lessening the formation of hierarchy by cutting the momentarily powerful down to size, while the diversity of rabbinic opinions and ease of forming alternative congregations further erodes the centralization of power. No one is beyond criticism in tribes, and no one fails to appreciate that, for a limited time, whoever controls the definition of the situation may direct the discussion and influence its outcome.

Decentralized religions and societies also have survival value. As we have noted, if you have a triangle and remove even a tiny bit from one of its points the geometric form will lose its distinctive character. But a wallpaper design can be almost totally destroyed yet the pattern can be regenerated. Because tribes do not depend on structure but on capabilities their essential elasticity can sustain otherwise devastating attacks. Moreover, tribes characteristically raise their god to a level of distanced action that leaves humans with the responsibility for many ethical issues. So, too, building a network within and beyond one's kinfolk is a very personal task. Thus, far from submerging the individual in some group mind tribes are intensely individualistic. Even more critically, as we have seen, a central feature of tribes is that no one can claim inherent moral superiority over others. In addition to undercutting hierarchy, the implications of this morality are felt in every domain, not least for Judaism in interpretations of religious law (*halakha*): Alternative interpretations not only underscore the challenge to certainty claimed by a single authority but reinforce the moral equivalence of each believer.

If the tribal ethos is one aspect of the equation then the other is surely the spirit of reciprocity. That spirit, as we have noted, embraces two elements. The first is an expectation of fungible return. What is given or bargained for creates a bond of indebtedness, social, and moral if not immediately economic. Chapter Twelve of the book of Leviticus exemplifies the stress on reciprocity, but that is certainly not the only source. As the late chief rabbi of the UK, Jonathan Sachs, in his essay entitled "The Chaos Theory of Virtue," noted:

> There is a most unusual blessing we make after eating or drinking something that requires the blessing of *shehakol*: ברוך נפשות תובר מחסרונם. We thank God for "creating many souls and their deficiencies." Normally we thank God for what we have. How can we thank God for what we lack? How can there be a blessing over a negation, a deficiency, something we do not have? The answer is that if we lacked nothing, we would never need anyone else. We would live in splendid isolation. And in Judaism, "It is not good for man to be alone." That is not how God wanted us to be. The very fact that He "created many kinds of souls" – that each of us is different – means that what I lack, you may have. What you lack, I may have. Each of us has something to give that someone else needs. One smile can rescue a person from depression. A single gesture of kindness, hospitality, can redeem a person from solitude. Not lightly did the Sages say: "Greater is hospitality than receiving the Divine Presence."[1]

The second element associated with tribal reciprocity is the proposition that equivalence is more appropriate than equality. In the tribal frame, treating everyone identically, regardless of category or personality, is inconsistent with the distribution of roles and undermines individuality. Indeed, individuals, far from being shackled by some uniform set of customs, are played up in tribal groups, each person's distinctive contributions being essential to the division of labor and creative adaptability that benefits all. So, too, in Judaism, justice is not, in fact, meted out to everyone without regard to who they are, who their actions affect, and determining the most appropriate remedy if they stray from what is expected of them. Justice as equivalence, like the differentiation of religious tasks, is personalized and equilibrated, with the result that the individual remains at the center of the moral code.

In any culture it is the integration of features across domains that holds its worldview together. Thus even concepts of time reflect and embody the tribal ethos. And nowhere is this more evident than in a culture's language. In Biblical Hebrew there are, essentially, no tenses: Actions are either completed or not, either without continuing effect in the world or of ongoing import. So, a matter that happened recently might be considered 'past' if it is of no persisting consequence while an act of the distant past may be considered 'recent' because it continues to have a noteworthy impact. In many tribal societies this temporal orientation couples with an emphasis on the pragmatic, the palpable, the rational. And not only does Hebrew embed this worldly orientation in its very grammar but, in its mode of narrating history, time reveals the nature of relationships and only loses its open texture when its implications for social relations are thought to be of no continuing effect.

The diffusion of power characteristic of the tribal ethos also incorporates a high degree of tolerance for ambiguity. In Judaism, Jacob can wrestle through the night with an angel, Job with God's trials, and each man with his conscience, the center being in each instance decentered, the opportunity to coalesce power across multiple domains curtailed, and the flexibility and personal creativity needed to adapt thus constantly reprised. This ambivalence even reaches to issues of gender identity. It is very common in tribal societies for a place to be found for those of mixed or alternative gender – often implying that the individual possesses medical, magical, or spiritual powers. Those of uncertain or mixed gender can shepherd society through the dangers of a liminal period to its indispensable replication or serve as a reminder that the ambiguity of the interstitial is not without creative power. So, too, there are passages in the Hebrew Bible that are readily interpreted as recognizing multiple genders. Max K. Strassfeld, in his *Trans Talmud: Androgynes and Eunuchs in Rabbinic Literature*, argues that nonbinary gender is central to understanding Jewish law.² As Rabbi Elliot Kukla, noting that intersexed individuals are referred to over 300 times in the Babylonia Talmud alone, summarizes the argument:

> There are four genders beyond male or female that appear in ancient Jewish holy texts hundreds of times. They are considered during discussions about childbirth, marriage, inheritance, holidays, ritual leadership and much more. When a child was born in the ancient Jewish world it could be designated as a boy, a girl, a "tumtum" (who is neither clearly male nor female), or an "androgynos" (who has both male and female characteristics) based on physical features. There are two more gender designations that form later in life. The "aylonit" is considered female at birth, but develops in an atypical direction. The "saris" is designated male at birth, but later becomes a eunuch.
>
> In the Mishna [e.g., Bikkurim 4], the oldest and most authoritative source of Jewish legal theory, composed in the second century, we learn that anyone who kills or harms an androgynos (either accidentally or on purpose) is subject to the exact same ramifications as someone who hurts a man or woman. That chapter ends with a conversation about whether the androgynos is more like men or women. One of the sages, Rabbi Yossi, suggests that "he is a created being of her own." This phrase plays with the gender in Hebrew grammar to poetically express the complexity of the androgynos's gender.³

Whether Judaism was born at a time of tribal life or was already bringing its tribal ethos to bear on paramount chiefdoms that morphed into anointed kingships, it is clear that later forms of Jewish life owed much to the continuing role of its earlier embodiments. Thus, Marshall Sahlins, in his *New Science of the Enchanted Universe*, notes: "Everything indicates… not that the 'tribals' got their gods from ancient 'high civilizations,' but that the civilizations inherited theirs from the tribes."⁴ When Judaism had a temple and a priesthood it did give way to hierarchy. But there still existed a countervailing force. Indeed, tribes commonly lift their primal god so high as to be beyond human grasp, the effects being left to intermediate and earthly figures imbued with divine directive or left to their own control. Placed at an elevated but not unapproachable level renders any human claim to full power of problematic legitimacy. Elements of the distrust of concentrated power may therefore remain, and in the Jewish case – particularly after the Temple was destroyed and there was no longer entrenched ranking – those elements have never been fully expunged. Indeed, the destruction of the Temple and its priesthood may have been the salvation of Judaism, the 'tribal' elements contributing to collective survival, while the individual – guided not through a hierarchy but a devolved rabbinate – was left free to question authority and concentrate on personal reason.

Some elements of a tribal ethos are not, of course, without their internal strains. Delight in ambiguity may engender creative debate over the proper category into which new practices should fit, but ambivalence may trigger the calcification of existing categories or the paralysis of choice in the face of threatening change. So, too, casting up an authoritative voice when clarity and purity seem at risk may suit the needs of the moment, but when does that moment end such that the forces that disperse power can be re-deployed? And if ritual reversals and joking patterns undercut the permanent consolidation of power, when do such practices reflect weakness in the face of charismatic authority? Balancing continuity and change, sustaining identity in the face of alteration, and undermining power without appearing weak nevertheless render the tribal ethos an ever-present alternative to these more rigid structures.

Tribalism is not, then, simply about territoriality and divisiveness – it never has been. Tribes try on one another's customs, retain their identity notwithstanding widespread adoption and intermarriage, share terrain as purpose suggests, and cherish the gambits of individual tactics. Jews are not a tribe in the misinformed sense of an inflexible structure or evolutionary stage, nor have tribes ever lacked histories or been the embodiment of some pure form. Indeed, there are no pure forms in social life – no democracies without the powerful, no saints without shame, no markets without advantage. We are all hybrids, mongrels, mutants – but no less resilient for partaking of such variation. Though loosed from the context of its birth, Judaism *is* a tribal religion – shaped to its circumstance, devolved from central control, focused on the relational, defined by its capabilities rather than its momentary shape. In a world that is ever more involuted and obdurate Judaism carries the elements of its tribal ethos into its changing circumstance, and with its flexibility intact resists the stasis that is anathema to its tribal core. Far from being lost, the tribal ethos continues to thread its way through the Jewish ethos and its overall engagement with the world.

Notes

1 Rabbi Jonathan Sachs, "The Chaos Theory of Virtue," *The Rabbi Sachs Legacy*, November 30, 2005, www.rabbisacks.org/archive/bella-wexner-memorial-lecture-on-the-chaos-theory-of-virtue/ (accessed June 16, 2015). See also, Rabbi Asher Meir, "Noach: Borei Nefashot," *Orthodox Union*, October 11, 2007. www.ou.org/life/torah/mm_borei_nefashot/ (accessed June 16, 2025).

2 Max K. Strassfeld, *Trans Talmud: Androgynes and Eunuchs in Rabbinic Literature*, Berkeley: University of California Press, 2022.
3 Rabbi Elliot Kukla, "Ancient Judaism Recognized a Range of Genders. It's Time We Did, Too," *New York Times*, March 18, 2023.
4 Marshall Sahlins, *The New Science of the Enchanted Universe*, Princeton: Princeton University Press, 2022, p. 173.

5
TRIBAL ENCOUNTERS
Colonialism, Corporations, and the Military

Tribes do not live in isolation. Notwithstanding Western fantasies, they are neither "lost" in time and space nor persistently isolated from other human contacts. As traders and explorers, nomads and seekers, tribesmen have long since spanned the globe, exchanging food and ornaments, ideas, and DNA all along the way. Their encounters, however, have often been trying, and often not of their own making. Whether it is with armies seeking their submission, colonists their land, corporations their resources, or missionaries their souls, tribal encounters with the world at large have yielded reciprocal effects transforming both parties. It is to these encounters that we must attend if, in the process of rethinking the concept of tribe, we are to grasp the place they have occupied in the course of history and our own times.

Colonial Encounters

"...one nation solemnly promised to a second the country of a third."
Arthur Koestler

Colonial empires by definition seek control of resources, primarily land. When others stand in the way they may (as in Australia) declare the land 'empty' (*terra nullius*, literally "nobody's land," because the populace was not settled) or (applying John Locke's concept to North America) "waste land" (vacuum domicilium, because the natives had not "subdued" it) and enshrine the concept in what they are pleased to agree among themselves to call international law.

They may ground their claims on a doctrine of discovery or they may simply conquer the territories of indigenous groups, employing military force or (even intentionally) the spread of deadly disease to achieve their ends.[1] And where it is a matter of addressing the presence of tribes who stand in their way they may, in addition to the use of sufficient force to secure territory, seek full-scale eradication of the resident population, temporary alliance, absorption into the invading population, political and geographic marginalization, or some mode of cultural domination. In each case, however, tribes may not only mold themselves to survive the new circumstance but so interact with the outside forces as to alter the latter as well.

> The basic conquest myth postulates that America was virgin land, or wilderness, inhabited by nonpeople called savages [whose] mode of existence and cast of mind were such as to make them incapable of civilization and therefore of full humanity. [As a result of their spread of disease] the American was more like a widow than a virgin. Europeans did not find a wilderness here; rather, however involuntarily, they made one.
>
> Francis Jennings, *The Invasion of America*,
> New York: W. W. Norton, 1976, pp. 15 and 30.

Eradication, alas, has taken many forms and yielded many consequences. It may, of course, mean trying to kill every man, woman, and child of the tribe, as when white settlers hunted down the aborigines of Tasmania or placed bounties on the scalps of Native Americans.

> If ever we are constrained to lift the hatchet against any tribe, we will never lay it down till that tribe is exterminated, or driven beyond the Mississippi...in war, they will kill some of us; we shall destroy them all.
>
> Thomas Jefferson

> All Indian men of that [Apache] tribe are to be killed whenever and wherever you can find them.

> General James H. Carlton's order to Colonel Kit Carson, October 12, 1862, Joint Special Committee, United States Congress, *Condition of the Indian Tribes*, Washington, Government Printing Office, 1867, p. 100, quoted in Redniss, *Oak Flat*, p. 41.

> If the savage resists, civilization, with the Ten Commandments in one hand and the sword in the other, demands his immediate extermination.
> Commissioner of Indian Affairs, *Report to the President by the Indian Peace Policy Commission*, Washington: Government Printing Office, 1868, p. 33, quoted in Redniss, *Oak Flat*, p. 107.

"Ethnic cleansing" of native populations is not limited to the past: Brazilian President Jair Bolsonaro, who took office in 2019, likened the indigenous people of the Amazon to animals in a zoo and supported programs resulting in the deaths of numerous members of the country's 308 tribes.[2] As recently as the 1960s and 1970s some 4500 Inuit women were subjected to involuntary sterilization by the Danish government in an attempt to limit the number of indigenous people in Greenland.[3] Longstanding animosities, exacerbated by colonial and post-colonial politics, have also led to intertribal warfare, as among the Nilotic tribes of the Sudan and various tribes in central and east Africa. At times such genocidal acts claim justification by recourse to holy text or by demonizing tribals as sub-human or beyond hope of redemption, thus making their elimination appear as a form of divine purification or natural improvement.[4] Often, too, the conqueror's justification has taken the form of *noblesse oblige*, as in the case of the Massachusetts Bay Colony whose emblem depicted a naked Indian begging the Europeans, in the borrowed wording of Acts 16:9, to "come over and help us."

Assimilation may also be forced through redefinition by the superior power of who is a tribal member and what is a tribe. By setting blood quantum as the criterion for inclusion in reservations or receipt of government benefits the state can limit the number of recognized natives or disrupt the tribe's own means of identification; by switching the criteria from time to time they can initially aid the tribesmen and, once they have become dependent, change the rules to suit the colonists' desires. We have already seen how the law dealt with the definition of a tribe in the Mashpee case; examples could also be cited that affect access in the U.S. to educational grants and treatment through the Indian Health Service. Similarly, the U.S. government in more recent years has offered a

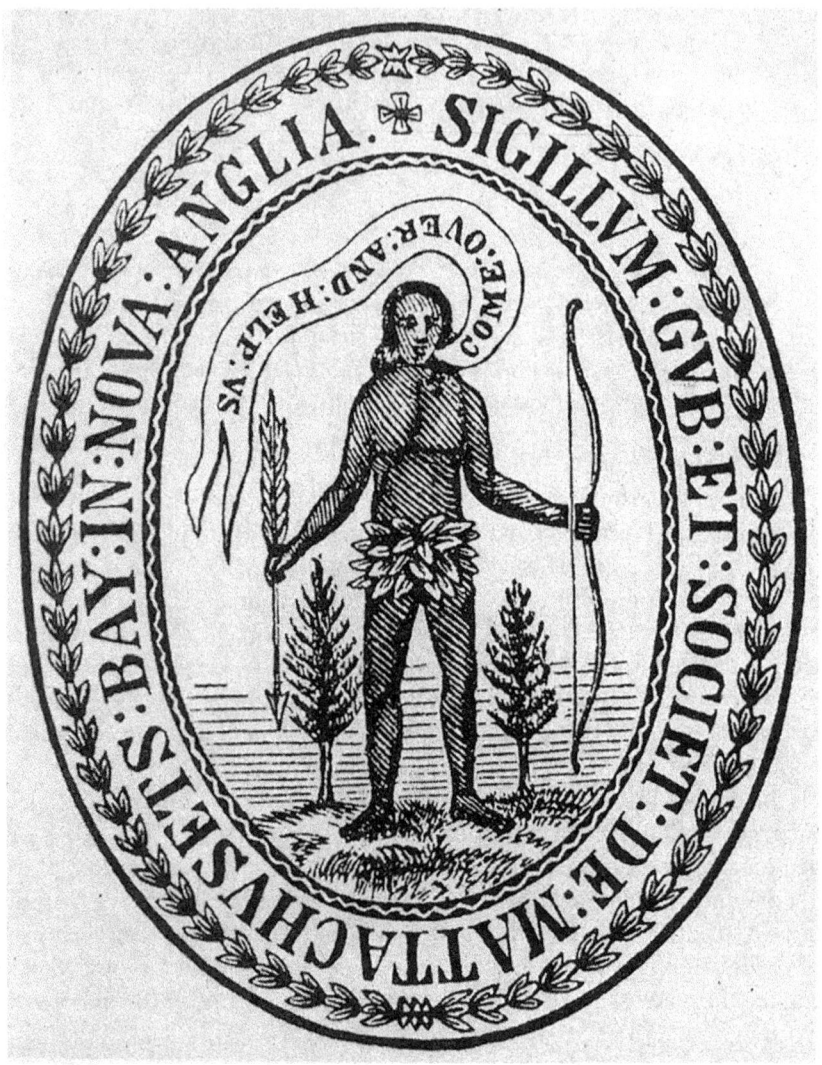

FIGURE 5.1 Seal of the Massachusetts Bay Colony, 1629 saying 'Come over and help us'.

path to federal recognition for tribes that were previously unrecognized. The criteria that were set up for inclusion, however, have emphasized proof of historic identity, the only acceptable records often being those of the conqueror or his subalterns.[5] As a result, a few tribes have indeed gained access to federal programs, but others have been denied their claims. Once again, this process may be a two-edged sword, insofar as a number of groups have used the recognition process to solidify their identity even if their application was ultimately unsuccessful.

Thus in a significant range of cases, even when threatened with utter destruction, tribes have often managed to adapt and survive. Earlier, it was suggested that tribes are shapeshifters, capable of rearranging themselves to accommodate changing circumstances. And even though it was suggested that structural forms are momentary solutions to governance and wellbeing, one enduring aspect of tribal structures does bear on their ability to adjust even to potential devastation. Here an analogy may be helpful. If you have a geometric figure like a triangle, for example, and you cut off even the tiniest bit from one of its points, whatever else may be true you no longer have a triangle. If, on the other hand, you have a wallpaper pattern design, one that is replicated endlessly, you can reduce it almost to the null point and still be able to revive the original motif. Tribal forms, being fluid and amoeboid, are more like the latter than the former: They are capable of regeneration in ways that rigidly structured entities are not. The views of some structural-functional anthropologists notwithstanding, we have seen that tribesmen are highly individualistic, make effective use of adoption and genealogical manipulation, form alliances through multiple devices, and can sequester their regenerative capabilities against considerable onslaught from the outside. Indeed, as we also saw in the Mashpee case, it is an error to look only at the structure of social and political relations to identify a tribe: If the capabilities for perpetuation are in place – the mechanisms for levelling and dispersing power, encountering each other as moral equals, etc. – the tribe may be able to survive even if its members now wear Western clothes and attend church services. In sum, despite the loss of many prior characteristics (linguistic, territorial, religious, economic), tribes can draw on their malleable, decentralized qualities – their ethos and their spirit – to face adversity, including colonial onslaught, with some chance of survival.

Colonizing powers operate through numerous agents – some working directly, some indirectly – and neither the policies nor the actions of those who implement them are identical across the board. Reactions have always varied. Individual tribes have disappeared or coalesced; military alliances have fragmented or been redirected; confederacies have expanded or melted away. Some of the "tribal empires" of history – whether those of the Moroccan Berbers who stormed into Spain or the Lakota and Comanche who dominated the Great Plains – built on their negotiable affiliations to garner forces sufficient for conquest. Others, like those of Genghis Khan or Attila the Hun, had morphed into paramount chiefdomships and, owing in part to the endemic capacity of subordinates legitimately to go their separate ways, fell apart soon after the death of the central figure. In whatever way, confronted by states and empires, tribes have had to address the presence of bureaucrats, missionaries, lawyers, anthropologists, and do-gooders as they have fashioned responses to the invading force.

It is not the military that always comes first. Traders and missionaries, scholars, and busybodies – those who are comfortable transgressing boundaries for gain or curiosity, glory, or salvation – often precede the states and empires that follow hard in their wake. They bring with them their conceptions of what tribal organization must be like or what is convenient to the colonists' interests. In their contacts with the Maori, for example, traders (like the missionaries and administrators) assumed that chiefs must exist – wasn't that true of all tribes, from Biblical times on? – and by favoring someone to deal with they convinced themselves they had found the real tribal leader. Traders bring goods that tribesmen may use to reinforce their own internal system of reciprocity, but the presence of such items as steel and guns have also transformed traditionally valued possessions held only by particular individuals or clans into new relationships – even hierarchic ones – that disturb existing patterns of reciprocity and levelling.[6] Worse, traders are often the first to bring disease, at rates that may be truly devastating, thus 'clearing' the way for those who come after. Between 1616 and 1619, to cite but one characteristic example, an estimated ninety percent of the tribesmen living just north of Narragansett Bay (in what is now part of the state of Rhode Island) died from diseases brought by Europeans. The ecological adaptation of a tribe may also change as overextended hunting and trapping to feed foreign demand alter the tribal economy, and the movement of people thus becomes a function of outside forces rather than localized adaptations.

But it is also true that by the time large numbers of outsiders arrive tribes may, instead of spiraling towards dissolution, have begun to reconfigure their lives without giving up the devices they have long employed to retain their identity. Examples are legion. Pushed by whites and enemy tribes (themselves pushed by colonists), groups from the upper Midwest gave up being agriculturalists, took up the horse, and moved out into America's Great Plains. Other groups in the Great Lakes made similar shifts with relative ease.[7] Numerous North African tribes, too, began a process of adaptation when confined or undercut by the European powers who divided the continent among themselves: Some Berber tribes in Morocco, for example, moved away from nomadism on the edge of the Sahara and were offered grazing and agricultural lands in return for protecting trade routes for the sultan. Thus, while many tribes may tread carefully as they adapt to new circumstances the idea that they remain timelessly attached to their pasts simply does not accord with all the known facts.

> [The Navajo's] pragmatism is especially revealed in their attitude toward change. They have little or no sentimental reservations about changing aspects of their way of life when better ways of doing things are known and accessible. Not being fearful of alien ways nor being highly sentimental about their own, they readily explore and experiment with new ways of doing things. This applies to the areas of religion and art, as well as to patterns of subsistence and economics.... They are not interested in change for the sake of change, only change for the sake of improvement and enhancement.... Navajos are careful and deliberate about the changes they make in their way of life. When they do change it does not usually involve the wholesale and unaltered adoption of alien ways, but a creative synthesis of alien ways with traditional modes.
> Gary Witherspoon, *Language and Art in the Navajo Universe*, p. 189.

Missionaries often come in train. Conversions of tribal peoples are quite common: We know of Berbers who became Jews, Asian tribesmen who became Muslims, Amazonians who became Evangelicals. A kind of cultural amalgamation was also common. Barred by missionaries and the laws of Canada and the United States from the conspicuous consumption of the potlatch, Northwest coast Indians discovered Christmas gift-giving and birthdays as a cover for continuing their traditions, while northeastern and southwestern tribesmen in the U.S. melded respected forebearers into the Catholic Church's hierarchy of the sainted .

Missionaries were frequently funded by the state: In 1819, with more support to follow, the U.S. Congress passed the "Civilization Fund Act" and appropriated $10,000 to pay specific denominations, in the words of the statute, "For the purpose of providing against the further decline and final extinction of the Indian tribes, adjoining the frontier settlements of the United States, and for introducing among them the habits and arts of civilization." Not only were native children forced to attend mission-run boarding schools set up in the U.S., Canada, and Australia but students were literally apportioned among the competing missions and designated one religion or another.[8] A century after President Grant divided reservation missionizing among various Christian sects, a student from the Navajo Nation told me about being lined up with the other children while a school official walked down the line designating every other child a Catholic or a Protestant. ('But for one,' he mused, 'I would be a Catholic!') In the U.S. it is estimated that hundreds of thousands of children were forcibly removed from their homes – some as young as four – and sent to one of over 500 schools in 37 states where they

FIGURE 5.2 Potlatch ceremony in the Northwest Coast.

were frequently subjected to physical and mental abuse, and where many died; in Canada the number taken from their homes exceeded 150,000; in Australia records are so poor that estimates are not possible. Only more recently, too, have the details of these schools been documented by various government investigations and painfully portrayed in such films as *Rabbit Proof Fence* (Australia), *Canada's Dark Secret*, and *Unseen Tears* (U.S.).[9] The Australian government issued a formal apology for these practices in 2008. It was not until 2024 that President Joe Biden formally apologized for the American government's role in these events, while Pope Francis, during his visit to Canada in 2022, poignantly apologized for the Church's role in the treatment of indigenous children in their care.[10] Yet here, too, in many cases the features of tribal identity remained present if not intensified even if, like an amoeba hunkering down, the tribal children's cultures had to be kept hidden or forced to lie dormant for years.

Alexis de Tocqueville, who witnessed firsthand the plight of the Choctaw on the Trail of Tears as they were forced across the Mississippi in the harsh winter of 1831, said it was the lawyers who presided at the theft of

FIGURE 5.3 Student at Indian boarding school forced to conform to White culture.

America: "In our day the dispossession of the Indians often works in a regular and so to speak wholly legal manner."[11] Whether by treaty or Constitutional provision – and notwithstanding U.S. Supreme Court opinions that occasionally acknowledged Indian rights – the legal profession served the interests of colonial expansion not only in America but in many parts of the European colonial world. In India the British wrote laws codifying what they chose to regard as the customs of "scheduled tribes," in New Zealand they agreed to the 1840 Treaty of Waitangi but did not begin to honor its implications until 1986, and in Canada it was not until 1999 that provision was made for an Inuit territory where native peoples could fashion some of their own laws. Throughout, many tribes did their best to adapt to the onslaught of legalism. The formation of legal aid groups pressing for native rights sustained both setbacks and victories, especially during the latter half of the 20th century. From the Australian decision in the Mabo case (asserting that Aboriginal title existed, and that the continent was not *terra nullius*) to American cases that reaffirmed native title and limited jurisdiction, legal cases brought attention to native rights and non-native depredations.[12] Even when unsuccessful, these legal cases did much to reinforce tribal identities and coalitions.[13]

166 Tribes

FIGURE 5.4 Native American leader George St. Gillette cries as government takes his tribe's land in 1948 to construct a dam.

Scholars, too, played their role in the response of tribes to colonial intrusion. Notwithstanding many examples to the contrary, it must be acknowledged that in some instances academics were effectively in league with the colonizing state. But two things need to be noted in this regard. First, when ethnographers moved in ahead of the colonial state they often grasped things about the local tribes that got distorted when the metropole later adopted a policy to which the tribes were subjected. So, for example, French ethnographers who studied tribes in North Africa often understood that they were not hermetically sealed off from one another, or that segmentation did not incorporate a rigid formula for alliance formation. Once the French sought to extend their colonial reach through a divide and conquer policy attention turned more to the issue of segmentarity, perhaps because those military and administrative personnel found in it a theory more compatible with their own aims. But when the struggle for independence began to fluoresce the attempt to fully separate Berbers and Arabs according to their legal systems only reinforced both groups' sources of common identity. So, too, early anthropology often countered the colonial justification by demonstrating the complex patterns of tribal life and thought. In Australia, to choose but one of numerous examples,

FIGURE 5.5 'Friends of the Indians' assist in dividing land under the Allotment policy.

telegrapher Francis Gillan worked with ethnologist Walter Baldwin Spencer to demonstrate, in *The Native Tribes of Central Australia* (1899), that the rituals of the Arrente people were highly sophisticated and peaceful.

Finally, there were the 'friends' of the tribes, those organizations, and individuals, often in touch with the missionaries and sympathetic legislators, who worked to better the situation of native peoples – or so they imagined. In the U.S. they were instrumental in several policy shifts, including passage of the Dawes Act of 1887 that conditionally allotted parcels of land to individual Indians – but which also opened the "excess" land to white settlers. Citizenship was offered piecemeal by treaty and legislation until being granted all American Indians in 1924.[14] Organizations such as The Friends of the Indian and do-gooders like Alice Fletcher assumed that this form of assimilation through ownership and citizenship would at least limit the destruction of the tribes. And even though the results of the allotment policy were catastrophic for the Indians and eventuated in yet another shift in American Indian policy, some of the tribes were able to reinforce or reconfigure themselves while retaining their distinctive qualities. Some were able to express their resistance quite effectively. For example, the Red Lake and Pembina bands of the Ojibwe supported their leadership in opposing allotment attempts by the federal government. "The Red Lake chiefs didn't just survive the encounter – they learned a valuable lesson from it: they needed to maintain strong leadership that worked to create

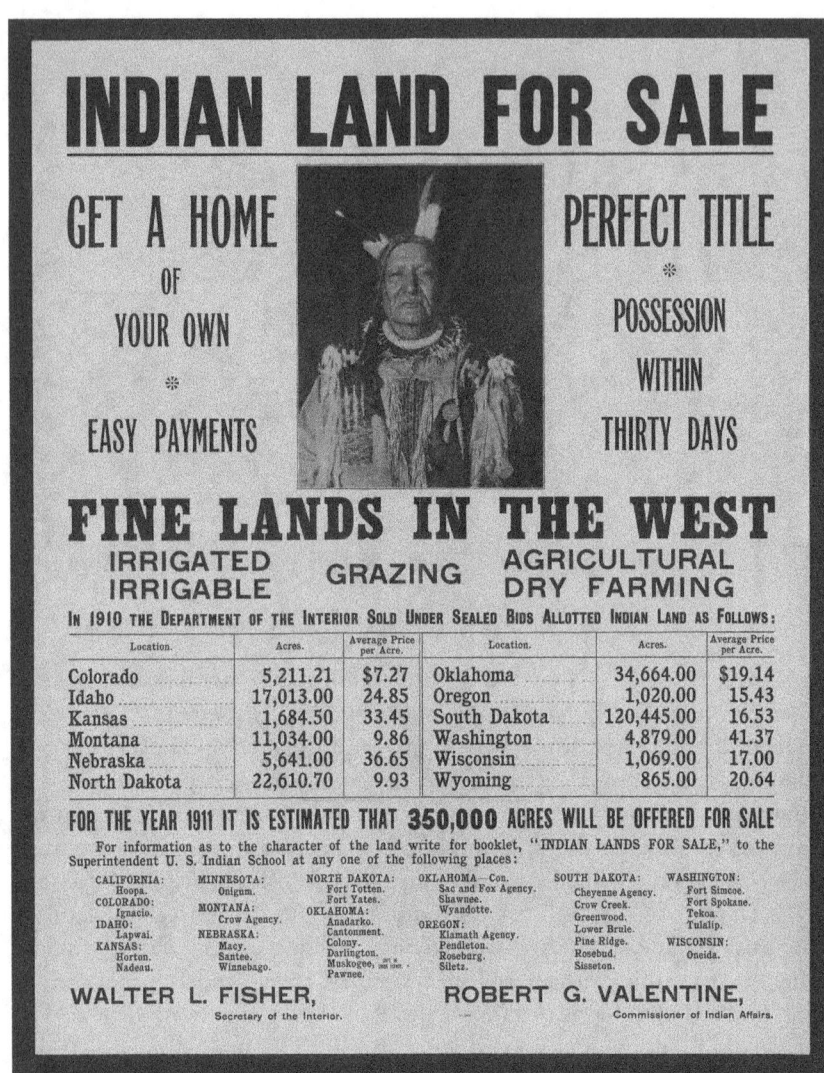

FIGURE 5.6   Poster offering Indian lands to white settlers, 1911.

consensus among the general population of the tribe."[15] By comparison, the Menominee revitalized and redirected some of their spiritual practices to create a forest management system, a practice that was partly responsible for their gaining support from Wisconsin Senator Robert La Follette in their efforts to retain tribal control of their own resources.[16] During the 1950s and 1960s the policies of many countries (e.g., the U.S., Israel) aimed at assimilating tribesmen through urbanization, policies, however, that had the reciprocal effect of stimulating increased unification and resistance on the part of the indigenous peoples.

> In 1963 Moshe Dayan said: "We should transform the Bedouins into an urban proletariat... Indeed, this will be a radical move which means that the Bedouin would not live on his land with his herds, but would become an urban person... His children would be accustomed to a father who wears trousers, does not carry a *shabaria* [the traditional Bedouin knife] and does not search for vermin ['nits in their hair,' in another translation] in public. This would be a revolution, but it may be fixed within two generations. Without coercion but with governmental direction... this phenomenon of the Bedouins will disappear."
> Quoted (from a 1963 interview in *Ha'aretz*) in Elena Boteach, et al., "The Indigenous Bedouin of the Naqab-Negev Desert in Israel," *Negev Co-Existence Forum for Civic Equality*, April 2008.

Through whatever agents, whatever mechanisms and policy shifts and incidents of brute force, states have, then, deeply affected tribes. But states are neither the inevitable creators of such entities nor have they invariably presided over their predicted demise. Earlier, we saw Morton H. Fried's argument that tribes only come into existence as a result of contact with states, that until then they are but a series of bands that may occasionally group together but that do not constitute a distinct stage in the evolution of social forms.[17] In many instances the impact of the state on tribal formation is indeed profound: As Alfred Kroeber noted in the case of Native North Americans, "our usual concept of tribe... appear[s] to be a White man's creation of convenience for talking about Indians, negotiating with them, administering them."[18] We have also seen that agents of the state may seek out a leader they can deal with or co-opt, and in the process reify that person's position well beyond its prior reach. However, the reverse may also occur when a tribe welcomes or seeks attachment to a central authority for purposes of protection or economic gain.[19] While on the surface this may appear as capitulation it can, to the contrary, work to maintain underlying tribal features that reappear when circumstances change. Within the tribe, for example, the authority of the government-appointed tribal "leader" may be consistently undercut by continuing mechanisms of levelling, thus constituting both a form of resistance to colonial practices and a means of retaining some of the mechanisms distinctive to tribal culture. Indeed, as James Scott notes: "a state often tries to find a collaborator and create a chiefdom. While it is usually in someone's interest to seize this chance, nothing prevents his would-be subjects from ignoring him."[20]

Kinship, too, may serve the tribe's need to adjust to colonial intrusion. Steven Webster, for example, points out that among the contemporary Maori "the ambiguous role of gender, the ambiguous number and size of concurrently accepted *iwi* or tribes (from twenty-some to more than fifty), and the ambiguity of *iwi* affiliation of many *hapuu* or 'subtribes, while internally consistent (and indeed thriving) are all inconsistent with the assumed segmentary and hierarchical traditional model."[21] As each grouping responds to changing economic and political circumstances new *iwi* are generated. Economically, as Webster notes, "The Maori have never been slow to adapt the trappings of free enterprise to the problem at hand."[22] The very definition of an *iwi* may appear problematic to outsiders but may, in fact, be integral to the amoeboid, shapeshifting we have seen to be so characteristic of the tribal ethos generally. Sometimes pedigree serves the state: In the Arabian peninsula various countries have sought to appropriate genealogical attachment as a vehicle for sorting out the largesse to be distributed by the state. Conversely, many of the Bedouin in the region assert their tribal lineages as a vehicle for resisting state control.[23]

By their economic impact states can certainly place preexisting modes of reciprocity at risk, if not wholly undermine them. By claiming to bring the rule of law to local tribes the colonizers may, whether by direct rule or through tribal intermediaries, draw custom into their own law or privilege some natives over others. Mahmood Mamdani, relying mainly on his reading of sub-Saharan Africa, can thus ask and answer the question: "What is a tribe? It is very largely a creation of laws drawn up by a colonial state which imposes group identities on individual subjects and thereby institutionalizes group life."[24] Referring to tribalism as "reified ethnicity," Mamdani, however, demonstrates that his is a rather particular definition of tribes when he further asks: "Did tribes exist before colonialism? If by 'tribe' we understand an ethnic group with a common language, the answer is yes. But tribe as an administrative entity, which discriminates in favour of 'natives' against 'non-natives', most certainly did not exist before colonialism."[25] Both Fried and Mamdani not only characterize tribes by their structures and outside contacts rather than their culturally distinctive capabilities but they fail to notice that tribes often reshape themselves in such a way that the colonizing force may imagine they have been defeated or assimilated when in fact more than identity as a distinctive ethnic or political entity may remain.

Other scholars have also regarded tribes as artifacts of state involvement. James C. Scott argues that, at least in the context of the hill areas of mainland Southeast Asia, nations "fabricate tribes in several ways." He regards them as "a political project – in dialogue and competition with other 'tribes' and states," and since all the world is becoming "administered space" Scott holds out little prospect for their independent survival.[26] He cites with approval the statement by Geoffrey Benjamin that "all historically and ethnologically reported tribal societies are secondary formations, characterized by the positive steps they have taken to hold themselves apart from incorporation into the state apparatus (or its more remote tentacles), while often attempting to suppress the knowledge that their way of life has been shaped by the presence of the state, or whatever represents its complexifying effects."[27] Scott concludes by clearly agreeing with Benjamin that "*tribality* in this context [as part of a political, not evolutionary, series] is simply a term applied to a strategy of state evasion."[28]

Once again we confront a particular view of tribes. Those who see them as artifacts of state contact are assuredly correct in noting that part of what tribes must frequently respond to is the presence of a state. But that is not the whole story. By downplaying instances of tribal integrity and resilience they render tribes as having no collective distinction beyond that which occurs through some external progenitor; by emphasizing only the moment of state contact they focus on just one direction of impact and fail to consider how many tribes have predated, existed alongside, and managed to survive state "creation" and assault. By saying that tribes have exercised choice but then asserting that such choices are simply expressions of state avoidance narrows the totality of tribal culture to its encounter with states. And by failing to realize that the distribution of power within tribes – and similar cultural features we have been addressing throughout – is directed only at avoiding states one fails to appreciate that tribes engage in this behavior in no small part to avoid the centralization of power *within* their own ranks, irrespective of the presence of any state. While it is necessary to consider in somewhat greater detail how indigenous states and the colonizing powers turned certain qualities of tribal culture against the tribes it is also imperative to consider how those same weaknesses are inherent in their own cultural scheme as well as having saved many tribes from destruction.

We have seen that tribes are composed of segmented (or more accurately, if more awkwardly, segmentable) groupings and that the theory of balanced opposition and segmentary coalescence made popular by the structural-functionalists found favor with colonial administrations for two main reasons: first, because it suggested that there were indigenous leaders with or through whom the colonizers could make deals or recruit a local administration, and, second, because segmentation implied an opening for a divide and conquer approach to the native population. Since both features of tribes were partly true, what was a tribal strength could often be turned against them. That is to say, tribes are indeed riven by segments as well as individually negotiated arrangements of kinship and alliance established in conformity with recognized cultural modes of association. Moreover, levelling practices and leadership by persuasion often make formation of lasting coalitions difficult to sustain, particularly when faced by powerful opponents.[29] No one who has ever worked with North American tribes can deny that factionalism is endemic. Such divisions may have seemed all but obvious to many Western analysts who accepted uncritically the notion that, as *New York Times* journalist Margaret Talbot has phrased it: "Ambivalence is a difficult state of mind to sustain; the temptation to replace it with a more Manichean vision is always close at hand." Such segmentation and levelling, of course, made it more possible for the colonial powers to insert themselves within these sociological crevices and pry apart the combinative forces that were also built into tribal systems. They did so, in part, by hooking tribesmen on the goods they could supply them and by treating tribal leaders who actually had limited if any authority to represent the tribe as the ultimate leaders of their group. The tribal emphasis on not allowing too much power in too few hands for too long contributed to their internal factionalism, and it was through this fault line that many states and empires were able to exploit the tribes. Moreover, when a tribal "big man" fashions a network of indebtedness he must constantly service his contacts, the least slippage encouraging others to either ridicule him as a leader or favor a competitor. By choosing to support one such individual over others the colonial administrator could insert the state into the system thus turning even balanced opposition into unbalanced dependence and situational leadership into privileged access to the dominating power.

But just as tribal segmentation and personalism could prove a weakness to tribes facing states so, too, other aspects of tribal culture could be drawn upon to sustain key elements of tribal integrity. Marshall Sahlins has said of the big men in Melanesian tribes: "The polity is unstable: in its superstructure a flux of rising and falling leaders, in its substructure of enlarging and contracting factions."[30] But what Sahlins takes as a weakness may also be a strength – of dissipating centralized power, of insuring that the wallpaper-pattern design of tribal society remains viable, and that even when the colonial power bolsters the position of a leader the followers will have their own ways of ameliorating the effects. At the same time, many tribes did what they had always done, namely cast up a leader of limited term, purpose, and power. Sometimes they did this by mimicking the conqueror's institutions. For example, the Chickasaw incorporated towns, elected individuals as mayors or councilmen, and built tribal-wide enterprises.[31] And just as a feature of tribal culture may be at once a weakness and a strength so, too, the colonizer often exhibits similar ambivalence that may simultaneously injure and bolster tribal survival.

The tribal encounter with the state often occasions ambivalence even among the conquerors themselves. Albert Memmi thus argues that many colonialists know that they are usurpers and may, therefore, be whiplashed between muted guilt and public self-justification.[32] That was surely the case for the large number of white Americans who signed petitions against the removal of the Indians from the American southeast in the 1830s or who, to this day, are reluctant to adopt a black child but do not hesitate to bring an Indian child into the heart of their families. And it was true for members of the Indian Claims Commission, charged with hearing even "moral claims" against the United States, who recognized that their forum had been created as part of an assimilation policy yet refused a clear directive to offset monetary awards with the value of inferior items supplied Indians under the treaties.[33] In a number of contexts colonizers thus exhibit a deep ambivalence towards the people whose lands they have stolen. Indeed, frequent changes in policies towards colonized tribes are an indication not only of shifting political attitudes in the metropole but recognition that no one policy necessarily fits the full array of emotions triggered by contact with tribal peoples.

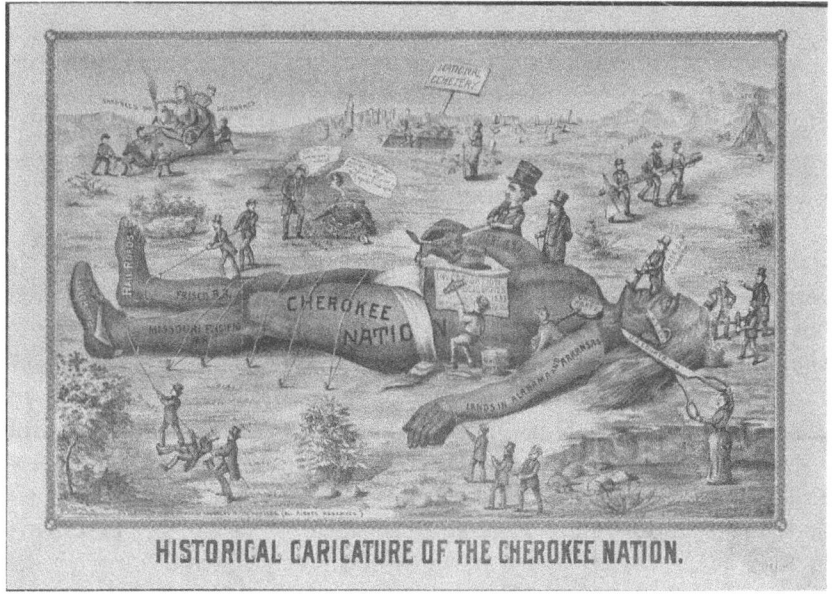

FIGURE 5.7   Caricature of the Cherokee Removal policy.

Conquest, however ambivalent, is often coupled not with elimination but with absorption into the conqueror's own society and polity. We have seen that in the case of the "tribes" of Europe absorption into Rome was not uncommon, and similar instances could be cited in the history of Asia as well. From the dominant entity's perspective such absorption may pull the teeth of an enemy force, but not without risk of undermining its own claims of internal purity. Here, too, tribal characteristics have often worked as both weaknesses exploited by the dominant force and strengths that have seen the tribes through to survival. Sometimes this presents a seeming paradox. On the one hand the presence of kin and allies who are more or less known entities makes absorption into an alien entity problematic at best and existentially threatening at worse. On the other hand, the fissiparous nature of tribes leaves the door open to just such new associations, particularly if the benefits clearly outweigh the costs. Segmentation, which may keep power from too few hands, may now work against the tribe or its confederated partners. As Francis Jennings has noted for the early colonial period in America:

> An Indian "emperor," or paramount chief, was head of a confederation of local governments and was obliged to exert his authority, whatever it may have been, through their means. Individually, the local chiefs were formally subordinate to the paramount chief; collectively, however, because of his dependence on them, they were his master. In this dependence lay a weakness in Indian confederations that exposed them to European manipulation. Lacking a standing army, a paramount chief had few alternatives when a subordinate chief chose to secede. Isolated secession seems to have been tolerated by custom...Indian tradition is full of stories of groups breaking away from parent communities to migrate and establish new tribes.[34]

Hybrid forms of tribal existence have posed special concerns. Intermarriage with non-tribesmen – as in the case of the Meti of Canada – has produced not simple absorption but a separate administrative or legal category more like that of full tribesmen. The colonial-era Canadian policy towards its native peoples was articulated in 1920 when Duncan Campbell Scott, the Canadian Deputy Superintendent General of Indian Affairs, said of his government's policy: "Our objective is to continue until there is not an Indian that has not been absorbed into the body politic, and there is no Indian question, and no Indian Department." But whether in Canada or elsewhere neither was the policy selflessly administered nor were the indigenous peoples prepared to relinquish their modes of association. Tribes, therefore, may transform themselves, but it is an open question whether forced assimilation has been carried out successfully in many colonial instances or not infrequently had the reverse effect of reinforcing tribal identity.

A third way in which colonizing states interact with tribes is by marginalizing but not eliminating them. This may take the form of establishing reservations, a process that not infrequently is connected with some sort of "civilizing" program that all too often results in everchanging boundaries or infusions of unrelated groups. Yet forced into reserves tribes have been able at times to resist the pressures of cultural assimilation and, hunkered down against moments when public opinion and policy may be more favorably disposed, have maintained and developed their cultures with less outside intrusion.[35] Legal regimes of the colonizer, too, have both pushed tribes to the margins of the state and, whether by design or not, allowed local modes of dispute resolution to quietly co-exist in a kind of plural law situation. The Hopi Tribal Court, the Navaho Peacemaker courts, the Pashtun jirga, and many other indigenous forums either survived colonial times or were reconstituted in later years. However, during the colonial period they were often manipulated. British indirect rule, for instance, involved having the locals do much of the state's work – criminal, extractive, and social welfare – with the colonizer overseeing matters at the

FIGURE 5.8 French colonial affairs officer oversees Berber tribal court in Morocco, 1954.

very top. In British colonies, customary law was limited by the requirement that laws not be repugnant to "natural law, equity, and good conscience," itself a provision that, in its actual application (particularly in Africa) was used as a means of insinuating the colonists' own law and controls on real property and social arrangements.[36] Nevertheless, local practices have often been able to subsist beneath the surface even when the use of indirect legal surveillance was not meant to grant such limited space.

Thus a more double-edged form of marginalization was at work in many parts of the colonial world. Using as examples the Apache and tribes of the Pakistani frontier, South Africa, and Argentina, Benjamin D. Hopkins argues that in such cases "frontier dwellers could be encapsulated in their own 'customs' and 'traditions' and exiled to the impoverished lands of little interest to the state and their land-hungry populaces."[37] Justifying their approach through 'the rule of law' and leaving its enforcement to an administrator with enormous discretionary powers, tribesmen were commonly forced or seduced into policing their own. Hopkins is undoubtedly correct to characterize this process as violent, extractive, and destructive. But in many cases tribes were not merely acted upon but were able to draw on some of their characteristic features to actively adapt. Hopkins refers to the states' control of their frontiers as "a regime of rule predicated on difference."[38] Rather than being able to exercise absolute domination over people on the frontier these states were effectively compelled to practice a form of "sovereign pluralism": "In such a realm, colonial authorities could indulge in the fiction of native sovereignty and independence – be it in the form of princely state or frontier tribes – without fundamentally contradicting their own all-encompassing pretensions to power."[39] And though the state may have tried to control the content of local custom, owing to the tribes' physical separation, the emphasis on difference and the inability of the state to dictate all aspects of local custom an opening was afforded for the retention of those tribal capabilities through which cultural preservation could be effected. By maintaining internal ties of reciprocity, by casting up multiple leaders for multiple purposes, and by limiting the powers of their own leaders through informal mechanisms of social control many tribes capitalized on their situation to maintain their integrity and identity. As we have seen, this is arguably the case for the Mashpee; it could as well be argued for the tens of thousands of Lumbee Indians of North Carolina (who for many years were not federally recognized) as well as many other small tribes in the United States.

Finally, colonizing states may engage in cultural appropriation. This, of course, may take many forms. One has grown all too familiar with images of native peoples in film, advertising, museum exhibits, and video games. Often the image conveys a feeling of "cultural cannibalism," in which the native is shown in what might be taken as a positive light – brave to the point of stoic, natural to the point of feeling nature's pain – only for the presentation to suggest that the conqueror has incorporated these strengths within his benevolent victory.

Reduced at times – quite literally – to objects of sexual fantasy, advertising come-ons, or mascots performing at an athletic event, the conqueror acts like a "cultural game warden" preserving what they imagine the benighted cannot or will not preserve for themselves. At still other times, the appropriation is one of apparent admiration: Picasso can adopt the Fang tribal mask to reveal the truth of a painted figure, aboriginal art can be hung in the finest of homes, and museums can display native pieces all out of context to emphasize that beauty is universal and we are all one big "family of man." American Indian museums, like that in Washington, DC, may, however, be compelled to arrange items by category (clothing, weapons, etc.) so no one tribe appears to be superior or more representative than another – but lose in the process the very contextual quality that is essential to their understanding. For the tribesman inclusion in such public displays often feels more like triumphalism than respect. Still, the Western appropriation of the tribal and the tribesman's accommodation through tourism and tourist art does have the reciprocal effect of contributing to the revivification of tribal identity.

The deleterious effects on tribes of colonialism have been enormous and can never be underestimated. But the reciprocal aspects of this history can also not be ignored. If it is true that the structure of a tribe is secondary to its cultural orientations and capabilities then tribes possess a quality that is less prone to being permanently fractured or transformed than structurally

FIGURE 5.9 Ecology poster.

based theories and policies would suggest. Indeed, these qualities have also played a key role in other encounters, particularly when Western military forces have invaded lands populated by tribesmen in the course of fighting world-wide terrorism.

Military Encounters

> "Yet I now ask of you—are you marauders or are you servants?
> Do you give power to others, or do you hoard it?
> Do you fight not to have something,
> but rather fight so that others might one day have something?"
>   Robert Jackson Bennett, City of Blades

To speak of military-tribal encounters during the colonial period is to call forth images of combat and, in most cases, ultimate state victory. But it is also to call forth the direct use of tribal peoples as trackers, spies, or soldiers attached to the conquerors' own forces. Thus in the early colonial period of North America tribes, such as the Iroquois, were sought by the English as allies against the French and vice versa, while in French colonial territories local tribes were often the shock troops sent against other tribes. Missionaries, whether Jesuits or Protestants, were often employed to recruit North American Indian tribesmen as allies, gifts from the European monarchs being used to grease the way. Although these modes of interaction were, from the state's perspective, often successful, it is also clear that distortions frequently occurred as a result of the misperception of tribal leadership and reciprocity, mistakes that not only appeared during the heyday of colonialism but that have persisted in tribal-military relations up to the present.

"Take me to your leader." In almost every cinematic or first contact fantasy of encounters with tribal peoples the demand to deal with someone in authority is a projection upon which Americans and Europeans have usually come to depend. The assumption that tribes have *a* chief, that once you convince (or convert) him all others will follow, and that it is only through such a figure that directives or agreements can be made has often led the military to seek a supreme native leader, whether or not one really exists. Sometimes the foreigners have known that designating such a figure is a dodge; sometimes they have been the victims of their own myth. The former was probably true, for example, when Governor Isaac Stevens rushed through the northwest coast of the United States in the mid-1850s forging treaties with whomever he could coerce or designate to sign on behalf of a tribe; the latter has probably been replicated innumerable times in the history of the Afghan wars. The practice of using native troops against new or traditional enemies has persisted well past colonial times: In southwest Africa, San (Bushmen) have been recruited to fight leftist rebels and in Southeast Asia Laotian hill tribes were engaged to fight the North Vietnamese.[40] In some cases military and intelligence officers have learned the local language and had a basic knowledge of local customs. All too frequently, however, Western forces have remained ignorant of important features of tribal life. Nowhere is this more noticeable than in the American military's approach to the tribes of Iraq and Afghanistan.

In 2003, when the U.S. reentered Iraq, little attention was paid to the country's tribes. Three-quarters of Iraqis identified with some tribe, but the U.S. viewed the tribes as unreliable for nation-building and avoided interaction with them. While the Iraqi tribes were less widespread and more hierarchic than among the Pashtun of Afghanistan and Pakistan, the lack of understanding about them was profound. Saddam Hussein, who came from the tribal region in and around Tikrit, had used and misused the tribes during his years in power, but after his capture in December of that year the U.S. continued to regard tribals as too prone to shifting alliances to be regarded as dependable partners.[41] Things were, however, to change just a few years later.

By 2006 the Sunni Muslims, who had benefited under Saddam, and the Shi'a, who were now empowered by the American presence, had turned on

FIGURE 5.10 American soldiers meeting with Afghan tribesmen.

one another with intense violence. Moreover, the tribes were growing very tired of al-Qa'ida fighters from abroad who had murdered many tribal leaders when the locals failed to follow the fundamentalists' dictates. With their lives and livings in jeopardy many of the Sunnis who had fought alongside the jihadists against the Americans – particularly those from the tribal regions – now began to switch their support away from al-Qa'ida. In the words of Colonel John Tien, stationed in one of the vital areas of the country: "People ask me what was the tipping point in Anbar Province. I would say 22 November [2006], the day Sheikh Jabbar [a key figure in the area] entered my tactical operations centre and said, 'I want you to help me take back my neighbourhood'."[42] The date is significant, since it was not until March of the following year that President George W. Bush ordered the infusion of 30,000 additional troops, under the command of General David Petreaus, in what came to be known as 'the surge.' But by then large payments were flowing to the tribesmen, former soldiers, and Shiite militias. By then, too, the actions of the tribes, known after a key province as the Anbar Awakening, had already had the effect of bringing the violence down considerably. In short, whereas previous to 2006 the tribes were seen as an inappropriate vehicle for building a democracy and whereas since 2007 the myth has taken hold that it was the surge that brought relative peace to Iraq for a period of time, it was, in fact, when the tribes came to the U.S., not the other way around, that, for a while, things began to quiet down.[43] Even then, however, the Americans once again decided who were the tribal leaders and paid them large sums of money to fight against al-Qa'ida. This reinforced the fact, as a reporter noted at the time, that "Throughout it all, tribal identity and traditions have reigned at the local level."[44] But it also had the subsequent effect of creating sheikhs who were not supported by their people but used the American recognition to extort monies from their fellow countrymen. As one reporter noted:

> Eight years after the American invasion put Iraq on a path to a more modern, democratic society, people here are increasingly resorting to the ancient process of tribal negotiations – called fassels, and conducted by tribal leaders or sheiks – to demand compensation for alleged injustices. While Iraqis have long joked about frivolous fasels, people say an especially degenerate version is now running amok, in which powerful sheiks are essentially extorting huge sums of money from professionals, especially doctors. The problem is partly a result of Iraq's weak legal system and the lack of official grievance processes, non-issues during Saddam Hussein's autocratic rule, when tyrannical order prevailed and malpractice complaints were handled through the courts. But many also blame a relic of the U.S. occupation: so-called 'fake sheiks' – including

'Condoleeza Rice sheiks,' named for the former secretary of state – who were paid by the United States to fight insurgents, a practice Prime Minister Nouri al-Maliki has continued."[45]

> Ask the same Anbari citizens why sometime in 2006 they began to turn against the by-then al-Qaeda-led insurgency, and the answer would be more direct. To them, their alliance with the radicals was a marriage of convenience to fight the U.S. occupation. Al-Qaeda brought dedication, organization, funding, and a willingness to die. Over time, however, it overplayed its hand and wore out its welcome by forcing an extreme Islamic agenda on a generally secular and very tribal culture. Al-Qaeda's campaign evolved from assistance, to persuasion, to intimidation, to murder in the most horrific ways, all designed to intimidate Anbari society—tribes and sheikhs alike—to adopt the most extreme form of Islam. At a certain point, al-Qaeda's agenda became too much for the average Anbari to bear. It was increasingly directed at the sheikhs themselves, and just as importantly, it began to have an impact on the business interests of tribal leaders.
>   John F. Kelly, at the time a major general, was later President Trump's Chief of Staff.
>   General John F. Kelly, "Foreword," in *Al-Anbar Awakening, Volume II, Iraqi Perspectives, From Insurgency to Counterinsurgency 2004–2009*, ed., Colonel Gary W. Montgomery and Chief Warrant Officer-4 Timothy S. McWilliams, Quantico, VA, Marine Corps University Press, 2009, p. viii. https://www.hqmc.marines.mil/Portals/61/Docs/Al-AnbarAwakeningVoIII%5B1%5D.pdf

In the case of Iraq, then, bias and ignorance in equal measure characterized the American approach to the country's tribes. Both the Bush and Obama administrations avoided involvement with the tribes. This is not to suggest that matters might have come out differently had they understood the nature of tribes more thoroughly. To the contrary, in all likelihood the divergence of interests and the lack of consistent, ongoing contacts probably doomed the relationship and its effects from the outset. That is why, when the counterinsurgency measures applied in both Iraq and Afghanistan began to incorporate field-based social scientists, the idea that such expertise could guide the Americans to what the Army Field Guide drawn up by General Petreaus called "a complex form of warfare [that] at its core is a struggle for the population's support" proved inapposite to the stated goals. Matters were to proceed no more favorably in America's next encounter with the tribes of Afghanistan.

Following the invasion of Afghanistan by American forces in October 2001 the focus on dislodging the Taliban incorporated no clear policy towards the nation's tribesmen. Tactics thought to be successful in Iraq were transferred to Afghanistan with little understanding of the differences involved. Some 150 major tribes span the Afghan-Pakistan border region and have often been described in segmentary terms as comprised of confederations (e.g., the Durani and Ghilzai) that break down into numerous tribes, sub-tribes, and family groupings.[46] Many in the military had seen the Iraqi tribes as hierarchical and as a result acted as though a deal at the top could bind the segments below. But the tribes are no more rigidly segmentary in Southwest Asia than anywhere else. Like those in Iraq, the Afghan tribes were not regarded as reliable allies or as the base upon which a democracy could be built. Indeed, American troops referred to the tribal regions as "Indian country." Although Americans had experience during the Viet Nam war with the hill tribes of the region, whatever may have been learned from that encounter did not translate to the new war. With only their understanding of tribes generally being based on the Iraqi experience military and intelligence efforts in Afghanistan were hesitant, confused, and based on faulty assumptions. Ultimately the experience with tribes in Afghanistan – and in the view of many, the entire war – was a complete failure.[47] Several stereotypes of tribes in particular led the Americans astray.

Once again the invaders looked for a single 'chief' of the tribe with whom to deal. Referring to a U.S. Army colonel meeting with an Afghan tribal leader, Lawrence Wright notes: "The meeting had allowed him to check off a couple of important boxes on the score-sheet of counterinsurgency doctrine, a 'key leader' engagement that offered an opportunity to secure greater control of a 'key terrain area'."[48] Like the British a century before, many of the American commanders thought that they could learn tribal traditions and thus recruit the tribesmen as allies. But like their predecessors, they seldom had command of the local languages, conjured various 'traditions' rather than grasping the range of cultural variation, and in many ways "rather than showing the sophistication of the military's cultural knowledge, merely demonstrate[d] to Afghans the coalition's poor understanding of local cultures."[49] This lack of understanding permeated encounters in numerous domains.

Quite aside from the vast amounts of cash ladled out to designated leaders, the military failed to understand that reciprocity within a tribal setting is not a one-off proposition but a long-term, often lifelong, association involving multiple aspects. Merely offering the occasional gift, far from establishing a relationship, only underlines the absence of ongoing ties, ties that for foreign invaders professing no desire to live permanently in their culture will never involve shared orientations and living arrangements, engaging in marital ties, or participating in a regularized cycle of ritual occasions.[50] Neither could the foreign military become embedded in the many stratagems by which the tribesmen disperse power: They were not positioned to be affected by joking, ridicule, or ritual reversals, nor were they likely to gain fluency in the style of language play so essential to both demonstrating and circumscribing another's place in the scheme of things. Instead of understanding that effective ties among tribesmen are not merely transactional, top American General David McKiernan could only envision "some sort of contract where the [tribal] community agrees and supports the idea of helping to provide security for its people" – as if security could ever be solely dependent on 'contracts' with an outside force.[51] Some 'contracts' were nevertheless made, as when the Shinwari tribe, representing 400,000 people in eastern Afghanistan, agreed to fight the Taliban and punish any of their own who aided them. American commanders gave the tribe $1 million in development projects – monies not channeled through Kabul. Whether the tribe made the agreement because the Taliban were cutting into their smuggling operations or because they were tired of the fundamentalists' intrusion, the American deal was not based on enduring involvement on a person-to-person level and was, therefore, founded only on a transactional, rather than cultural, foundation.[52]

> "...the Americans who arrived in their midst [in Afghanistan] could have been from Mars.... To the tribesmen, the Americans who came from nowhere in flying machines no one had seen before and abruptly disappeared with their catch were seen as aliens, with their abnormally large frames covered in strange padding, protruding wires, protective helmets, and peculiar weapons. These invaders could see at night through their glasses, speak into those wires, and command deadly airstrikes while resting on the ground. They appeared to have few social skills and neither offered nor received hospitality. Americans were loud, rude, and violent and expressed no interest in the land or its people."
> Akbar Ahmed, *The Thistle and the Drone: How America's War on Global Terror Became a Global War on Tribal Islam*, Washington: Brookings Institution Press, 2013, p. 5.

Similarly, the invaders failed to grasp that the characteristic dispersal of power in the tribal societies of Southwest Asia also involved an ambiguous feature found in many tribes, namely that on the one hand anyone claiming a degree of power had, from time to time, to give some indication of its possession while at the same time not overplaying his hand since power was, in fact, both limited and not to be too extravagantly touted. Ernest Gellner said of the former that sometimes you had to light a match not to burn something but to show you still had some matches that worked, while in Afghanistan "politics meant convincing people you had power by forestalling any event that might reveal you didn't."[53] Since the tribal leaders the invaders cultivated were not actually hereditary chiefs but persons simultaneously constrained by local levelling and propped up by momentary access to external resources, the idea that one could use them as state-builders in an environment where the writ of the state neither ran nor was welcome was only one more instance of failing to understand the nature of the tribes with whom the military were dealing.

Wedded nevertheless to their nation-building goals yet realizing their need for help from the local population in developing the country, the Americans characteristically turned to "experts." There were, however, few people who knew the tribes of Afghanistan and fewer trained in the social sciences who were prepared to assist. Funds from the Department of Defense were authorized to recruit experts and after two years of a pilot program $40 million was allocated to implement the project through every military unit in Afghanistan.[54] From 2010 until the drawdown of forces in 2014 what was designated as the Human Terrain Project operated alongside military operations advising on how best to relate to the local population. Members of the teams helped assess who were the leaders, what to make of the locals' body language, the impact of assassinations on tribal divisions, and which development projects would find favor with the tribesmen and villagers. But the questionable qualifications of the project's personnel and opposition from such professional organizations as the American Anthropological Association only highlighted the poor quality of the advice being offered. The original members of the team were soon replaced, Congressional hearings raised doubts about the project's effectiveness, and the deaths of several team members in the field brought the entire scheme into question even before the troop withdrawal. Like its predecessor programs in Vietnam, the Human Terrain Project's failure owed much not only to the poor quality of its work but to the fraught issue whether such wars are won by capturing minds and hearts with anthropological nets or whether only force has a chance of achieving such an end to hostilities.[55]

During those years military leaders at the highest level did come to realize how faulty was their understanding of the local tribes of Afghanistan. Perhaps claiming more credit for the Iraqi experience than is supportable,

General David A. Petraeus, the top allied commander in Afghanistan at the time, was reported as indicating that "unlike in Iraq, the U.S. has long lacked a detailed knowledge of the motivations and allegiances of various Afghan tribes and tribal elders."[56] His successor, General Stanley McChrystal, too, later said that the U.S. began the war with a "frighteningly simplistic" view of the country, the military never having made "an effective effort" even to learn the country's languages.[57] Moreover, the tribes had good reason to believe that not only would the Americans never be long-term residents of their country but that the Americans' ignorance was matched only by their untrustworthiness. After all, it was the Americans who backed the young "holy warriors" against the authority of their tribal elders when the U.S. sought the younger religionists' help in combating the Russian invasion of Afghanistan in the 1980s and it is the Americans who were seen as consistently supporting corrupt officials in Kabul. Nor in all the years of its presence had the coalition found a way to reconcile support of the tribes with the view of those Afghans who, as David Rohde reported, "see the tribes as inherently anachronistic, sexist and corrupt – a system that further undermines the already extraordinarily difficult task of creating multiethnic, merit-based national institutions."[58]

The military have, then, been quite literally the tip of the spear in many state-tribal relations, both colonial and in the more recent quest to build a friendly state in terrorist territory. In the Middle East, in particular, nations like Jordan, the Gulf states, and Saudi Arabia have not grown out of tribes in some straightforwardly evolutionary sense but have seen the employment of modern weaponry and communications as vital aids in the assertion of dominance over individual tribes.[59] Moreover, many of the rulers of the independent countries of the Middle East and North Africa have either played tribes against one another, favored their own and repressed others, or exploited the ambiguities of tribal attachments for their own ends.[60] And just as the state and the tribal may, in such cases, continue to be interwoven, so, too, are the tribes of the world often affected by the activities of foreign corporations and the reorganization of their own economies along corporate lines.

The Corporations and the Tribes

"How can you buy or sell the sky, the warmth of the land?
The idea is strange to us.
If we do not own the freshness of the air and the sparkle of the water, how can you buy them?"

Chief Seattle

The exploitation of indigenous resources involves more than land: It may also concern medicinal, artistic, and intellectual property. As tribes were pushed to marginal lands colonial powers and investors usually thought they had also been confined to locales containing little of commercial value. But what was once regarded as worthless land often turned out to be immensely valuable for its uranium, oil, coal, or copper. In many cases governments and corporations have worked hand in hand using legislation, government leases, and blatantly corrupt practices to obtain access to resources or exacerbate native impoverishment to coerce concessions. Examples, historic and contemporary, are legion. In the 1920s oil interests were responsible for creating a Navajo leader in order to have someone who could sign leases.[61] More recently, in the upper Great Plains oil pipelines that affect Indian lands have been the subject of numerous protests and lawsuits. Mining conglomerate Rio Tinto and its partners destroyed an aboriginal ancestral site at Juukan Gorge in Australia in their quest for minerals and more recently have threatened the off-reservation sacred site of the San Carlos Apache with a copper mining scheme.[62] The Brookings Institution has documented innumerable instances of corruption involved in the exploitation of indigenous resources in many parts of the world.[63]

Tribes have undoubtedly suffered from the machinations of those corporations that have preyed on their assets. But such predation has also precipitated tribal responses, whether in the form of coalition building, protest, or litigation – all of which have at times strengthened tribal solidarity, even when encountering setbacks. Divisiveness within tribal communities has also shown itself when the choice is between traditional practices and commercial gain. This is particularly visible in the clashes over gambling on American Indian reservations. Following a U.S. Supreme Court ruling that effectively permitted gambling on tribal lands, Congress passed legislation regulating such enterprises. Some tribes rejected the exploitation of reservation gambling outright, but many others were riven by factions when the question was presented. Non-Indian casino operators were quick to object to the fact that Indians did not pay state taxes and might, therefore, have a competitive advantage. Donald Trump famously testified before Congress in 1993 claiming that Indians dressed in suits and running multimillion-dollar establishments in competition with his own casinos were not real Indians.[64] However, by 2022, Indian casinos took in nearly forty-one billion, from more than five hundred gaming operations in twenty-nine states.

> I'll tell you what, if you look – if you look at some of the reservations that you have approved – you, sir, in your great wisdom, have approved – will

> tell you right now, they don't look like Indians to me, and they don't look like Indians. Now maybe we say politically correct or not politically correct. They don't look like Indians to me, and they don't look like Indians to Indians, and a lot of people are laughing at it, and you are telling how tough it is, how rough it is, to get approved.
> Donald Trump, Congressional testimony, 1993.

More distressing, a number of tribes that have been able to sell their mineral resources or establish casinos have sought to revoke tribal membership to long-standing members of the tribe in a blatant attempt to increase the political power and per capita income of those still enrolled. What may once have been a common mechanism for sloughing tribal members in order to form external alliances and maintain an internal balance of resources was now turned against many individuals who had regarded themselves as tribesmen all their lives.[65] Moreover, the division of power that served tribesmen well when it forestalled transition to a more centralized regime now revealed its weakness as a form of internal factionalism in the face of an outside force.

In some instances tribes have chosen or been coerced into mimicking the very structure that at other times has worked to their detriment. The Native Alaska Claims Settlement Act of 1971, for example, set up regional and village corporations eligible for access to 44 million acres of land and a $963 million fund. The native corporations have certain tax and contracting benefits and though some of the nearly two hundred corporations have been unsuccessful others have developed sport and commercial fishing, mining, and oil drilling projects yielding annual revenues in excess of one billion dollars each.[66] Participants have had to learn the complexities of corporate law and may risk losing control to non-native shareholders. Similarly, in New Zealand, Maori have organized many of their enterprises in the form of corporations.[67] In 1992 the government of New Zealand and the Maori reached a cash settlement on the basis of which the tribal corporations purchased approximately twenty percent of the country's commercial fishing, which has since grown to some thirty percent.[68] In each instance, the choice of adopting a Western form has the advantage of linking native enterprises to the laws and practices of others so that whatever protections are afforded any individual or corporation are also afforded them. Nevertheless, being subject to additional laws specific to tribes and compromising claims to governmental sovereignty may negate some of these advantages.

Faced with limited access to resources some tribes have also sought to market their special status. In the United States, in addition to gambling

FIGURE 5.11A Tamati Waka Nene, a traditional Maori warrior with facial tattoos, was probably born in the 1780s.

casinos, tribes have used their state tax free status to sell tobacco at lower prices than non-reservation competitors. Drug manufacturing also enters the picture. The Saint Regis Mohawk tribe negotiated a deal with Allergen, a large pharmaceutical company that was trying to stave off loss of its patent on a particular drug by selling the license to the tribe in the expectation that the tribe's sovereign immunity would shield the corporation from an adverse decision by the patent office. However, the U.S. Supreme Court affirmed dismissal of the tribe-corporate arrangement that lower courts had characterized as a sham.[69]

Tribal intellectual property has also become a highly contentious issue in recent years. Whether it is claims of exclusive control over the wild rice cultivated in their region or the design of an artifact sold to

FIGURE 5.11B   Professor Te Kahautu Maxwell with facial tattoos and business suit.

tourists, tribesmen in many parts of the world face issues of copyright and patent their predecessors had not encountered.[70] Recall that a quarter of contemporary pharmaceuticals are based on the knowledge of indigenous peoples and that over two hundred such remedies continue to be listed in the official *United States Pharmacopeia*.[71] Under such circumstances the pressures on tribal peoples to commercialize their knowledge can be intense. Many tribes have coalesced, usually in opposition, to the use of their DNA by researchers and pharmaceutical companies.[72] Similarly, the return of human remains and cultural artifacts from museums has galvanized tribes in pursuit of newly conceptualized rights, often serving to revitalize the solidarity and identity of their societies. Thus, in a wide range of instances tribes have once again been challenged and invigorated by the various ways in which corporate organization has entered, complicated, and extended their adaptation to the wider world.

* * *

There is a story told of an anthropology graduate student who had just returned from the field when he encountered one of his professors, a leading figure in the discipline, in the quadrangle. The professor asked how long the student had been in the field. "Two years," replied the student. "Oh," said the professor, "that will take you decades to make sense of."

Anyone who has worked extensively in a tribal setting – unless they simply apply a pre-existing explanation like a cookie cutter – realizes that one cannot reduce to a simple formula the complexities of what they have encountered. It is easy to criticize colonialists and soldiers, politicians, and NGOs for getting a lot wrong about tribes and, in carrying their ignorance into action, then finding themselves flummoxed when matters do not go as expected. But if, as we have suggested throughout, one approaches tribal life not as an array of structural forms or evolutionary stages then the complexity, the subtlety, the sheer adaptability of tribes can be seen as challenging the observer's comprehension while demonstrating the subject's capacity to withstand enormous strain. No form of human life, no cultural precept or belief or orientation is impervious to change or destruction; no tribe is invulnerable to dissolution, whether from within or without. But given the qualities of their ethos and spirit tribes, quite remarkably, do manage to endure in the face of assault with remarkable frequency. And when they do their relationship to the larger nations within which they now exist raises the question of the distribution of powers that should apply. It is to this problem of empowerment and sovereignty that we must, finally, turn our attention.

Notes

1 Though often phrased in the singular, the doctrine of discovery should perhaps be seen as embracing several different concepts that were operative in colonial practice: See, Douglas Lind, "Doctrines of Discovery," *Washington University Jurisprudence Review*, vol. 13, no. 1 (2020), pp. 1–64.
2 For a sampling of Bolsonaro's comments on indigenous peoples see, Survival International, "What President Bolsonaro Says about Brazil's Indigenous Peoples," September 14, 2022. https://survivalinternational.medium.com/what-president-bolsonaro-says-about-brazils-indigenous-peoples-470665154955 (accessed September 8, 2025).
3 Miranda Bryant, "'I Was Only a Child': Greenlandic Women Tell of Trauma of Forced Contraception," *The Guardian*, March 29, 2024.
4 For the Old Testament, see Deuteronomy 20:16-18 ("You must completely destroy them – the Hethite, Amorite, Canaanite, Perizzite, Hivite, and Jebusite") and 1 Samuel 15:3 ("Now go and attack the Amalekites and completely destroy everything they have. Do not spare them. Kill men and women, infants and nursing babies, oxen and sheep, camels and donkeys"); for the New Testament, see Luke 19:27 ("But as for these enemies of mine, who did not want me to reign over them, bring them here and slaughter them before me."); for Islam, see Quran 9:5 ("But when the forbidden months are past, then fight and slay the Pagans wherever you find them, and seize them, beleaguer them, and lie in wait for them in every stratagem [of war].")

5 For the criteria of eligibility for recognition, see 25 Code of Federal Regulations 83.7 (a-g) (2011).
6 On trade with Europeans in the early colonial period in America see, Francis Jennings, *The Invasion of America*, New York: W. W. Norton, 1976, pp. 85–104.
7 On the tribes' ability to alter their structures and identities, devolve into autonomous local units, and shift their subsistence strategies see, Richard White, *The Middle Ground: Indians, Empires, and Republics in the Great Lakes Region, 1650-1815*, Cambridge: Cambridge University Press, 2011, pp. 16–20.
8 There were 523 such boarding schools in the US: See, https://boardingschoolhealing.org/list/ (accessed June 7, 2025) See generally, David Wallace Adams, *Education for Extinction: American Indians and the Boarding School Experience*, Lawrence: University Press of Kansas, 1995.
9 See, Dana Hedgpeth and Sari Horwitz, "More Than 900 Native American Children Died at U.S. Boarding Schools," *Washington Post*, July 30, 2024. For the full report see, www.bia.gov/sites/default/files/media_document/doi_federal_indian_boarding_school_initiative_investigative_report_vii_final_508_compliant.pdf (accessed September 8, 2025).
10 Apologies have been forthcoming in other countries as well. For example: "Taiwan is also home to about 580,000 people who belong to one of 16 officially recognized tribes, descendants of Austronesian people whose presence on the island dates back thousands of years.... Recently, leaders such as Taiwanese President Tsai Ing-wen, who is a quarter [indigenous tribal] Paiwan, have promoted Taiwan's Indigenous identity. In 2016, Tsai issued the first official apology to Indigenous groups for centuries of mistreatment, including the seizure of ancestral lands and assimilation policies that banned Indigenous languages and traditions." Lily Kuo and Alicia Chen, "Taiwan's Han Chinese Seek a New Identity among the Island's Tribes," *Washington Post*, March 4, 2022.
11 Alexis de Tocqueville, *Democracy in America, Vol. One*, trans. by Harvey C. Mansfield and Delba Winthrop, Chicago: University of Chicago Press, 2000, chapter 10, p. 311.
12 *Mabo v. Queensland* (No. 2) [1992] HCA 23; (1992) 175 CLR 1.
13 See, for examples, the documentary film *First Australians: The Untold Story of Australia*, 2008.
14 While Australian aborigines are citizens for many purposes they are still subject to powers of the federal government distinctive to them: See, "The 1967 Referendum," Parliament of Australia. www.naa.gov.au/explore-collection/first-australians/other-resources-about-first-australians/1967-referendum (accessed September 8, 2025).
15 David Treuer, *The Heartbreak of Wounded Knee*, New York: Riverhead Books, 2019, p. 165.
16 Treuer, *The Heartbreak of Wounded Knee*, pp. 169–72.
17 "[S]tates created tribes rather than having evolved from them. However much the thought may disturb us, all human societies larger than the immediate band or village were of the vaguest dimensions and boundaries, with memberships that shifted for any number of reasons. The nascent state then turned to its hinterland and began to transform the societies it encountered there into parts of itself or partial replicas or at least organized it into something that could feed some of its needs. It is time to dispense with the myth and acknowledge tribes for what they are – products and servants of the state." Morton H. Fried, "The Myth of Tribe," *Natural History*, vol. 84, no. 4 (April 1975), pp. 12–20 (ellipses removed).

18 Quoted in Eleanor Leacock, "Ethnohistorical Investigations of Egalitarian Politics in Eastern North America," in Elizabeth Tooker, ed., *The Development of Political Organization in Native North America*, Philadelphia: The American Ethnological Society, 1983, pp. 17–31.
19 See, e.g., James Howe, "How the Cuna Keep Their Chiefs in Line," *Man*, New Series, vol. 13, no. 4 (December 1978), pp. 537–53, at 539.
20 James C. Scott, *The Art of Not Being Governed*, New Haven: Yale University Press, 2009, p. 210.
21 Steven Webster, "Escaping Post-Cultural Tribes," *Critique of Anthropology*, vol. 15, no. 4 (1995), pp. 381–413, at 396.
22 Webster, *Escaping Post-Cultural Tribes*, p. 397.
23 See, e.g., Nadav Samin, *Of Sand and Soil: Genealogy and Tribal Belonging in Saudi Arabia*, Princeton: Princeton University Press, 2015.
24 Mahmood Mamdani, "What Is a Tribe?" *London Review of Books*, September 13, 2012; see also, his *Define and Rule: Native as Political Identity*, Cambridge: Harvard University Press, 2012.
25 Mamdani, "What Is a Tribe?" He continues: "Like race, tribe becomes a single, exclusive identity only with colonialism. Above all, tribe was a politically driven, totalizing identity. As such, it looks very much like a subset of race."
26 James C. Scott, *The Art of Not Being Governed*.
27 Geoffrey Benjamin and Cynthia Chou, eds., *Tribal Communities and the Malay World: Historical, Cultural, and Social Perspectives*, Singapore: Institute for Southeast Asian Studies, 2002, p. 9. See generally, the materials in their Chapter 2, "On Being Tribal in the Malay World," pp. 7–76.
28 Scott, *The Art of Not Being Governed*, p. 183 (original italics).
29 For example, Timothy J. Shannon (*Iroquois Diplomacy on the Early American Frontier*, New York: Viking, 2008, pp. 178–79) says of the Iroquois Confederacy: "Since its inception, the Iroquois League had always lacked any powers other than persuasion when it came to influencing its member nations. The Six Nations had never been especially centralized or uniform in pursuing politics and diplomacy, but the divisions among them were more pronounced in 1775 than perhaps at any previous time in the colonial history."
30 Marshall Sahlins, *Tribesmen*, p. 90.
31 See, Treuer, *The Heartbreak of Wounded Knee*, pp. 168–69.
32 Albert Memmi, *The Colonizer and the Colonized*, New York: Orion Press, 1965.
33 Members of the Indian Claims Commission, who refused to deduct from awards the value of such "gratuitous offsets" as the blankets supplied to the Native Americans, may have taken heart from the sardonic comment of one mid-19th century observer who wrote:

> The blankets, to be sure, were very thin, and cost a great deal of money in proportion to their value; but, then, peculiar advantages were to be derived from the transparency of the fabric. By holding his blanket to the light, an Indian could enjoy the contemplation of both sides of it at the same time; and it would only require a little instruction in architecture to enable him to use it occasionally as a window to his wigwam. Nor was it the least important consideration, that when he gambled it away, or sold it for whisky, he would not be subject to any inconvenience from a change of temperature. The shirts and pantaloons were in general equally transparent, and possessed this additional advantage, that they very soon cracked open in the seams, and thereby enabled the squaws to learn how to sew.

J. Ross Browne, *Crusoe's Island*, New York: Harper & Brothers, 1864, p. 293.

34 Jennings, *The Invasion of America*, pp. 115–16.
35 Examples are vividly portrayed in the film *First Australians: The Untold Story of Australia* (2008).
36 See, e.g., Kwame Affuko, "Equity in Colonial West Africa: A Paradigm of Juridical Dislocation," *Journal of African Law*, vol. 50, no. 2 (2006), pp. 132–44; T. O. Elias, "Customary Law: The Limits of Its Validity in Colonial Law," *Journal of African Studies*, vol. 13, nos. 3-4 (January 19, 2007), pp. 97–107. Damen Ward, "Legislation, Repugnancy and the Disallowance of Colonial Laws: The Legal Structure of Empire and Lloyd's Case," *Victoria University of Wellington Law Review*, vol. 41 (2010), pp. 381–402; and Lauren Benton, *Law and Colonial Cultures: Legal Regimes in World History, 1400–1900*, New York: Cambridge University Press, 2002.
37 Benjamin D. Hopkins, *Ruling the Savage Periphery: Frontier Governance and the Making of the Modern State*, Cambridge: Harvard University Press, 2020, p. 4.
38 Hopkins, *Ruling the Savage Periphery*, p. 8.
39 Hopkins, *Ruling the Savage Periphery*, p. 19.
40 For the Bushmen see, Robert Gordon and Stuart Sholto-Douglas, *The Bushman Myth: The Making of a Namibian Underclass*, 2nd edn., Boulder: Westview Press, 2000.
41 The elaborate, multicolored chart showing Saddam's connections was called the Mongo Link by its developers. An example of network analysis, it was started in June 2003 with four names and eventually contained more than 9000, emphasizing contacts within the five main clans of the Tikrit area. Yossef Bodansky, *The Secret History of the Iraq War*, New York: Regan Books/HarperCollins, 2005, pp. 471–72. See also, Chris Wilson, "Searching for Saddam," *Slate*, February 21, 2010; and Eric Schmitt, "How Army Sleuths Stalked the Adviser Who Led To Hussein," *New York Times*, December 20, 2003.
42 Sam Collyns and James Jones, "'America Used to Be Our Enemy No. 1. But Now It's al-Qa'ida,' Say Former Insurgents," *The Independent*, September 29, 2010.
43 See, Peter Beinart, "The Surge Fallacy," *The Atlantic*, September 2018, pp. 13–15. David Kilcullen, General Petraeus's counterinsurgency and troop surge adviser, has also stated that "the tribal revolt was arguably the most significant change in the Iraqi operating environment in several years." David Kilcullen, *The Accidental Guerrilla: Fighting Small Wars in the Midst of a Big One*, Oxford: Oxford University Press, 2009, p 179. Andrew Bacevich - a West Point graduate, veteran of the Gulf War, and professor of history - says: "The surge…functions chiefly as a smoke-screen, obscuring a vast panorama of recklessness, miscalculation and waste that politician, generals, and sundry warmongers are keen to forget." Quoted in Frank Rich, "Freedom's Just Another Word," *New York Times*, September 5, 2010, p. WK5. In the words of Lieutenant General Daniel Bolger: "The surge didn't 'win' anything. It bought time." Quoted and discussed in Alex Kingsbury, "Why the 2007 Surge in Iraq Actually Failed," *The Boston Globe*, November 17, 2014. The prestigious Afghanistan Study Group (*A New Way Forward: Rethinking U.S. Strategy in Afghanistan*, 2010. www.afghanistanstudygroup.org/read-the-report/ [accessed June 14, 2025]), in its list of "Myths and Realities in the Afghan Debate," states categorically that the surge failed in most respects. A member of Congress who at the time served on two intelligence committees also told me in a private phone conversation: "The surge was not what turned things

around." See also, Michael E. Silverman, *Awakening Victory: How Iraqi Tribes and American Troops Reclaimed al-Anbar and Defeated al-Qaeda in Iraq*, Havertown, PA: Casemate Publishers, 2011. On the possible use of the tribes by American forces at the time of the invasion in 2003, see Amatzia Baram, "The Iraqi Tribes and the Post-Saddam System," Brookings Institution, July 8, 2003. www.brookings.edu/research/the-iraqi-tribes-and-the-post-saddam-system/ (accessed June 6, 2025). On the subsequent loss of Anbar to ISIS see, Carter Malkasian, *Illusions of Victory: The Anbar Awakening and the Rise of the Islamic State*, Oxford: Oxford University Press, 2017.

44 Tim Arango, "In New Iraq, Tradition of Tribal Chiefs' Power Holds Firm," *International Herald Tribune*, March 15, 2012, p. 2.
45 Stephanie McCrummen, "Tribal Lawsuits, 'Fake Shieks' Threaten Iraqi Doctors," *Washington Post*, April 6, 2011.
46 See, e.g., the chart and comments in Ruhullah Khapalwak and David Rohde, "A Look at America's New Hope: The Afghan Tribes," *New York Times*, January 31, 2010, p. WK3.
47 See former combat veteran officer, who served in Iraq and Afghanistan, Timothy Kudo, "The Truth that Iraq and Afghanistan Veterans Know," *New York Times*, November 24, 2020 ("those of us who served in the military have long realized: We lost.")
48 Lawrence Wright, "The Double Game," *The New Yorker*, May 16, 2011.
49 Benjamin D. Hopkins and Magnus Marsden, "Ten Years In, Afghan Myths Live On," *New York Times*, October 7, 2011, p. A19. See, e.g., the development projects that failed owing to a misunderstanding of local practices described in Noah Coburn, *Bazaar Politics: Power and Pottery in an Afghan Market Town*, Stanford: Stanford University Press, 2011; and his *Losing Afghanistan: An Obituary for the Intervention*, Stanford: Stanford University Press, 2016, esp. pp. 173–99.
50 A good example is supplied by the attempt, on the part of a former marine hired as an expert on the local tribes of Iraq, to offer ceremonial swords to cooperative tribals, without understanding that what matters is the long-term relationship that such a singular gift could not instantly effect. See, Greg Jaffe, "To Understand Sheiks in Iraq, Marines Ask 'Mac'," *Wall Street Journal*, September 10, 2011, p. A1.
51 Community Editor, "Petraeus: Afghan Tribes Could Fight Militants," *Military Times*, November 6, 2008.
52 See, Dexter Filkins, "Afghan Tribe, Vowing to Fight Taliban, to Get U.S. Aid in Return," *New York Times*, January 28, 2010.
53 Alexander Star, "Applied Anthropology," *New York Times Book Review*, November 20, 2011, pp. 16–17, at 17.
54 The program was implemented to a much more limited extent in Iraq.
55 *Compare* Bing West, *The Wrong War*, New York: Random House, 2011 (program was a failure) *with* Christopher Lamb, et al., *Human Terrain Teams: An Organizational Innovation for Sociocultural Knowl3dge in Irregular Warfare*, Washington, DC: Institute of World Politics Press, 2013 (notwithstanding problems, program was largely valuable). For comments by former members of the teams see, Corey Flintoff, "Marines Tap Social Sciences in Afghan War Effort," April 5, 2010. www.npr.org/templates/story/story.php?storyId=125502485 (accessed September 8, 2025); and Montgomery McFate, "The Military Utility of Understanding Adversary Culture," *Joint Force Quarterly*, Issue 38, July 2005, pp. 42–48. For anthropological critiques of the program see, Roberto González, *American Counterinsurgency: Human*

Science and the Human Terrain, Chicago: Prickly Paradigm Press 2009; and Network of Concerned Anthropologists, *The Counter-Counterinsurgency Manual*, Chicago: Prickly Paradigm Press, 2009. See generally, Lawrence Rosen, "Anthropological Assumptions and the Afghan War," *Anthropological Quarterly*, vol. 84, no. 2 (March/April 2011), pp. 535–58.

56 Julian E. Barnes, "Petraeus: U.S. Lacks Afghan Tribal Knowledge," *Wall Street Journal*, September 2, 2010.

57 Associated Press, "Former US Commander in Afghanistan Says US Lacked Understanding of the Country from Day 1," *Washington Post*, October 6, 2011.

58 Ruhullah Khapalwak and David Rohde, "A Look at America's New Hope."

59 See, e.g., the examples in Uzi Rabi, ed., *Tribes and States in a Changing Middle East*, Oxford: Oxford University Press, 2016.

60 See, e.g., the Libyan case under Col. Qadhafi, Elena Vismara, "The Contemporary Nature of Tribalism: Anthropological Insights on the Libyan Case," CMI (The Christian Michelsen Institute for Science and Intellectual Freedom, Norway) Working Paper WP 2018:12. www/cmi.no/publications/6695-the-contemporary-nature-of-tribalism (accessed accessed August 1, 2025).

61 Carole Goldberg-Ambrose, "Of Native Americans and Tribal Members: The Impact of Law on Indian Group Life," *Law and Society Review*, vol. 28, no. 5 (1994), pp. 1123–48, at 1131.

62 See, Annette McGivney, "Revealed: Trump Officials Rush to Mine Desert Haven Native Tribes Consider Holy," *The Guardian*, November 24, 2020. See generally, Lauren Redniss, *Oak Flat: A Fight for Sacred Land in the American West*, New York: Random House, 2020, pp. 191–92 (on Rio Tinto's corrupt practices).

63 Carter Squires, Kelsey Landau, and Robin J. Lewis, *Uncommon Ground: The Impact of Natural Resource Corruption on Indigenous Peoples*, Brookings Institution, August 7, 2020. www.brookings.edu/blog/up-front/2020/08/07/uncommon-ground-the-impact-of-natural-resource-corruption-on-indigenous-peoples/ (accessed September 8, 2025).

64 Trump spent over a million dollars surreptitiously funding an ad campaign against Indian gambling. However: "What Trump did not mention during [one radio] interview was that he had been trying to partner with a tribe near Palm Springs, Calif. Trump personally called the chairman of the Agua Caliente band of the Cahuilla Indians and visited the tribe's administrative offices in an unsuccessful attempt to manage the tribe's proposed casino, according to a statement the chairman later gave to federal lawmakers." Shawn Boberg, "Donald Trump's Long History of Clashes with Native Americans," *Washington Post*, July 25, 2016. See also, Joseph Tanfani, "Trump Was Once So Involved in Trying to Block an Indian Casino that He Secretly Approved Attack Ads," *Los Angeles Times*, June 30, 2016. During his second presidency Trump demanded that the Washington and Cleveland sports teams revert to the former names ('Redskins' and 'Indians') that both Native Americans and others had found deeply offensive. Erica L. Green, "Trump Urges Washington and Cleveland Sports Teams to Revert to Former Names," *New York Times*, July 20, 2025.

65 See, e.g., the example of a California tribe who built a casino after their status was reinstated: Anonymous, "Chukchansi Tribe Starts Disenrollment Proceedings against More Than 60 Citizens," *Indians.com*, June 27, 2019. www.indianz.com/News/2019/06/27/chukchansi-tribe-starts-disenrollment-pr.asp (accessed September 8, 2025); and Linda Geddes, "Tribal Wars," *New Scientist*, vol. 210, issue 2817 (June 15, 2011), pp. 8–10. See also, Judith

M. Stinson, "When Tribal Disenrollment Becomes Cruel and Unusual," *Nebraska Law Review*, vol. 97, no. 3 (2019), pp. 820–859; John K. Crawford, "Disenrollment as Citizenship Revocation: Promoting Tribal Sovereignty by Embracing International Norms," *Yale Law Journal*, vol. 134, no. 4 (2025) pp. 1359–1453.

66 For example, the annual gross revenue in 2019 of the Arctic Slope Regional Corporation was $3.7 billion, the Bristol Bay Native Corporation $1.7 billion, NANA $1.6 billion, and Lyndon $1.05 billion. See, Joaqlin Estus, "Alaska Native Corporations Dominate List of State's Top Businesses," *Native American News*, October 5, 2020. www.indianz.com/News/2020/10/05/indian-coun try-today-alaska-native-corporations-mean-business/ (accessed September 8, 2025). Collectively the twelve native corporations had revenues of $10.5 billion in 2018.

67 See, Gwendolyn J. Gordon, "Bones, Breath, Body, The Life of an Indigenously Owned New Zealand Corporation," unpublished Ph.D. Dissertation, Princeton University, Department of Anthropology, 2014; and her "Legal and Cultural Construction of the Maori Corporate Person," *Law and Social Inquiry*, vol. 48, no. 1 (February 2023) pp. 50–63.

68 On recent efforts, ultimately unsuccessful, to abrogate the Treaty of Waitangi (and limit special programs and representation for Australian Aborigines) see, Natasha Frost, "In Rightward Shift, New Zealand Reconsiders Pro-Maori Policies," *New York Times*, December 16, 2023.

69 See, Katrina G. Geddes, "Sovereign Immunity for Rent: How the Commodification of Tribal Sovereign Immunity Reflects the Failures of the U.S. Patent System," *Fordham Intellectual Property, Media and Entertainment Law Journal*, vol. 29, no. 3 (2019), pp. 767–802. For the background and an argument favoring such corporate-tribe deals see, Daniel C. Kennedy, "Strange Bedfellows: Native American Tribes, Big Pharma, and the Legitimacy of Their Alliance," *Duke Law Journal*, vol. 68 (2019), pp. 1433–68.

70 The White Earth Band of Ojibwe in Minnesota have even passed a tribal law recognizing the rice's right to exist and flourish. They hope the principle will be accepted by a state court to help in its protection against proposed pipelines that may ruin the crop. On the Ojibwe's dispute with the University of Minnesota concerning the latter's attempts to genetically modify the crop see, Aurelien Bouayad, "Wild Rice Protectors: An Ojibwe Odyssey," *Environmental Law Review*, vol. 22, no. 1 (April 2019), pp. 25–42.

71 See, Virgil J. Vogel, "American Indian Influence on the American Pharmacopeia," Paper presented at the American Association for the Advancement of Science, February 24, 1976. https://files.eric.ed.gov/fulltext/ED138390.pdf (accessed September 8, 2025).

72 See, e.g., Jessica W. Blanchard, Simon Outram, Gloria Tallbull, and Charmaine D. M. Royal, "'We Don't Need a Swab in Our Mouth to Prove Who We Are': Identity, Resistance, and Adaptation of Genetic Ancestry Testing among Native American Communities," *Current Anthropology*, vol. 60, no. 5 (October 2019), pp. 637–55.

6
ANOMALOUS SINGULARITIES
Tribes and Sovereignty in the Modern World

"[I]t may well be doubted whether those tribes which reside within the acknowledged boundaries of the United States can, with strict accuracy, be denominated foreign nations. They may, more correctly, perhaps, be denominated domestic dependent nations. [T]hey are in a state of pupilage. Their relation to the United States resembles that of a ward to his guardian."
Chief Justice of the United States Supreme Court John Marshall, *Cherokee Nation v. State of Georgia*, 30 U.S. 1 (1831)

"Indian tribes are "distinct, independent political communities, retaining their original natural rights" in matters of local self-government. Although no longer "possessed of the full attributes of sovereignty," they remain a "separate people, with the power of regulating their internal and social relations." They have power to make their own substantive law in internal matters, and to enforce that law in their own forums."
Associate Justice of the U.S. Supreme Court Thurgood Marshall, *Santa Clara Pueblo v. Martinez*, 436 U.S. 49 (1978)

"[A]boriginal title to land exists in relation to those lands indigenous nations held exclusively (either de facto or de jure according to their own legal traditions) at the time when the Crown asserted sovereignty, and where it continues to exist today it represents a sui generis communal property right that, although inalienable except to the Crown, permits title holders to use the land for any purpose that does not destroy their cultural attachment to it."
Chief Justice Joseph Lamer, Supreme Court of Canada, *Delgamuukw v. British Columbia* [1997] 3 SCR 1010

The issue of self-governance poses "the problem of tribe" in its boldest terms. If tribes are to possess some control over their own lands and members then this will most often take place nowadays within the context of the nation-state. Indeed, the state has become the irreducible unit in the international political scheme. As a sort of political atom it is seen as fractured only at the risk of releasing forces that may spin out of control – whether in Yugoslavia (which imploded upon dissolution), in Belgium, Spain, and the U.K. (where it has resulted in devolution and could spell national fission), in Iraq (where some coalition members feared that the country's fractionation could justify their own dismemberment), or in Russia (where Vladimir Putin seeks the Soviet Union's reassembly). For most present-day tribes, then, the foundational question is how self-governance is to be managed while living within the borders of a theoretically indissoluble nation-state.

Practical answers to this question entail numerous issues. First, a workable concept of tribe must itself be established so one can determine which groups qualify for whatever distinctive status is to apply. The definition of tribe for these purposes need not be that presented here: If tribes are not exclusively territorial or politically autonomous that does not mean that for governmental purposes these features might not be of central concern. Indeed, in the present-day order of things it is difficult to imagine a form of tribal governance that would not, for example, require some defined territorial base.[1] Similarly, it is unlikely that states will agree to allow tribes to define membership in such a way that people could buy into a tribe or be adopted solely to escape jurisdiction by the larger polity. Once again, though, the definition of tribe for these purposes may set boundaries and criteria that are more rigid than we have suggested for tribes generically yet be constructed in such a fashion as to allow the cultural features we have discussed to play out within the tribe itself. To ask in what ways tribal cultures should be more or less independent is thus to partake of an ongoing debate over the core meaning of sovereignty and, indeed, whether it is appropriately applied to tribal-state relations.

Sovereignty has been the governing concept since at least the 17th century. Treaty of Westphalia rendered it integral to the characterization of any nation-state. On its face it would appear to be an absolute: Either you have full sovereignty, or you do not. Often conceived in the West as supreme authority within territorial bounds, different political philosophers have appended a wide range of powers and potential limitations to the concept, ranging from Martin Luther's distinction between the worldly and spiritual jurisdictions of the Church, to Jean Bodin's emphasis on superordinate laws of God or nature (rather than territoriality) that limit the sovereign, to Carl Schmitt's more contemporary notion that "the sovereign is he who decides on the exception."² Yet, as Lauren Benton has shown, as Europeans moved out across the oceans the idea of sovereignty that trailed along with them was characterized less in terms of fully circumscribed territories than as personal subjection to an authority. "Territorial control," she writes, "was a contingent element of imperial rule, not a property firmly associated with sovereign jurisdiction, and subjecthood was defined by a set of political and legal relationships shaped by strategic maneuvering and interpretation, and subject to challenge."³ Historically, then, not only has sovereign power actually been fragmented and discontinuous but that fact suggests a less-than-absolutist set of possibilities for tribal-state relations.

> [S]overeignty is often more myth than reality, more a story that polities tell about their own power than a definite quality they possess. Most boundaries are porous, and many are contested, and states cannot consistently enforce laws to regulate activities across and within borders.... [T]erritory plays tricks....Political space everywhere generates irregularities: polities and subpolities secure exemptions from legislation, jurisdictions guard their autonomy, and subjects and citizens seek to expand or protect extraterritorial legal rights. Peculiar forms of attenuated and partial sovereignty are as common to political life as acts of corruption, and they are politically more far reaching in their effects.
>
> Lauren Benton, *A Search for Sovereignty*, Cambridge University Press, 2009, p. 279.

Indeed, when it comes to the relation of tribes and colonizing powers these historic ambiguities and intermittent applications have produced a number of anomalies. At times, the colonial authorities have treated tribes as equivalent nations, often assuming, however, that they were insufficiently evolved or civilized, thus justifying limitations on their sovereignty to the benefit of the colonizing power. When, as we have seen, Chief Justice John Marshall characterized the relation of the United States to its Indian tribes – with whom the Europeans and their American successors had already been dealing for two hundred years – he had to reach for concepts like "domestic dependent nations" and "guardian/ward" to capture this anomalous relationship. In the process he also sought to place some limitations on the powers the state could exercise over them, phrasing this in terms of correlative duties rather than limitations of national sovereignty. Even though such limits never fully challenged what Congress could do in its plenary power, the idea of inherent sovereignty was destined to lie dormant for many years until it was reawakened in the legal cases of the past half century. The experience of other nations demonstrates a wide range of responses to claims of full or limited tribal sovereignty, including greater recognition of treaty rights in New Zealand, realistic restraint by Pakistan in trying to control the tribes of its border regions, and Canada's limited recognition of an Inuit province. Thus divisible sovereignty, now found among nations and to some extent between nations and tribes, has led to a more elaborated array of possible accords between these two kinds of political entities.

The distribution of governing powers among states and tribes might be based on any number of arrangements. Without claiming to have covered all possibilities or their corollaries it may be useful to consider several such arrangements – keeping clearly in mind that one approach need not suit all possible instances. These approaches include total independence of the tribe; some form of federalism; contractual sovereignty based on treaties or other instruments of agreement; dual citizenship with residence or subject matter determining jurisdiction; and some form of human rights regime that would take precedence over portions of nation-state control.

Total independence would seem the most clear-cut solution: Tribes would refer to themselves as nations (as many already do, e.g., the Navajo Nation) and would possess all the powers of such an entity in the eyes of the world. Indeed, given that so many tribes have sustained past injustices, ranging from restrictions on their land to outright genocide, it might seem that the nation within which they are currently placed – and indeed the whole human rights community – owes them a duty of full recognition that neither partial compensation nor limited authority can satisfy. More broadly, one may argue that it is their very diversity that warrants protection by others if we are not to allow superordinate states to smother all difference. Not all commenters, however, would agree. Michael Walzer, for example, states that "majorities have no obligation to guarantee the survival of minority cultures.... [There] is no reason to come to their rescue; they have a claim, indeed, to physical but not to cultural security." Every individual and every group, he argues, should emphasize more than one feature of their identity, concluding that "our common humanity will never make us members of a single universal tribe. The crucial commonality of the human race is particularism."[4]

Yet the problems this poses, both morally and politically, are not insignificant. It may be one thing if the rules and values of the nation and those of the encompassed tribe coincide. But if the practices of another culture – particularly one whose members are also citizens of the surrounding nation-state, as well as being entitled to certain universal human rights – are unduly restrictive or discriminating (say, against women), what does the nation or world community owe to the indigenous group? When, as in the *Martinez* case cited above, the child of a tribal woman who marries an outsider man is not regarded as a member of the tribe whereas the child of a man who marries an outsider woman is, should tribal sovereignty trump an American citizen's right to equal protection, as the U.S. Supreme Court ruled? If tribal law in Pakistan permits a child from a murderer's group to be sent as replacement for the child killed, does deference to their practice, national law, or a human rights accord govern?[5] If all solutions are, in a sense, imperfect, is it just a matter of brute power who gets to decide the outcome or is there a universal set of procedures for making such determinations that is not the product of a just one cultural tradition? And at the risk of sounding paternalistic, is it really to the benefit of another culture to risk freezing an indigenous entity in place by recognizing its full independence in its present form when the opportunity for change is no less of an entitlement for them as for all people? Indeed, although international law tends to disfavor it, should a tribe have the right to secede from the surrounding nation or (as has been the argument of many Iroquois) may indigenous individuals refuse to have the citizenship of the dominant state imposed on them?

> [M]ulticulturalism requires a political society to recognize the equal standing of all the stable and viable cultural communities existing in that society. This includes the need for multicultural political societies to reconceive themselves. There is no room for talk of a minority problem or of a majority tolerating the minorities. A political society, a state, consists—if it is multicultural—of diverse communities and belongs to none of them. While the relative size of the different communities affects the solutions to conflicts over resources and public spaces among them, none of them should be allowed to see the state as its own, or to think that the others enjoy their standing on sufferance.... While incorporating policies of non-discrimination, liberal multiculturalism transcends the individualistic approach which they tend to incorporate, and recognizes the importance of unimpeded membership in a respected and flourishing cultural group for individual well-being.
>
> [M]ulticultural measures...should not aim to preserve the pristine purity of different cultural groups. They should aim to enable them to adjust and change to a new form of existence within a larger community, while preserving their integrity, pride in their identity, and continuity with their past and with others of the same culture in different countries.
>
> Joseph Raz, *Ethics in the Public Domain*, Oxford University Press, 1995, pp. 174, 189; and his "Reform or Destroy?" *Boston Review*, October/November 1997.

Full independence for tribes is an unlikely solution in the vast majority of cases. In the tribal regions of Pakistan it may be a fact on the ground, if not in the law, and indeed there are those who would argue that given the tribes' own codes of honor and the long history of their resistance to state control it would be the course of wisdom to permit them the *de jure* independence they largely possess in any event.[6] But even here not only is the Pakistani state unwilling to give up sovereignty over any portion of its territory but the maintenance of that control is seen as indispensable to averting yet other claims that might fractionate the state. Others may be caught up in local state-tribal power struggles. For example, the governments of several Muslim countries convinced American officials that it was the tribes who were helping terrorists, the goal of such claims being to use the Americans in their own pursuit of greater control over tribal resources and populations.[7] Even in so isolated a place as one of the Andaman Islands, where, particularly since the killing of John Chau, a 26-year-old uninvited American missionary, the Indian state has thrown up a cordon around the island and essentially left the tribesmen to their own devices, the central government has not foresworn its right to exercise ultimate control over the area.[8] As in much of the world, any division of powers among tribe and state is, however, more likely to lead to peaceful relations if, instead of being fashioned in absolutist terms, the plan rests on some form of enforceable mutual agreement.

Agreement necessitates compromise. Particularly in the current international order the powers of any state are almost always limited to some degree. This may result from agreements by which each entity gives up some form of absolute control in exchange for what it deems to be economic, security, or legal benefits. In theory that was true for treaties signed with the indigenous people of the United States: Until 1871 such treaties were the common mode of engagement between the federal government and the Native American tribes. In the early years of the republic, when the tribes were the more powerful force, such treaties were signed by the federal government out of national necessity; later they served as a fig-leaf for what was in fact constant intrusion into Indian lands. Two seemingly contradictory rules of international practice make any treaty-making problematic: (1) that all nations must honor their treaties and (2) that any nation may abrogate its treaties if it is in its national interest to do so. In the American case, not only were many treaties to which a tribe acceded never ratified by Congress, but the provisions of valid treaties were frequently contravened (rather than formally abrogated) by subsequent federal legislation, whereas the tribes rarely went back on their word. Nevertheless, many tribes insist on the federal government honoring their treaty provisions, particularly since some features – such as the Choctaw's

FIGURE 6.1 Signing of the Treaty of Fort Laramie, 1868.

right to send a representative to Congress – have never been implemented. While some have called for the strict enforcement of existing treaties and others for opening new treaty-making, serious concerns persist about the relative costs and benefits of this form of tribal-state engagement. Among the detractions are: the agreement can be tossed aside even though parties have acted in reliance on it; the state may pass laws that contradict treaty provisions thus constituting de facto abrogation; the weaker party may effectively have to compromise its rights in the negotiating process because of the costs involved in refusing to agree to the terms set forth; the structure of the agreement may make revisions occasioned by changing circumstances very cumbersome; and parties may be frozen in place, thus adversely affecting the groups' internal dynamics. Recent threats to the Treaty of Waitangi between the government of New Zealand and the Maori underscore the dependence of such arrangements on the vicissitudes of electoral politics.[9] On the other hand, the recent decision by the highest court in Canada finding that violations by the central government of its treaty obligations – characterized by the court as "longstanding and egregious" – may constitute an effective backdrop for renewed negotiations.[10]

Moreover, as we have seen in the discussion of tribal modes of engagement and their contacts with the military, tribesmen commonly conceive of such agreements as relational rather than transactional. That is, they regard them as artifacts in an ongoing process, not a one-off contract for a limited purpose. Long-term personal interaction, reciprocity, and engagement in the rituals of negotiation are the indicators of reliability, not the written terms of the agreement. As such, the *process* of treaty-making not just the actual treaty provisions are often at the heart of any relationship, and if the non-tribal party does not see the engagement in those terms the deal has a good chance of ultimately going sour. This is as true for the early colonial period in the United States as it is in the dealings between the American military and the tribes of Iraq or Afghanistan in more recent times.

> Colonial Americans attended treaty conferences to achieve specific ends – such as a promise of alliance, trade concessions, or a land purchase – which could be documented and archived in a written record of the proceedings. Europeans thought of Indian treaties as texts, contracts that recorded in black and white deals reached with America's indigenous inhabitants. The ceremonies, speech-making, and gift-giving that went on at such meetings were merely steps to achieving this end, a document that could be sent to superiors in London, Paris, or colonial capitals, filed away, and cited as necessary to prove a binding agreement.
>
> The Iroquois did not see it that way at all. The vast majority of those who participated in treaty conferences were not literate, and they talked disparagingly of what [Iroquois leader] Canasatego called the "pen and ink work" that went on at treaty conferences. They knew that the written records of such proceedings could exaggerate, manipulate, and outright fabricate what had transpired there, and years of experience with such chicanery had taught them to place little faith in such documents. Instead, they valued the process of treaty-making: the reception hosts provided their guests, the exchange of ritual objects at the council fire, the give and take of speechmaking, and the distribution of presents at the treaty's conclusion. To the Iroquois, linking arms together was not a contractual agreement that once entered into became forever binding. On the contrary, linking arms committed the participants to mutual obligations that could only be met through a perpetual process of negotiation and renewal.
>
> Timothy J. Shannon, *Iroquois Diplomacy on the Early American Frontier*, New York: Viking, 2008, p. 81.

> Procedure usually called for the English to read the document aloud to the Indians before the signing, and they did not always read what was on the paper. The Indians signed for what they heard. The English held them to what was written.
>
> Francis Jennings, *The Invasion of America*, W. W. Norton, 1975, p. 24.

On the international front, of course, treaty-making has gained importance in recent decades, particularly as concerns trade. Whether it is general trade pacts or regional associations, all of the benefits and flaws of this form of agreement – witness the controversies over Brexit, the Pacific Trade Pact, and NAFTA – remain of concern. However, few governments of the world are currently prepared to employ the treaty as a preeminent vehicle for their dealings with tribal groups, not least because the form itself constitutes a recognition of nation-to-nation dealing that may have implications reaching well beyond the formal contents of a particular pact. Nevertheless, there are a number of other forms tribe-state agreements can take.

In the U.S., for example, agreements (called compacts) are not uncommon between federally recognized tribes and states. Such agreements may cover the cross-deputization of police (so they can pursue a suspect across state/reservation boundary lines) or environmental compacts (because neither pollution nor endangered species recognize borders). Both sides need to have a clear idea of which jurisdictional issues are most vital to their respective sense of well-being. Control over matters of personal status (marriage, divorce, filiation, child custody, etc.) are often key to a tribe's sense of being able to preserve its identity, whereas states may have a vested interest in criminal jurisdiction for major felonies and, at the national level, full control of foreign affairs. Tribal judges, who may serve more than one tribe, and mechanisms for allowing non-tribesmen to represent tribal members before tribal courts may also be worked out by mutual agreement.

Federalism is practiced in a number of tribal-state relations. It may take the form of a native parliament modeled somewhat along that of the nation – as is the case with the Sami in several Scandinavian countries – or it may take the form of rendering tribes equivalent to other entities within the federal system, whether that of a municipality, county, parish, or other governmental unit. This may have the advantage of making tribal law-ways more palatable to the national government while maintaining tribal control over procedures and aftereffects. If, to take an example, it is incest on one side of the river for first cousins to marry but not in the state on the other side of the river ought not equivalent differences between tribal and state family law be easily tolerated? The Canadian creation of a separate Inuit province suggests that in some instances large tracts of land can be under indigenous control, though the precise level of qualified independence the Inuit province will actually be able to exercise remains to be seen.

Indeed, there is understandable concern that without some form of federalism tribes will always remain at the whim of the state. Kouslaa

T. Kessler-Mata, one of whose parents comes from a federally recognized U.S. tribe and another from a tribe that lacks recognition, argues that, at least where American Indians are concerned, full independence still relies on an imbalance of power with the central government and limited recourse from arbitrary harassment. She details, in the sphere of tribal casino operations and resource control, how tribes could, however, be the functional equivalent of individual states, thus positioning themselves more favorably for agreements with other states and the federal government. Sovereignty as autonomy, she concludes, simply does not address the actual distribution of power affecting nation-tribal relations, and no amount of skillful lawyering within the existing framework of federal Indian law can address those imbalances, particularly when Congress can invoke its court-sanctioned plenary power to affect the status of recognized tribes.[11] How state-like status could be worked out for more than five hundred recognized Native American tribes and hundreds more that would like to be recognized remains only one of many impediments to the implementation of such a solution.

Vine Deloria, Jr. once said of Native American tribes: "What we need is a cultural leave-us alone agreement, in spirit and in fact."[12] If we take this not to mean full jurisdictional sovereignty but, instead, we stress the cultural aspect of his remarks, it might be possible to acknowledge certain distinctively cultural rights for tribes – for example, those pertaining to intellectual property. In addition to forums that would specialize in such matters one could apply national and international law to recognize control over indigenous art and design, sacred symbols, local medicinal plants, and personal DNA. Arrangements have been made in a number of instances for exclusive rights to the marketing of tribal products beyond what might be covered by ordinary copyright and patent laws, and additional protections may be afforded by agreement to the resale price of native items, much as some countries (and California) have begun protecting the pass-on value for artists generally. Similarly, assigning native groups as stewards of national parks – and permitting them to set their own standards for that care – would allow a significant degree of dominion without constituting ultimate sovereignty over key territories.

International accords might seem an especially useful vehicle for safeguarding certain tribal powers. However, few of the existing accords carry effective sanctions. The U.N. Declaration on the Rights of Indigenous Peoples was long opposed by countries such as Brazil and the United States, who claimed that it would undermine their own sovereignty, and even where grudging approval has been forthcoming the Declaration is lacking in enforceability. Other accords are similarly couched in rather general terms, may address groupings besides tribes and hence are not shaped for the tribes' special needs, and, so long as states regard any international body trenching on dealings with their internal populations as an attack on their own sovereignty, it is unlikely that broad-scale programs of this sort will ever have a major impact. Rather, accords on specific subjects (environmental, copyright, etc.) can include recognition of distinctive tribal concerns and, if also linked to protections for all citizens, may be fashioned to have real teeth.

Given the qualities of tribal life that have been suggested, is there, then, a set of principles to which one could point concerning how states ought to interact with the tribes living among them? If tribes are perfectly competent to make their own choices and adaptations perhaps the simplest principle would be to leave them alone. A guarantee of protection against direct attack is vital. What constitutes a direct attack, of course, is key to such a proposal, and – whether in international conventions like that of the International Labor Organization or various United Nations and regional accords – attempts to lay out such parameters risk being drawn either too specifically to gain broad acceptance or too generally to get down to cases. Even so, non-interference can be the first line of defense for tribes and can include, at a minimum, control over their own membership, legal protections for collective lands that are at least as great as those afforded any individual or voluntary association within the nation, full jurisdiction over matters of personal status, and the freedom of all members either to remove themselves from the tribe or not to be barred from inclusion having once met the criteria of membership.

The second principle would be that of the negotiated compact. Here, the parties would have to deal with one another face-to-face. Mandatory negotiation would be required, no party being able to refuse to meet for discussion. Here, too, the inducement to negotiate can be contained in the proposition that, if the state refuses to bargain, the last offer placed on the table by the tribe prevails, a provision that got people to the table when on-reservation gambling legislation took effect in the U.S. However, it might be valuable for one or more mediators also to be involved, individuals who could assist both sides to consider all aspects of their potential arrangement and bring comparative examples to the attention of the contracting parties. Indeed, the negotiations over mediation styles might be a useful preamble to the actual bargaining, the lessons of early treaty making processes and indigenous customs being particularly helpful in formulating the eventual procedures. Once again, linking these agreements to enforceable contracts within the superordinate nation may help ensure that they are actually implemented, since violations of their terms would endanger the viability of anyone else's contracts within that jurisdiction.

Finally, specialized forums may be desirable to settle disputes between the parties. These too might take the form of arbitration or mediation panels rather than formal courts of law and might draw on features of indigenous dispute resolution mechanisms no less than those through which other sectors of the nation address their differences. Examples would be forums that address issues of tribal intellectual property rights, custody of children living away from the tribe but clearly attached to it, the repatriation of human remains, access to sacred sites, and environmental issues that might benefit from the advice of a panel of native and scientific experts.[13]

No one approach will fit all situations, of course. Nor will everyone be pleased with all outcomes: Corporations will protest agreements that cut their profits, human rights advocates will protest tribal practices that fail to treat women as exact equals, federated states will protest the possible dilution of their influence. But if the foundational principle is one of mutual respect for difference, if measures are taken to counter national stereotypes of tribal populations, if mechanisms are in place to clarify jurisdiction, and if forums are available that build a distinctive body of experience in mediating disputes, at least the most harmful disproportion of power may be ameliorated. Beyond that, whether by avoiding state intrusion or compromising with its ineluctable presence, the world's tribes may just have a chance to do what they have done best throughout history – shape-shift enough to survive and preserve their ethos of moral equality and individuality without sacrificing their spirit of collective integrity. Tribes are, in the contemporary political order, anomalous indeed, oddities that in their singularity challenge the categories, the claims, the myths, and the pretensions of the states that surround them. But in their offer of the tribesmen's sense of balance and the cosmopolite's willingness to find common ground both parties may be able to focus attention on how difference may be accommodated and other ways of viewing the world accorded due respect.

Notes

1 Notwithstanding a territorial base recognized by the state in which they are situated, tribal jurisdiction over non-tribal individuals is often denied and hence the power to control the actions of outsiders on tribal lands may be severely hampered. See, e.g., the discussion in L. Scott Gould, "Tough Love for Tribes: Rethinking Sovereignty after *Atkinson* and *Hicks*," *New England Law Review*, vol. 37, no. 3 (2003), pp. 669–93. More recently, in *Oklahoma v. Castro-Huerta,* 142 S. Ct. 2486 (2022), the Supreme Court, by a 5-4 vote, held that Oklahoma and the Indians have concurrent criminal jurisdiction over non-Indians on Indian lands, thus undermining exclusive Indian jurisdiction over such outsiders. See generally, Kirke Kickingbird, "The Jurisdictional Landscape of Indian Country after the McGirt and Castro-Huerta Decisions," *Human Rights Magazine*, vol. 48, no. 4, July 26, 2023; and Michael D.O. Rusco, "Oklahoma v. Castro-Huerta, Jurisdictional Overlap, Competitive Sovereign

Erosion, and the Fundamental Freedom of Native Nations," *Marquette Law Review*, vol. 106, no. 4 (2023), pp. 889–947.
2 Carl Schmitt, *Political Theology: Four Chapters on the Concept of Sovereignty*, Chicago: University of Chicago Press, 2005, p. 5.
3 Lauren Benton, A *Search for Sovereignty*, Cambridge: Cambridge University Press, 2009, p. 288.
4 Michael Walzer, "The New Tribalism," *Dissent*, Spring 1992, pp. 164–71, at 168 and 171.
5 In one such case the tribal *jirga* (council of male elders) handed over an eight-year old girl in an inter-tribal murder case; in another, the tribal council ordered a ten-year old boy to pay a fine for having sex with a thirty-year old married woman even though national law denies such councils the right to render such decisions.
6 See generally, Akbar Ahmed, *The Thistle and the Drone: How America's War on Terror Became a Global War on Tribal Islam*, Washington: Brookings Institution Press, 2013.
7 Ahmed, *The Thistle and the Drone*, 2013.
8 See, J. Oliver Conroy, "The Life and Death of John Chau, the Man Who Tried to Convert His Killers," *The Guardian*, February 3, 2019. The issue of state versus universal rights was at the heart of debates over passage of the United Nations Declaration on the Rights of Indigenous Peoples, and the refusal of a number of nations to adopt its terms.
9 Eva Corlett and Jamie Tahana, "'Dangerous' and 'Retrograde': Māori Leaders Sound Alarm over Policy Shifts in New Zealand," *The Guardian*, July 28, 2024. The Treaty Principles Bill, as it was called, failed passage in April 2025.
10 "For well over a century, the Crown has shown itself to be a patently unreliable and untrustworthy treaty partner," Justice Mahmud Jamal wrote. "It has lost the moral authority to simply say 'trust us'." Accordingly, the court ruled, one "must consider both the words of a treaty and the historical and cultural context" and take into account how the agreement would have been understood by each party at the time. Frances Vinall, "Canada Owes First Nations for Treaty Breaches, Top Court Rules," *Washington Post*, July 28, 2024. The full decision is available at https://decisions.scc-csc.ca/scc csc/scc csc/en/item/20554/index.do (accessed September 8, 2025).
11 Kouslaa T. Kessler-Mata, *American Indians and the Trouble with Sovereignty: Structuring Self-Determination through Federalism*, Cambridge: Cambridge University Press, 2017. An earlier legal commenter's conclusion still has currency:

> Tribal sovereignty in any form is so precarious within American jurisprudence today that it often seems too dangerous for Indians to vent their concerns about tribal legitimacy 'in public.' And there is at present no international institution with the mandate and stature necessary for it to offer meaningful redress.

Carole Goldberg-Ambrose, "Of Native Americans and Tribal members: The Impact of Law on Indian Group Life," *Law & Society Review*, vol. 28, no. 5 (1994), pp. 1123–48, at 1139.
12 Vine Deloria, Jr., *Custer Died for Your Sins*, Norman: University of Oklahoma Press, 1988, p. 34.
13 See, Lawrence Rosen, *The Rights of Groups*, New York: New York University Press, 2024, pp. 90–99.

AFTERWORD

"We're Still Here"

> "Had it been our intention we could have made you all the same."
>
> *Quran* 5:48

To most people, "tribe" may be no more than a metaphor or an anachronism. Just as we may dilute the term "evolution" when it is applied to the development of an idea or personality rather than restricting it to a specific biological process so, too, use of the word "tribe" may seem an innocuous surrogate for truculence and exclusivity. But putting the analogue ahead of the referent can be distorting. When we call our politics tribal we project a sense of confinement and premonitory violence where the reverse, seen from the perspective of actual tribes, is more often the case; when we call our clubby behavior or prickly political groupings tribal we create an image of humankind as instinctively hostile to outsiders whereas actual tribes are usually far more accommodating. And when we apply the fraught image of tribes uncritically we risk limiting their economic and political development – as well as distorting our theories of power – by assessing their lives from a statist, top-down view of political order. Far from being inoffensive, perpetuating such images has thus been misleading and injurious.

But imagine that in place of these negative attributes we characterize tribal relationships – without in any way romanticizing them – as possessing a sense of moral equality or openness to others' orientations; imagine that the story we tell of our evolution is not one of the struggle that left other tribes (or indeed other hominin species) in our dust but one that bespeaks a process in which large parts of our DNA and cultural heritage have been quietly incorporated from our alter selves; imagine that when we place bounds around our groupings we do not create a wall to be defended but a semi-permeable membrane that enables as much as it hinders and sifts as much as it impedes. Would our vision of the tribal as a mode of life and metaphoric extension not, then, have to be revised for the better? And would our scholarship on the question of social form versus cultural process not benefit from thinking in terms of flexible concepts rather than rigidified shapes? Indeed, would such a shift also remove the romanticized stereotype of tribal people as "spiritual" or "at one with Mother Earth" and replace it with the more fitting images of limited powers and rituals of equilibration? One need hardly subscribe to a Marxist world view to realize that in such an instance turning the world upside down to set it right side up is both the sensible and the moral thing to do.

Human social structures and modes of conceptualizing the world meld into one another notwithstanding that the feckless quest for purity of form can be highly seductive. Just as evolution cannot go forth without "mistakes" of transcription so, too, social change would seem to require random departures from the expected or moments when the intentional "rage for chaos" is aimed at keeping alive our conceptualizing apparatus as the preeminent vehicle by which we adapt to changing circumstances. Anthropologists are as vulnerable as any others to hindsight bias – the process of assuming, after the fact, that things were predictable, when they were not – and to simply ignoring the role of chance and luck in social life. Yet if the range of variation allowable within existing confines is itself enormous a framework such as that of the tribe may contain alternatives, responding to "mistranslation" and "chaos" without loss of identity, far more successfully than less pliable social solutions. Indeed, as has been suggested throughout this study, it is the nature of the cultural constructs to which tribes bear witness – their ways of dividing up and combining the categories of created experience – that is their greatest strength and their surest asset for survival. To see tribal orientations as emergent in particular settings – a repertoire that can be called upon to address a wide range of situations; a malleable tool for responding to circumstance and fortune, individual innovation, and collective constancy – is to contend with the sheer improvisational creativity such cultures have nurtured across thousands of years of human history.

The practical implications of seeing tribes in this more realistic way are also attractive. For if it is true that tribes tend to be shape-shifters then the idea that they can accommodate themselves more readily to outside influence means that their interactions with state structures need not be envisioned as inherently rigid and antagonistic. Like any other human construct tribes may succeed or fail; they may be so transformed as to become unrecognizable or adamantly preserve elements of their identity, even clandestinely, in the face of overwhelming opposition. When, therefore, states confront tribes in war zones or resource competition either mutual misunderstanding or reluctance to be drawn into open-ended negotiation frequently results in the retreat to stereotypes, just as – particularly in the Western linear view of history – tribes are expected to gracefully assimilate or be escorted from the scene. The result is to stultify comprehension and communication, with the predictable outcome that the image of tribal obstinacy becomes self-fulfilling.

Academics may be no less susceptible than others to using tribes to ratify the presumptions with which their studies were begun. As suggested earlier, the evolutionists who assume that the human psyche was formed in an imagined tribal phase and has remained the same ever since are, at a minimum, unable to prove their case. But they may come close to a more telling point – that tribes have long served as a cauldron in which the essential ingredients of human cultural life have continued to simmer, and from which tribes have served as both generative force and reservoir of possibility for the social and cultural lives of all humankind. More flexible than chiefdoms and states, more immune to destruction than isolable families, tribes have harbored and begat not fixed forms and unyielding constructs but the very ability to create the classifications by which a people may attend to the world and render it comprehensible.

Tribes are, of course, not perfect embodiments of adaptability. Like the rest of us they have, at times, ruined their own environments, battled one another into oblivion, or lacked the knowledge to fend off devastating famine or disease. Others, holding on to ways that are untenable in a changing climate or having melded into other groupings, have disappeared from view. Yet, as an approach to life, as systems that give shape to belief and substance to an effervescent sense of something greater than the self, tribes have come through history with their amoeboid flexibility and their contribution to the human condition bruised but intact.

It is also possible that tribal life, under the pressures of the outside world, has in many cases devolved into a tribal ethos and, like the Protestant ethos, loosed from earlier forms of design, has become a disembodied, almost ethereal avatar of its earlier configuration, a placeholder in which the spirit of skepticism about power and its attendant modes of levelling become a background murmur more noted when absent than prized when dominant. Indeed, is it the inability to carry over these features to other types of organization that forces some tribes to retain or recapture their distinctive form, even when an amalgamation of ethos and acculturation may hold out the allure of momentary benefit? Or is it that, for tribes, structure and value are so tightly linked that the destruction of the one must of necessity lead to the destruction of the other?

It is easy for those who have grown up in the West – heirs to Rousseauian ideas of the noble savage, Christian visions of time as directional, or colonial images of primitive communism – to see tribesmen through a distorted lens. But without idealizing or demonizing we can instead grasp the wisdom of the tribe as one in which, to elaborate on the Barotse saying, life does not move straight as cattle do to water, but one in which our zig zag course creates choice at every step, forms crevices in power to provide a handhold for diversity, and employs mutual indebtedness to level relationships rather than solidify an imbalance of power.

Much remains to be understood about tribal ways; much remains to be revised if the history of antipathy to them – and with it our own self-image – is not to be perpetuated. Responsibility towards the world's tribes, then, lies both in the comprehension and the actions – at home and abroad – taken in the name of each of us.

"We are still here," say many tribal peoples.

And by their being so, it may yet be so for us all.

INDEX

Note: Endnotes are indicated by the page number followed by 'n' and the endnote number e.g., 20n1 refers to endnote 1 on page 20.

Aborigines (Australia) 25, 43, 46, 74, 78, 80, 90–1, 133, 136, 164–5, 186
anthropology, defined 11, 51

'Barbarian' tribes of Europe 49–50
Barth, Frederik 38
Boas, Franz 33, 42
Brooks, David 6–7, 18n26, 92, 133
Bushman/San 74–5, 78–9, 129, 138–9

Chagnon, Napoleon 20, 28
Cherokee 41, 197
Cheyenne 31–2, 89, 98, 100
chiefdoms 28, 30, 32, 34, 48, 50, 76, 98, 174

Dawes (Allotment) Act 167–8
Diamond, Jared 28, 33

epigenetics 24; dual inheritance and 24–5
Eskimo/Inuit 128, 159, 205; and Native Alaska Claims Settlement Act 187
Evans-Pritchard, E. E. 39–40, 51, 54–5, 105n6, 124
exchange and reciprocity 115–30, 152, 182–3

First Nations (Canada) 83, 197, 203
Fox, Robin 23
Fried, Morton 8, 35, 50, 56
Friedman, Thomas J. 7, 126

Geertz, Clifford 137, 142, 149
Gellner, Ernest 54–5, 184
gifts *see* exchange and reciprocity

Ibn Khaldun 39, 53–5
Indigenous peoples: in Taiwan 191n10
intention *see* persons, construction of

joking relations 81–3, 90
Judaism, as tribal religion 149–56

kinship 22–3, 25, 28, 37–41, 48, 52, 54–5, 89–90, 118–21, 170
Kuhn, Thomas 52

law, tribal 99–102, 131, 175–6, 197, 205
Leach, Edmund 37, 42, 95
levelling *see* Judaism, as tribal religion; tribes, distribution of power
Lévi-Strauss, Claude 53

Maori 96, 116, 165, 170, 187, 203
Mashpee Indians 7, 13, 42, 73

Native Americans 40; treaties and 202–5
Navajo 40–1, 63n45, 75, 89, 132–3, 163, 186

Obama, Barack 7, 18n28, 27

persons, construction of 130–4
Pinker, Steven 20n39, 28
potlatch 80–1, 163–4

Radin, Paul 56, 74, 82, 87–8, 94, 119, 125, 130, 136–7
rituals and ritual knowledge 75, 92, 136; *see* tribes, religion and

Sahlins, Marshall 24, 33, 39–40, 49, 54–5, 62n34, 78–9, 94, 116, 118, 130–1, 135, 137, 154, 172
sovereignty 197–209

time, concepts of 134–5, 153
treaties *see* Native Americans
tribal art 132
'tribal' as political term 3–5, 14, 73, 210
tribal ethos 13, 44, 114–15, 140–1, 155
tribes, adoption and 95–6; amoeboid metaphor for 72; anthropologists on 7; archaeology and 21–2, 28–31, 96, 106n20; autocracy and 4, 18, 23; colonialism and 157–78, 199; corporations and 185–9; cultural evolution and 7–8, 22–37, 48, 52, 212; distribution of power in 73–93; federal recognition of 160–1; historically viewed 51–7; human nature and 6–7, 9, 23, 26–7, 30; Human Relations Area File and 10; Human Terrain project and 184; identity changes and 1; Indigenous scholars' views of 11–12; individualism and 6, 38–41, 56, 76, 119, 123, 125, 132–3, 153; intellectual property and 188–9, 206, 208; international law and 201, 205–7; Iraq and Afghanistan 179–85; language and 42, 45–7, 75; leadership and 93–9; level of biological taxonomy and 9; military and 13–14, 178–85; missionaries and 163–4, 178, 202; moral equivalence and 13, 49, 124–30, 153; political organization and 47–51; property and 77, 119, 135, 199; religion and 24, 134–40; rhetorical skills and 83–4; segmentarity and 49, 121, 123, 171–2; sexuality and 6, 153–4; states and 8, 12–13, 169–71, 176, 198, 209; territory and 42–4, 133; theoretical approaches to 9–13; usefulness of concept of 8–9, 12; violence and 14, 26–35, 49, 83, 96–7; women's powers and 80, 89, 91–3, 201; writing and 55–6
trickster 82–3, 89, 93, 125–6
Trump, Donnald 186–7

White, Leslie 33–5
Wilson, E. O. 26
witchcraft accusations 91, 131

For Product Safety Concerns and Information please contact our EU representative GPSR@taylorandfrancis.com
Taylor & Francis Verlag GmbH, Kaufingerstraße 24, 80331 München, Germany

www.ingramcontent.com/pod-product-compliance
Lightning Source LLC
LaVergne TN
LVHW012014060526
838201LV00061B/4301